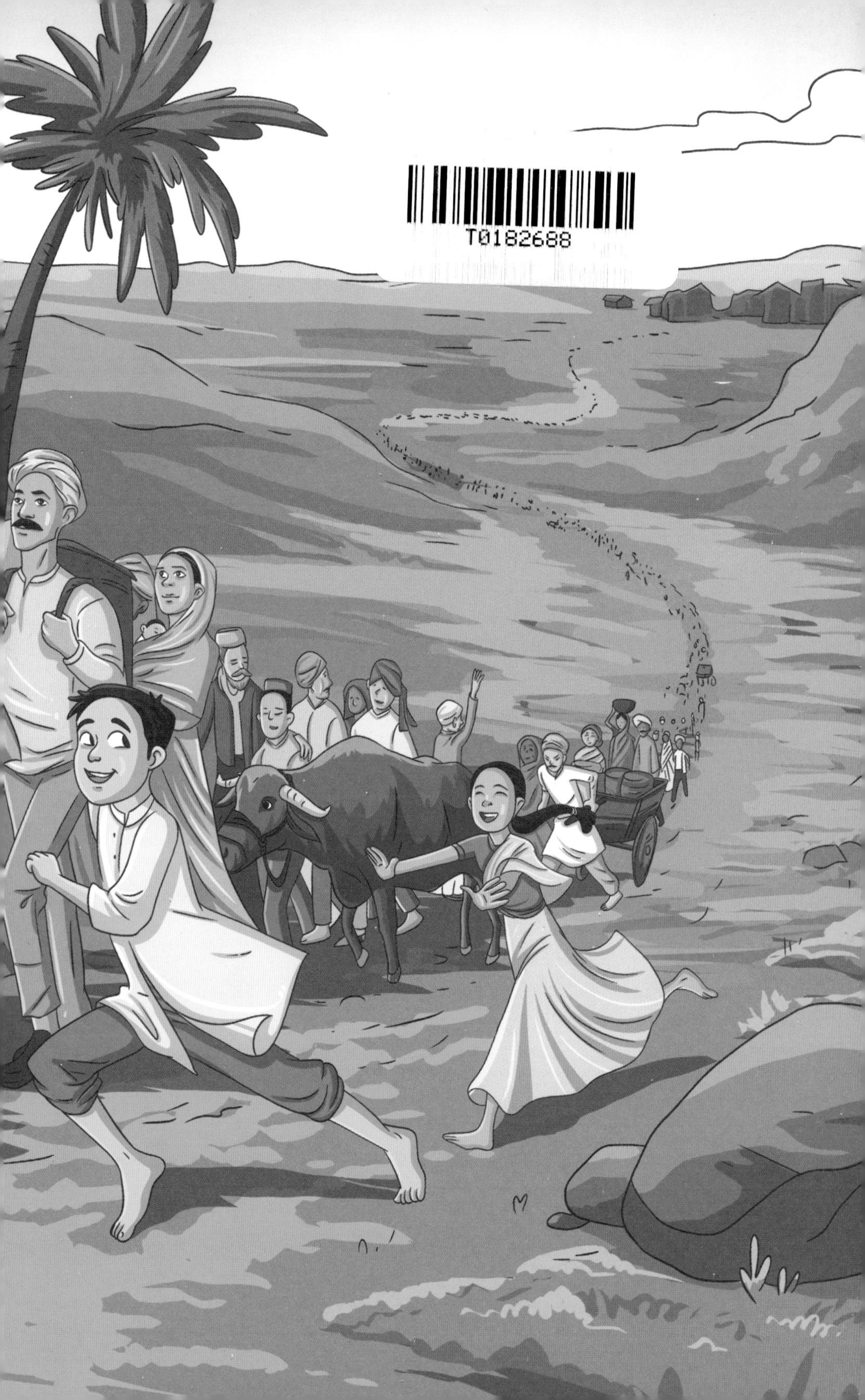

SHOW ME HISTORY!

GANDHI

The PEACEFUL PROTESTER!

BY
JAMES BUCKLEY JR.

ILLUSTRATED BY
CASSIE ANDERSON

LETTERING & DESIGN BY
SWELL TYPE

COVER ART BY
IAN CHURCHILL

PORTABLE PRESS

SAN DIEGO, CALIFORNIA

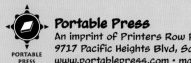

Portable Press
An imprint of Printers Row Publishing Group
9717 Pacific Heights Blvd, San Diego, CA 92121
www.portablepress.com • mail@portablepress.com

Printers Row Publishing Group is a division of Readerlink Distribution Services, LLC. Portable Press is a registered trademark of Readerlink Distribution Services, LLC.

Correspondence regarding the content of this book should be sent to Portable Press, Editorial Department, at the above address. Author and illustrator inquiries should be sent to Oomf, Inc., www.oomf.com.

Portable Press
Publisher: Peter Norton • Associate Publisher: Ana Parker
Senior Developmental Editor: April Graham Farr
Editor: Stephanie Romero Gamboa
Production Team: Julie Greene, Beno Chan, Rusty von Dyl

O•MF Produced by Oomf, Inc., www.Oomf.com
Director: Mark Shulman
Producer: James Buckley Jr.

Author: James Buckley Jr.
Illustrator: Cassie Anderson
Inks and colors: Vineeth Vijayan Kallemvalli
Assistant Editor: Michael Centore
Lettering & design by Swell Type: John Roshell, Forest Dempsey,
    Sarah Jacobs, Drewes McFarling, Miles Gaushell
Cover illustrator: Ian Churchill

Library of Congress Control Number: 2021930582

ISBN: 978-1-64517-409-7

Printed in Singapore

25 24 23 22 21   1 2 3 4 5

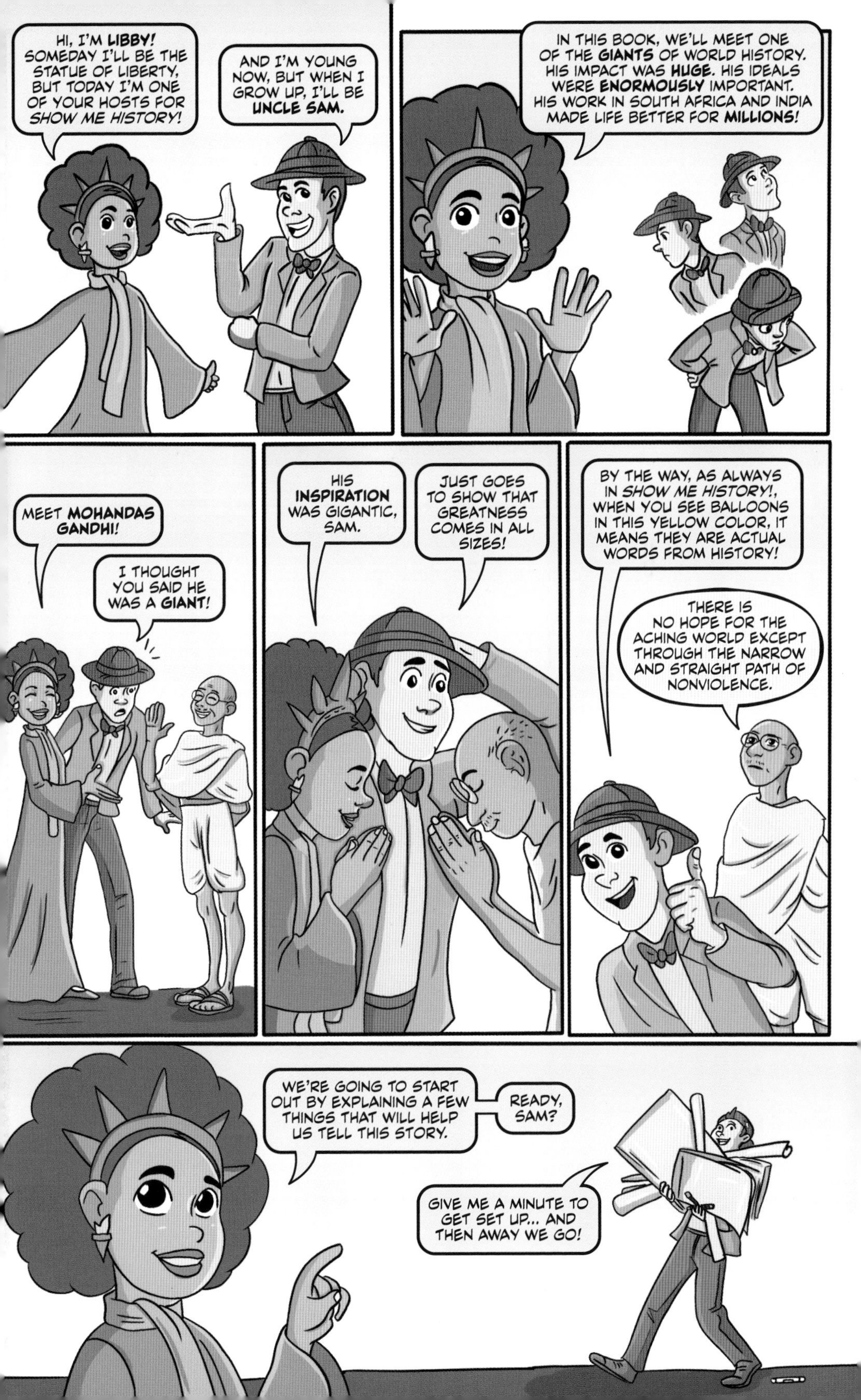
HI, I'M LIBBY! SOMEDAY I'LL BE THE STATUE OF LIBERTY, BUT TODAY I'M ONE OF YOUR HOSTS FOR SHOW ME HISTORY!
AND I'M YOUNG NOW, BUT WHEN I GROW UP, I'LL BE UNCLE SAM.
IN THIS BOOK, WE'LL MEET ONE OF THE GIANTS OF WORLD HISTORY. HIS IMPACT WAS HUGE. HIS IDEALS WERE ENORMOUSLY IMPORTANT. HIS WORK IN SOUTH AFRICA AND INDIA MADE LIFE BETTER FOR MILLIONS!
MEET MOHANDAS GANDHI!
I THOUGHT YOU SAID HE WAS A GIANT!
HIS INSPIRATION WAS GIGANTIC, SAM.
JUST GOES TO SHOW THAT GREATNESS COMES IN ALL SIZES!
BY THE WAY, AS ALWAYS IN SHOW ME HISTORY!, WHEN YOU SEE BALLOONS IN THIS YELLOW COLOR, IT MEANS THEY ARE ACTUAL WORDS FROM HISTORY!
THERE IS NO HOPE FOR THE ACHING WORLD EXCEPT THROUGH THE NARROW AND STRAIGHT PATH OF NONVIOLENCE.
WE'RE GOING TO START OUT BY EXPLAINING A FEW THINGS THAT WILL HELP US TELL THIS STORY.
READY, SAM?
GIVE ME A MINUTE TO GET SET UP... AND THEN AWAY WE GO!

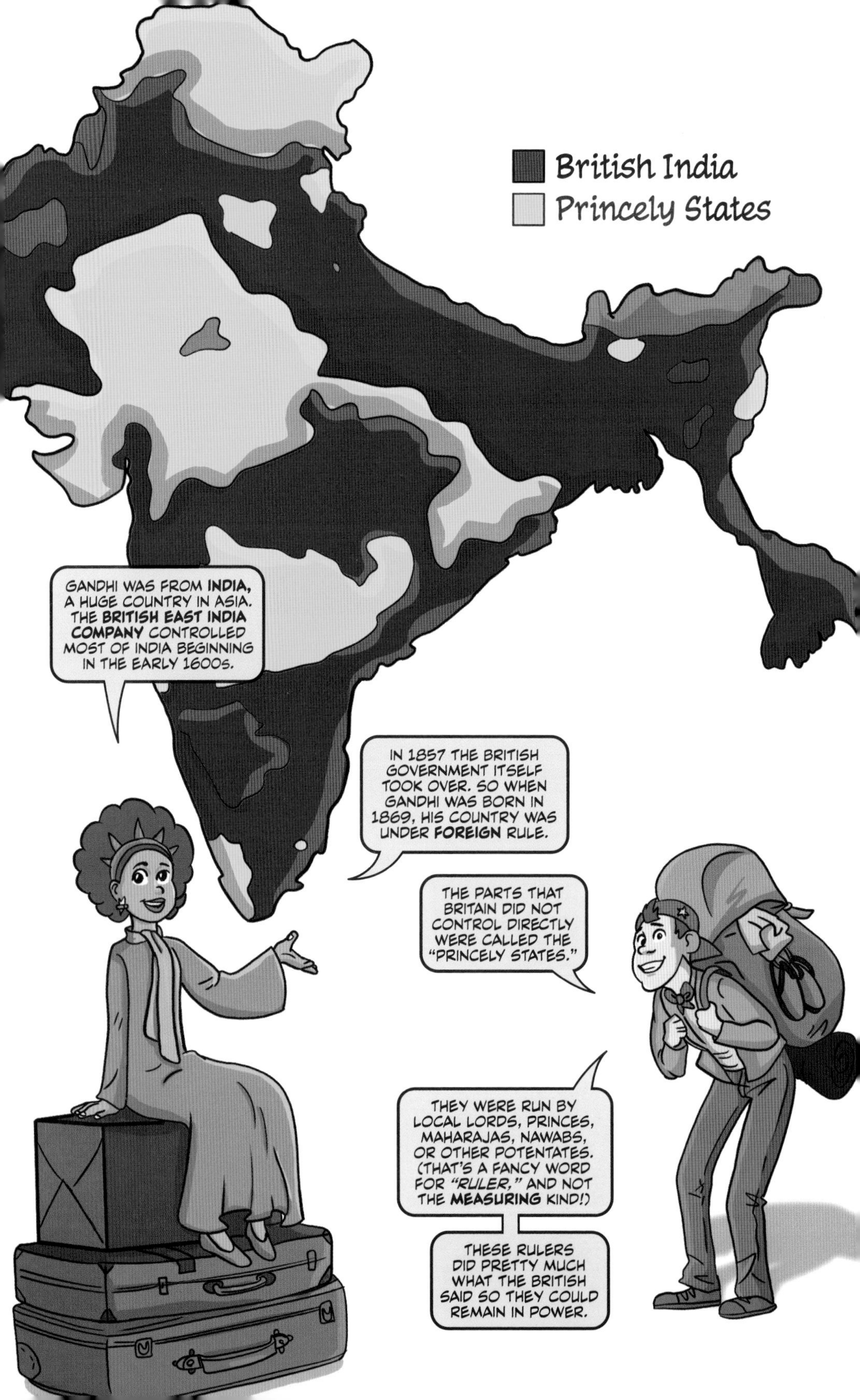
British India
Princely States
GANDHI WAS FROM INDIA, A HUGE COUNTRY IN ASIA. THE BRITISH EAST INDIA COMPANY CONTROLLED MOST OF INDIA BEGINNING IN THE EARLY 1600s.
IN 1857 THE BRITISH GOVERNMENT ITSELF TOOK OVER. SO WHEN GANDHI WAS BORN IN 1869, HIS COUNTRY WAS UNDER FOREIGN RULE.
THE PARTS THAT BRITAIN DID NOT CONTROL DIRECTLY WERE CALLED THE "PRINCELY STATES."
THEY WERE RUN BY LOCAL LORDS, PRINCES, MAHARAJAS, NAWABS, OR OTHER POTENTATES. (THAT'S A FANCY WORD FOR "RULER," AND NOT THE MEASURING KIND!)
THESE RULERS DID PRETTY MUCH WHAT THE BRITISH SAID SO THEY COULD REMAIN IN POWER.

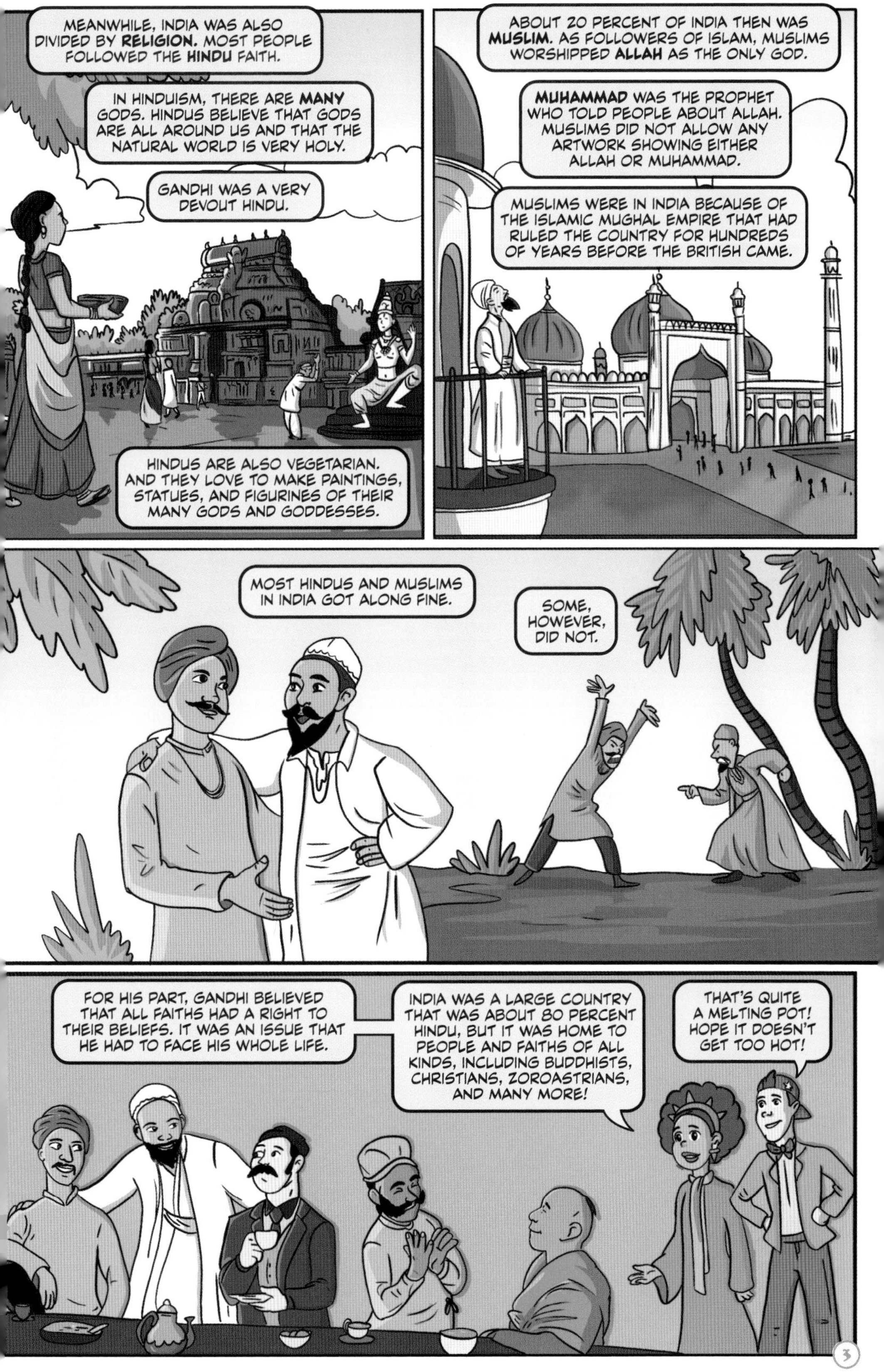
MEANWHILE, INDIA WAS ALSO DIVIDED BY **RELIGION.** MOST PEOPLE FOLLOWED THE **HINDU** FAITH.
IN HINDUISM, THERE ARE **MANY** GODS. HINDUS BELIEVE THAT GODS ARE ALL AROUND US AND THAT THE NATURAL WORLD IS VERY HOLY.
GANDHI WAS A VERY DEVOUT HINDU.
HINDUS ARE ALSO VEGETARIAN. AND THEY LOVE TO MAKE PAINTINGS, STATUES, AND FIGURINES OF THEIR MANY GODS AND GODDESSES.
ABOUT 20 PERCENT OF INDIA THEN WAS **MUSLIM.** AS FOLLOWERS OF ISLAM, MUSLIMS WORSHIPPED **ALLAH** AS THE ONLY GOD.
MUHAMMAD WAS THE PROPHET WHO TOLD PEOPLE ABOUT ALLAH. MUSLIMS DID NOT ALLOW ANY ARTWORK SHOWING EITHER ALLAH OR MUHAMMAD.
MUSLIMS WERE IN INDIA BECAUSE OF THE ISLAMIC MUGHAL EMPIRE THAT HAD RULED THE COUNTRY FOR HUNDREDS OF YEARS BEFORE THE BRITISH CAME.
MOST HINDUS AND MUSLIMS IN INDIA GOT ALONG FINE.
SOME, HOWEVER, DID NOT.
FOR HIS PART, GANDHI BELIEVED THAT ALL FAITHS HAD A RIGHT TO THEIR BELIEFS. IT WAS AN ISSUE THAT HE HAD TO FACE HIS WHOLE LIFE.
INDIA WAS A LARGE COUNTRY THAT WAS ABOUT 80 PERCENT HINDU, BUT IT WAS HOME TO PEOPLE AND FAITHS OF ALL KINDS, INCLUDING BUDDHISTS, CHRISTIANS, ZOROASTRIANS, AND MANY MORE!
THAT'S QUITE A MELTING POT! HOPE IT DOESN'T GET TOO HOT!

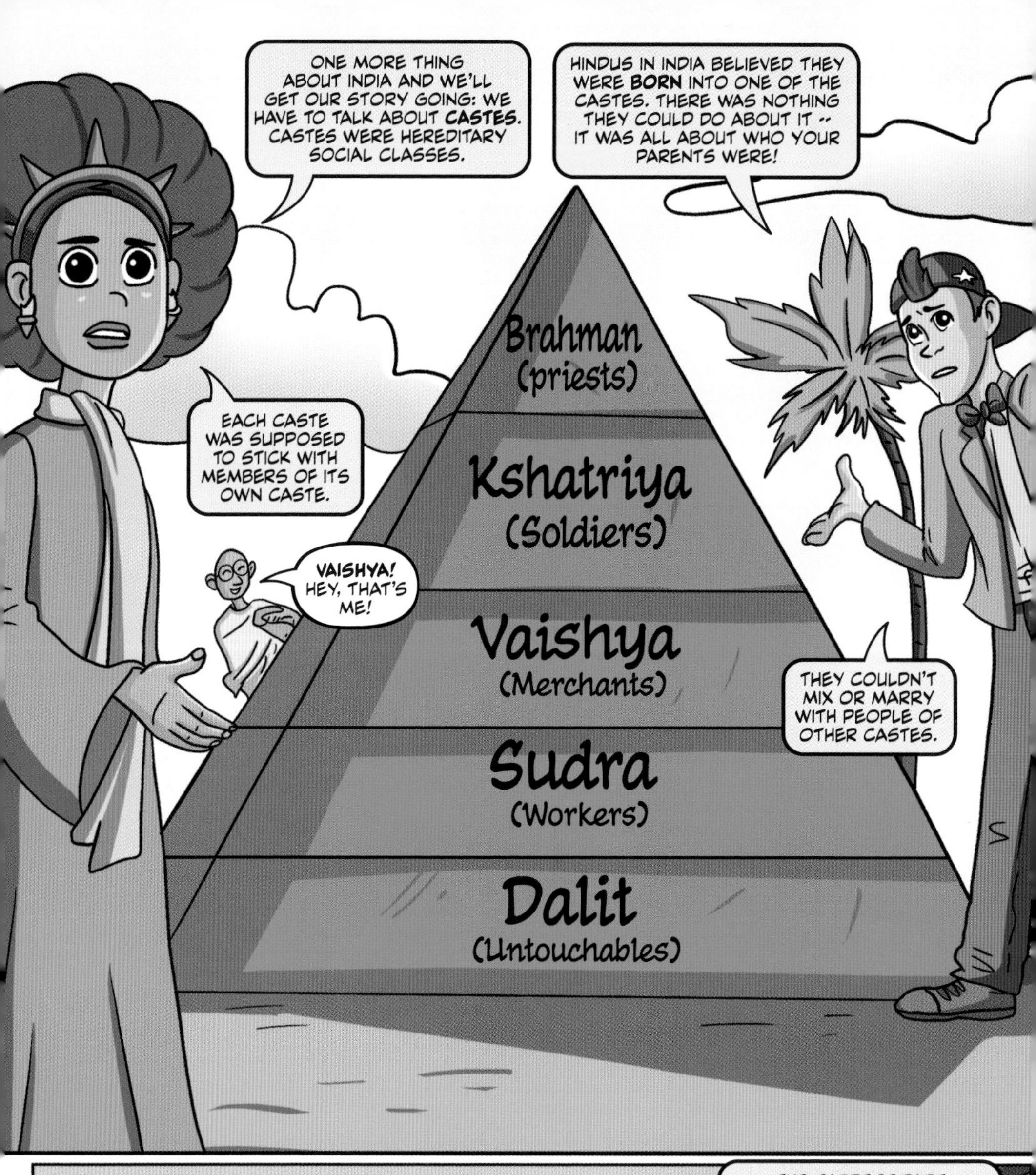
ONE MORE THING ABOUT INDIA AND WE'LL GET OUR STORY GOING: WE HAVE TO TALK ABOUT **CASTES**. CASTES WERE HEREDITARY SOCIAL CLASSES.
HINDUS IN INDIA BELIEVED THEY WERE **BORN** INTO ONE OF THE CASTES. THERE WAS NOTHING THEY COULD DO ABOUT IT -- IT WAS ALL ABOUT WHO YOUR PARENTS WERE!
Brahman (priests)
Kshatriya (Soldiers)
Vaishya (Merchants)
Sudra (Workers)
Dalit (Untouchables)
EACH CASTE WAS SUPPOSED TO STICK WITH MEMBERS OF ITS OWN CASTE.
VAISHYA! HEY, THAT'S ME!
THEY COULDN'T MIX OR MARRY WITH PEOPLE OF OTHER CASTES.

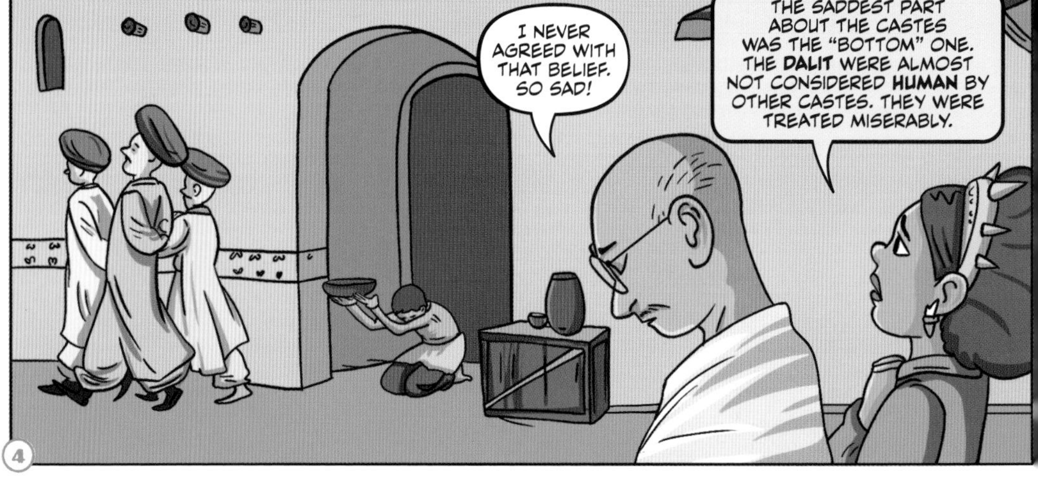
I NEVER AGREED WITH THAT BELIEF. SO SAD!
THE SADDEST PART ABOUT THE CASTES WAS THE "BOTTOM" ONE. THE **DALIT** WERE ALMOST NOT CONSIDERED **HUMAN** BY OTHER CASTES. THEY WERE TREATED MISERABLY.

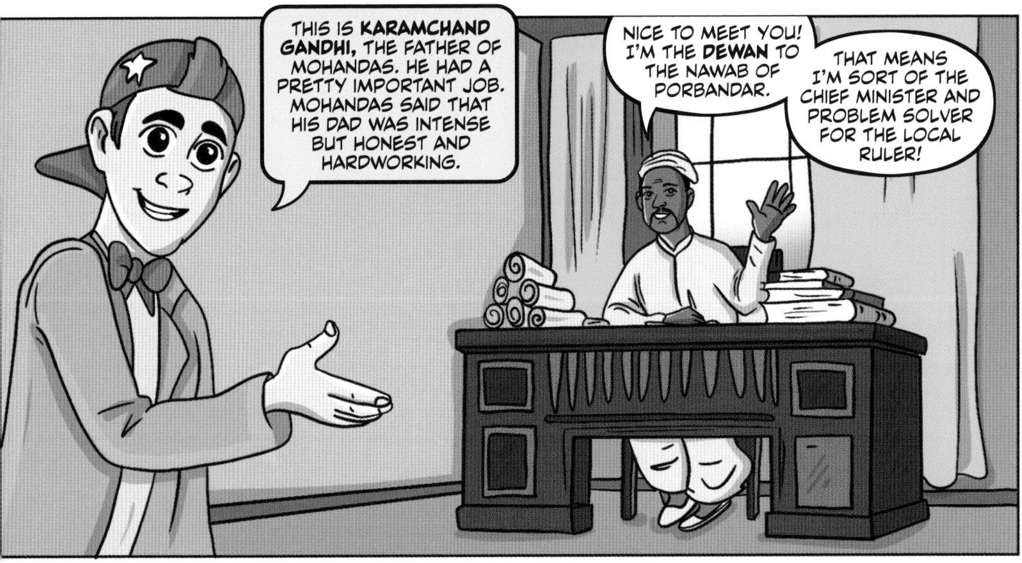
THIS IS **KARAMCHAND GANDHI,** THE FATHER OF MOHANDAS. HE HAD A PRETTY IMPORTANT JOB. MOHANDAS SAID THAT HIS DAD WAS INTENSE BUT HONEST AND HARDWORKING.
NICE TO MEET YOU! I'M THE **DEWAN** TO THE NAWAB OF PORBANDAR.
THAT MEANS I'M SORT OF THE CHIEF MINISTER AND PROBLEM SOLVER FOR THE LOCAL RULER!

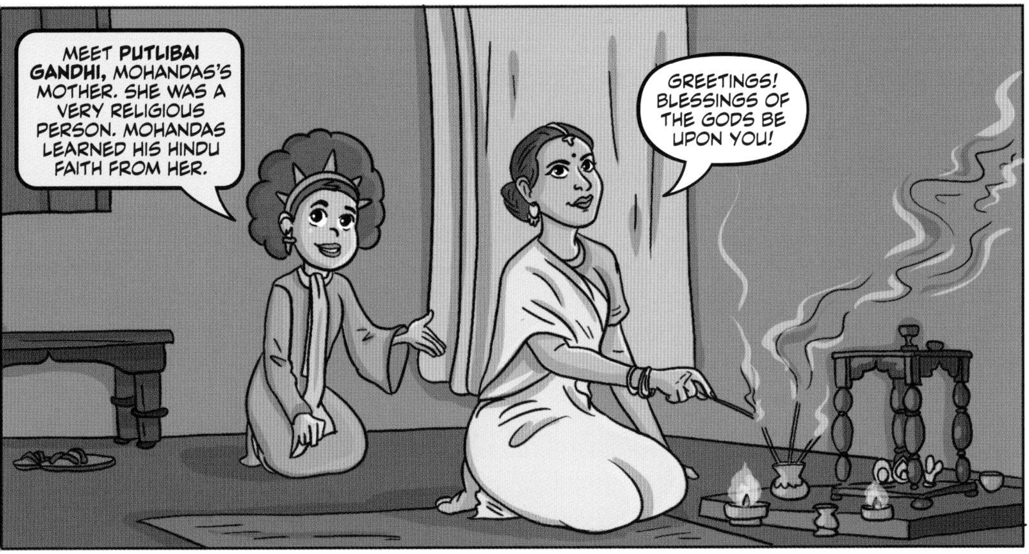
MEET **PUTLIBAI GANDHI,** MOHANDAS'S MOTHER. SHE WAS A VERY RELIGIOUS PERSON. MOHANDAS LEARNED HIS HINDU FAITH FROM HER.
GREETINGS! BLESSINGS OF THE GODS BE UPON YOU!

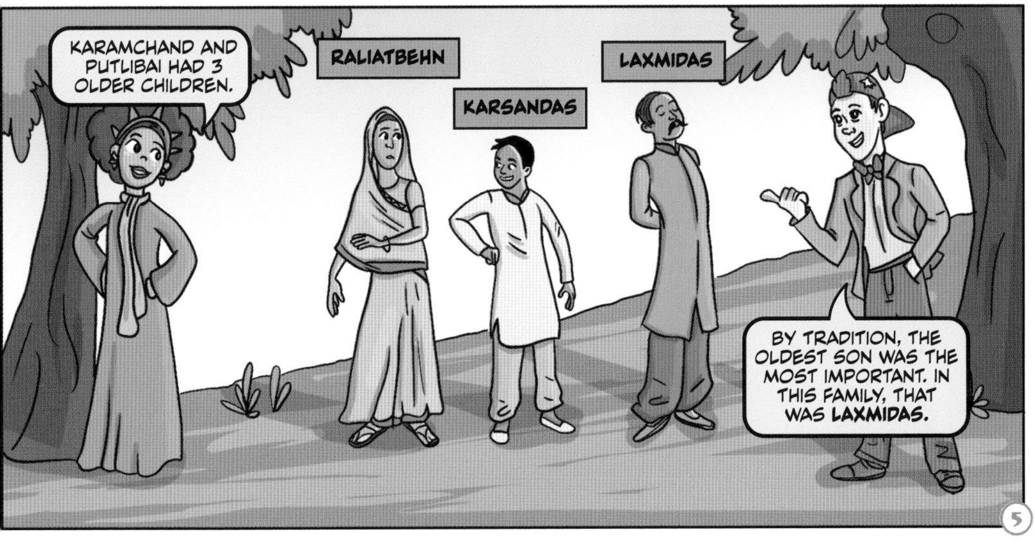
KARAMCHAND AND PUTLIBAI HAD 3 OLDER CHILDREN.
RALIATBEHN
KARSANDAS
LAXMIDAS
BY TRADITION, THE OLDEST SON WAS THE MOST IMPORTANT. IN THIS FAMILY, THAT WAS **LAXMIDAS.**

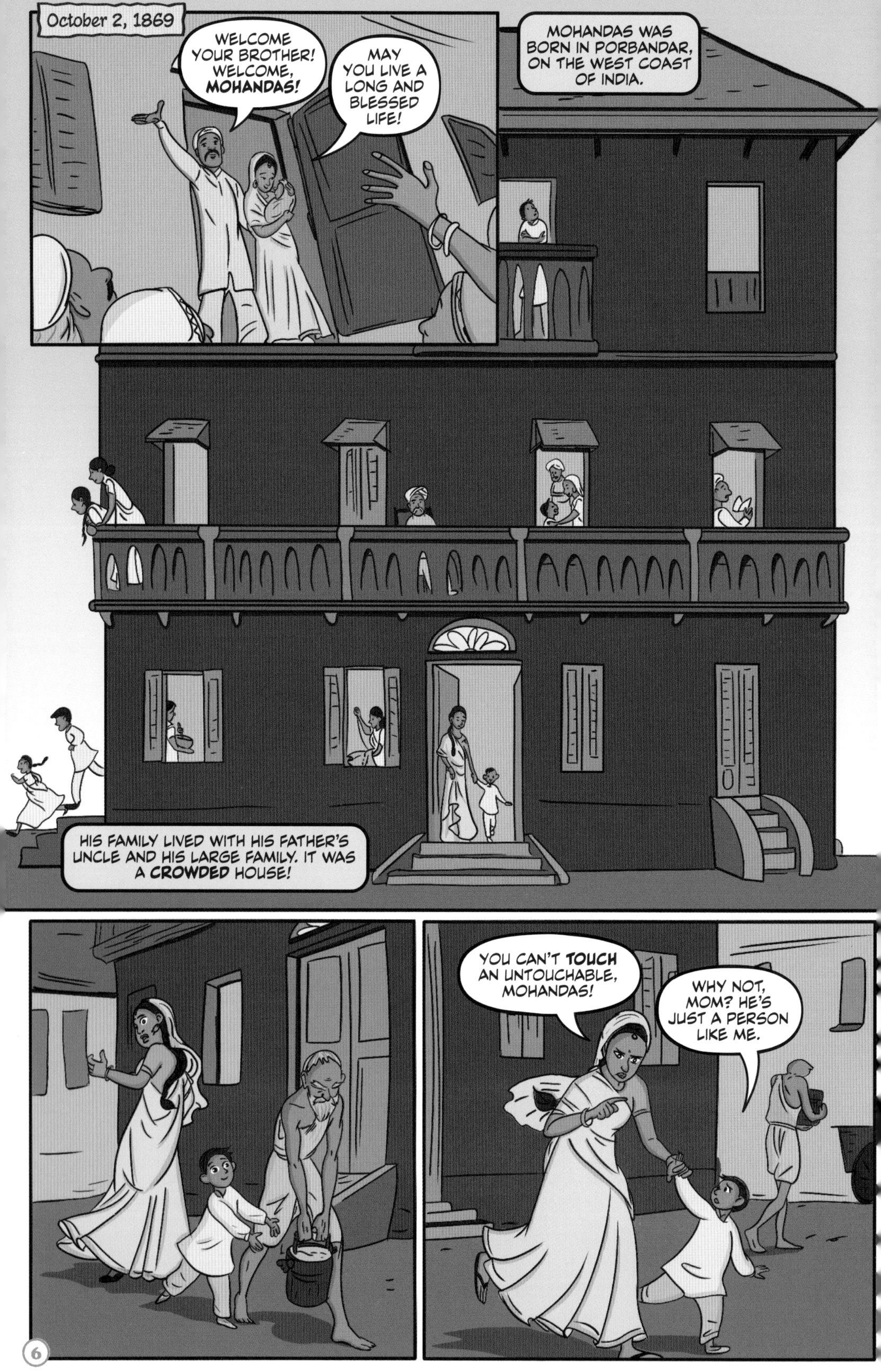
October 2, 1869
WELCOME YOUR BROTHER! WELCOME, **MOHANDAS!**
MAY YOU LIVE A LONG AND BLESSED LIFE!
MOHANDAS WAS BORN IN PORBANDAR, ON THE WEST COAST OF INDIA.
HIS FAMILY LIVED WITH HIS FATHER'S UNCLE AND HIS LARGE FAMILY. IT WAS A **CROWDED** HOUSE!
YOU CAN'T **TOUCH** AN UNTOUCHABLE, MOHANDAS!
WHY NOT, MOM? HE'S JUST A PERSON LIKE ME.

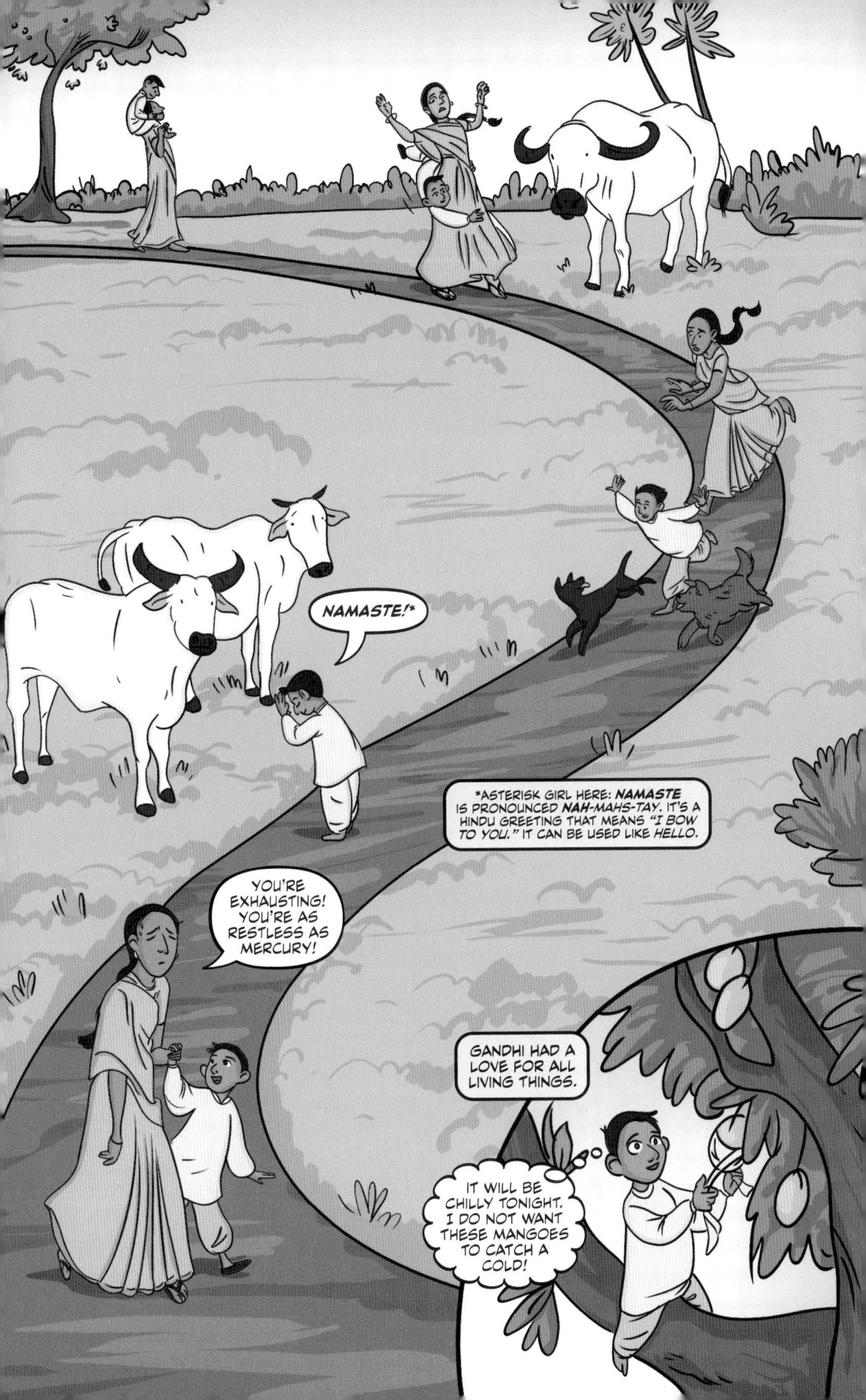
NAMASTE!*
*ASTERISK GIRL HERE: NAMASTE IS PRONOUNCED NAH-MAHS-TAY. IT'S A HINDU GREETING THAT MEANS "I BOW TO YOU." IT CAN BE USED LIKE HELLO.
YOU'RE EXHAUSTING! YOU'RE AS RESTLESS AS MERCURY!
GANDHI HAD A LOVE FOR ALL LIVING THINGS.
IT WILL BE CHILLY TONIGHT. I DO NOT WANT THESE MANGOES TO CATCH A COLD!

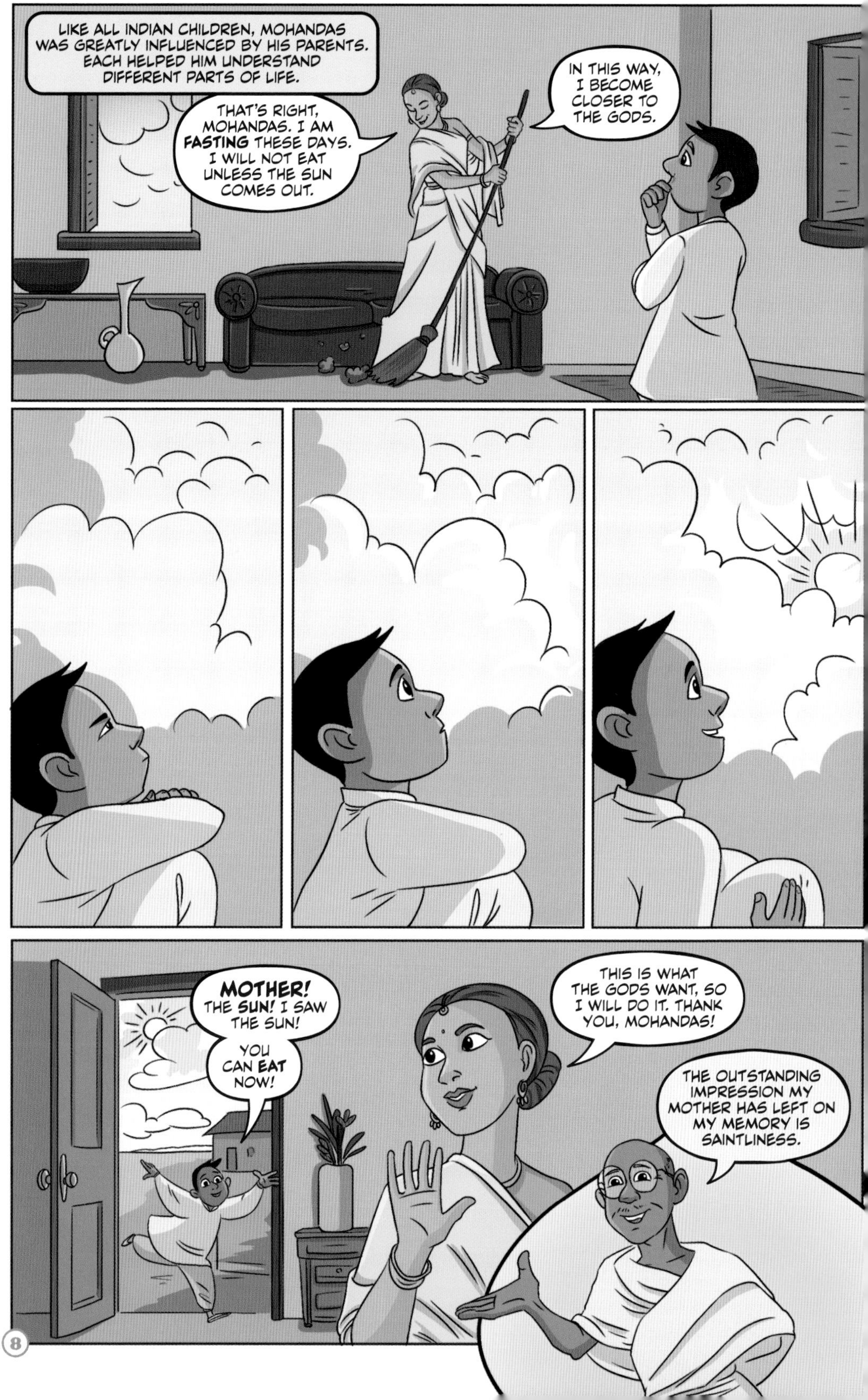

LIKE ALL INDIAN CHILDREN, MOHANDAS WAS GREATLY INFLUENCED BY HIS PARENTS. EACH HELPED HIM UNDERSTAND DIFFERENT PARTS OF LIFE.
THAT'S RIGHT, MOHANDAS. I AM **FASTING** THESE DAYS. I WILL NOT EAT UNLESS THE SUN COMES OUT.
IN THIS WAY, I BECOME CLOSER TO THE GODS.
MOTHER! THE **SUN!** I SAW THE SUN!
YOU CAN **EAT** NOW!
THIS IS WHAT THE GODS WANT, SO I WILL DO IT. THANK YOU, MOHANDAS!
THE OUTSTANDING IMPRESSION MY MOTHER HAS LEFT ON MY MEMORY IS SAINTLINESS.

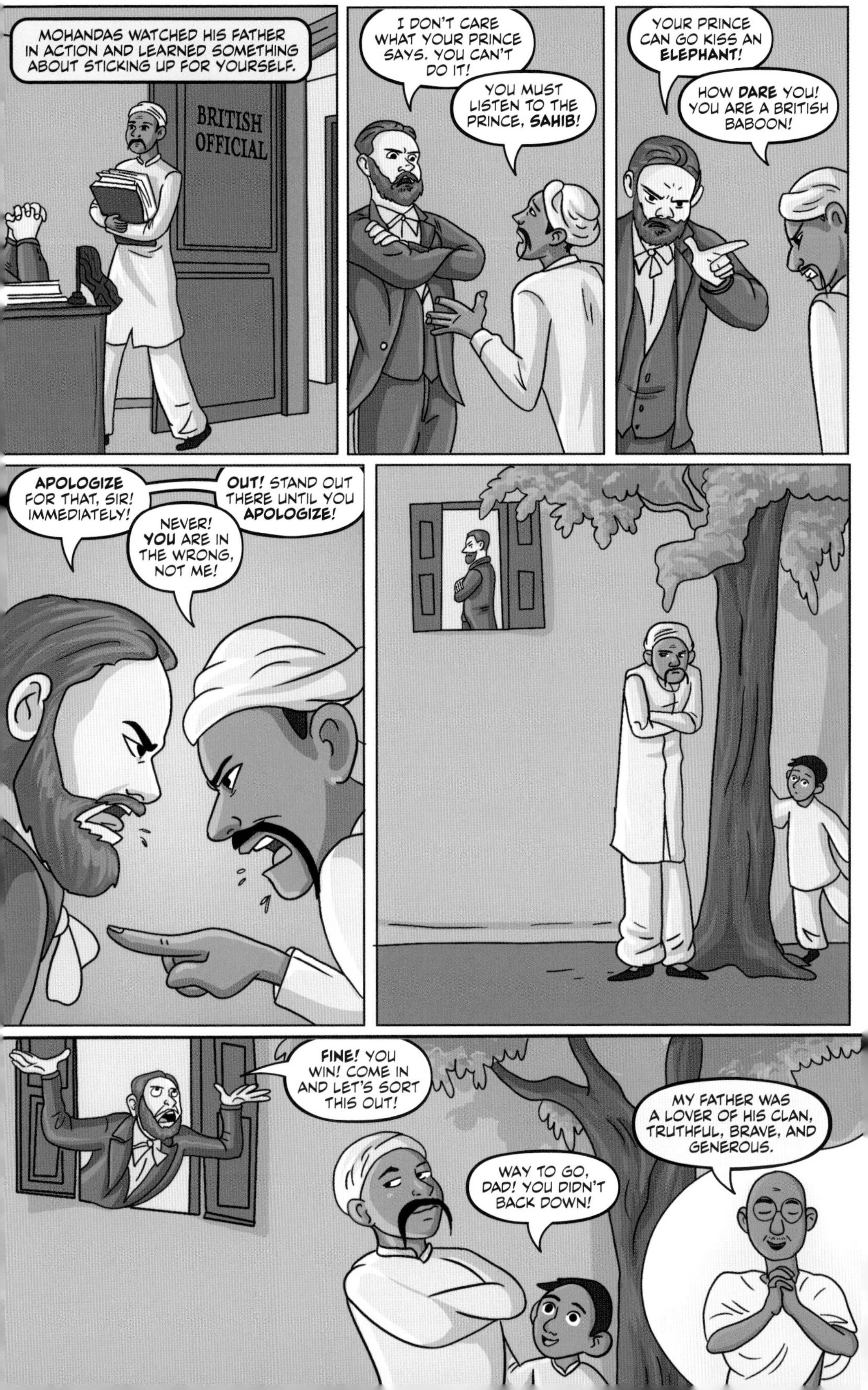
MOHANDAS WATCHED HIS FATHER IN ACTION AND LEARNED SOMETHING ABOUT STICKING UP FOR YOURSELF.
BRITISH OFFICIAL
I DON'T CARE WHAT YOUR PRINCE SAYS. YOU CAN'T DO IT!
YOU MUST LISTEN TO THE PRINCE, SAHIB!
YOUR PRINCE CAN GO KISS AN ELEPHANT!
HOW DARE YOU! YOU ARE A BRITISH BABOON!
APOLOGIZE FOR THAT, SIR! IMMEDIATELY!
NEVER! YOU ARE IN THE WRONG, NOT ME!
OUT! STAND OUT THERE UNTIL YOU APOLOGIZE!
FINE! YOU WIN! COME IN AND LET'S SORT THIS OUT!
WAY TO GO, DAD! YOU DIDN'T BACK DOWN!
MY FATHER WAS A LOVER OF HIS CLAN, TRUTHFUL, BRAVE, AND GENEROUS.

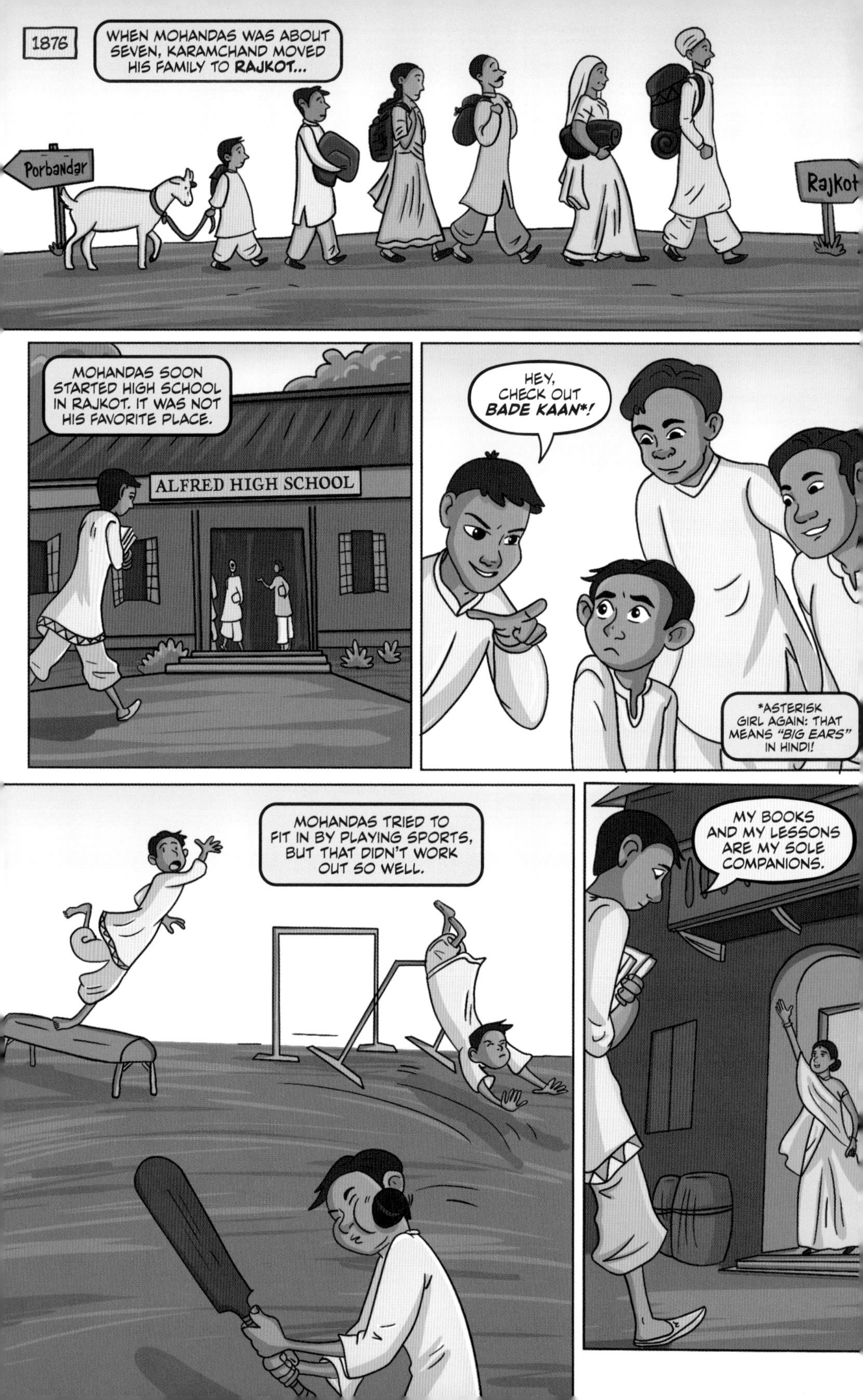
1876
WHEN MOHANDAS WAS ABOUT SEVEN, KARAMCHAND MOVED HIS FAMILY TO **RAJKOT...**
Porbandar
Rajkot
MOHANDAS SOON STARTED HIGH SCHOOL IN RAJKOT. IT WAS NOT HIS FAVORITE PLACE.
ALFRED HIGH SCHOOL
HEY, CHECK OUT ***BADE KAAN*!***
*ASTERISK GIRL AGAIN: THAT MEANS *"BIG EARS"* IN HINDI!
MOHANDAS TRIED TO FIT IN BY PLAYING SPORTS, BUT THAT DIDN'T WORK OUT SO WELL.
MY BOOKS AND MY LESSONS ARE MY SOLE COMPANIONS.

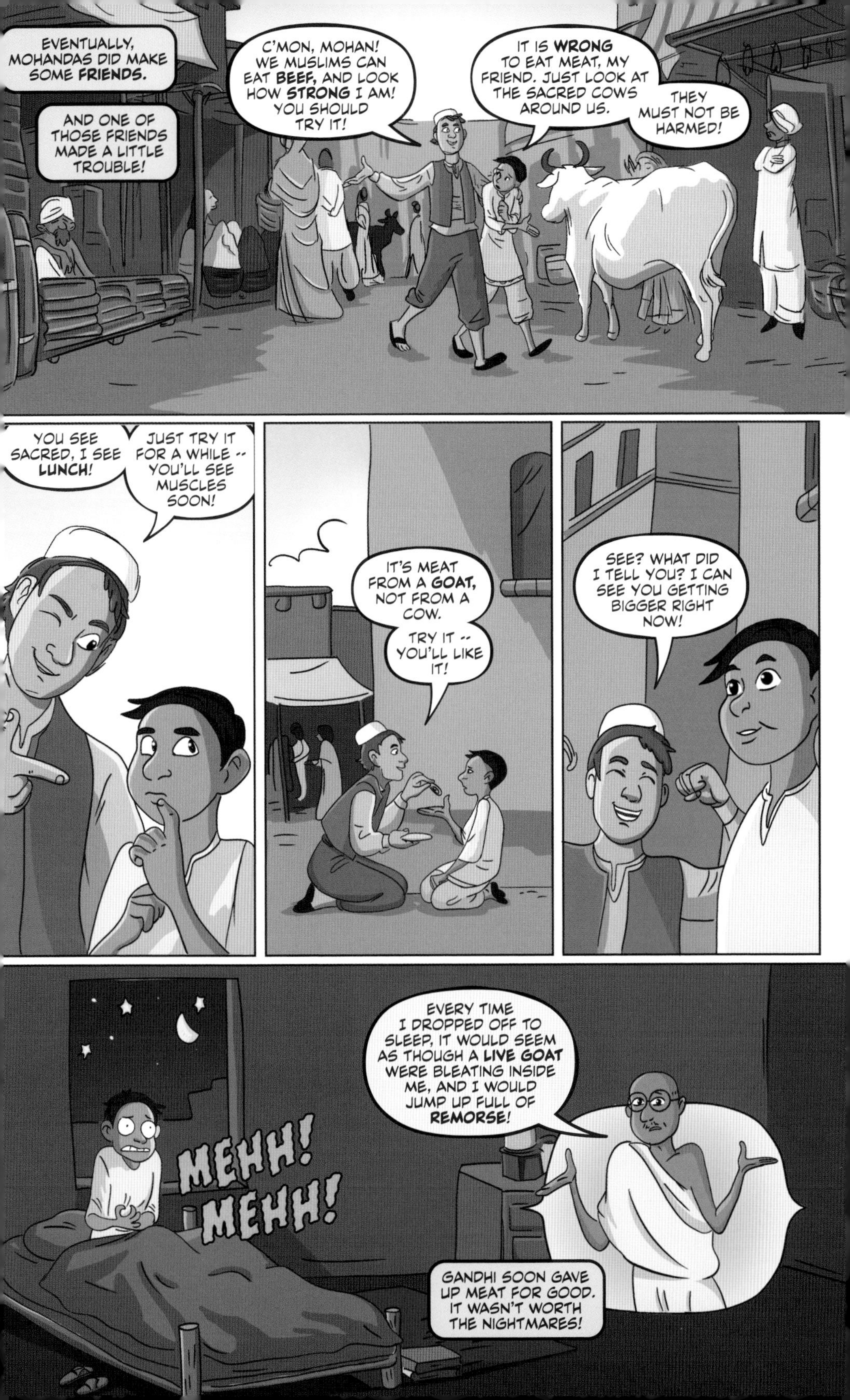

EVENTUALLY, MOHANDAS DID MAKE SOME FRIENDS.
AND ONE OF THOSE FRIENDS MADE A LITTLE TROUBLE!
C'MON, MOHAN! WE MUSLIMS CAN EAT BEEF, AND LOOK HOW STRONG I AM! YOU SHOULD TRY IT!
IT IS WRONG TO EAT MEAT, MY FRIEND. JUST LOOK AT THE SACRED COWS AROUND US.
THEY MUST NOT BE HARMED!
YOU SEE SACRED, I SEE LUNCH!
JUST TRY IT FOR A WHILE -- YOU'LL SEE MUSCLES SOON!
IT'S MEAT FROM A GOAT, NOT FROM A COW.
TRY IT -- YOU'LL LIKE IT!
SEE? WHAT DID I TELL YOU? I CAN SEE YOU GETTING BIGGER RIGHT NOW!
EVERY TIME I DROPPED OFF TO SLEEP, IT WOULD SEEM AS THOUGH A LIVE GOAT WERE BLEATING INSIDE ME, AND I WOULD JUMP UP FULL OF REMORSE!
MEHH! MEHH!
GANDHI SOON GAVE UP MEAT FOR GOOD. IT WASN'T WORTH THE NIGHTMARES!

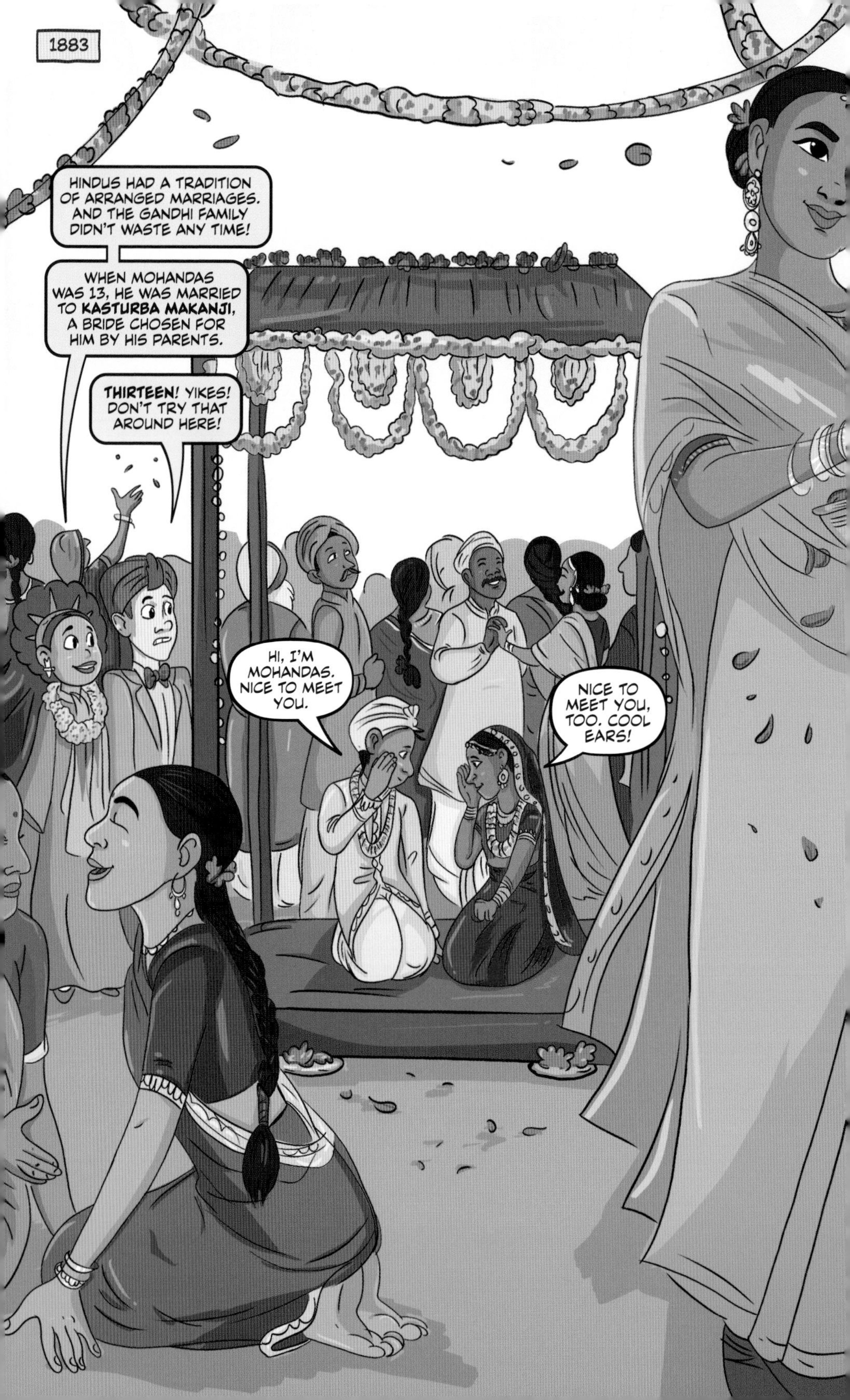
1883
HINDUS HAD A TRADITION OF ARRANGED MARRIAGES. AND THE GANDHI FAMILY DIDN'T WASTE ANY TIME!
WHEN MOHANDAS WAS 13, HE WAS MARRIED TO **KASTURBA MAKANJI**, A BRIDE CHOSEN FOR HIM BY HIS PARENTS.
THIRTEEN! YIKES! DON'T TRY THAT AROUND HERE!
HI, I'M MOHANDAS. NICE TO MEET YOU.
NICE TO MEET YOU, TOO. COOL EARS!

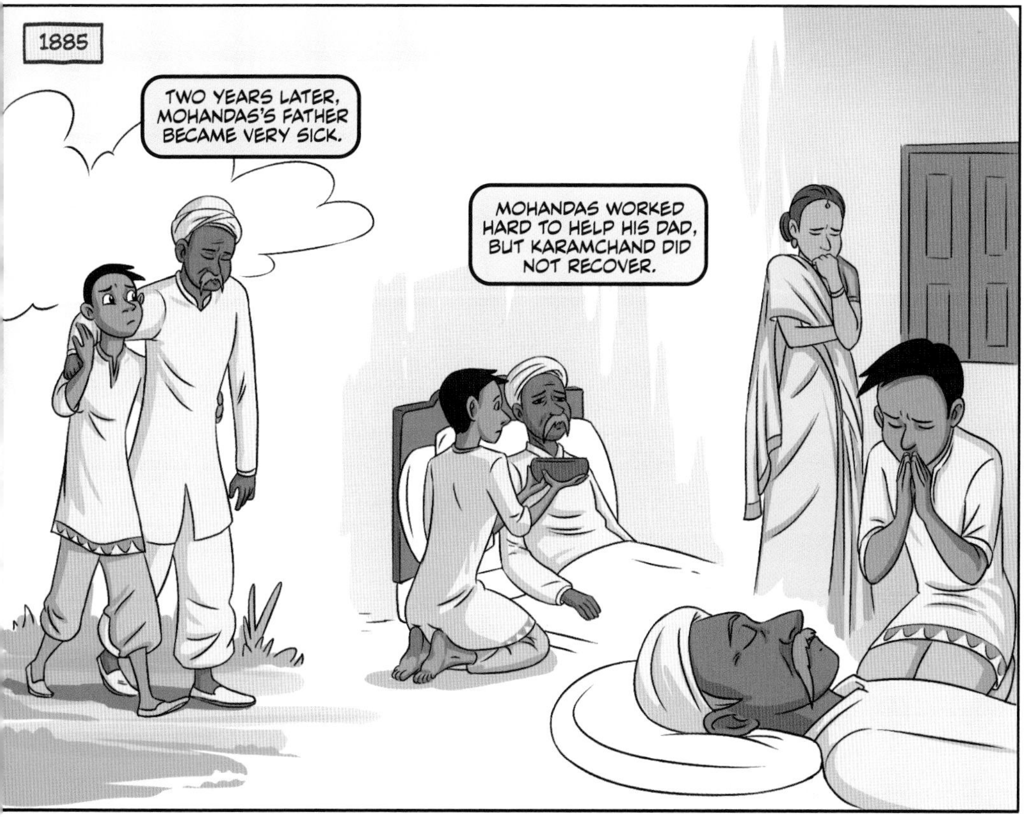
1885
TWO YEARS LATER, MOHANDAS'S FATHER BECAME VERY SICK.
MOHANDAS WORKED HARD TO HELP HIS DAD, BUT KARAMCHAND DID NOT RECOVER.

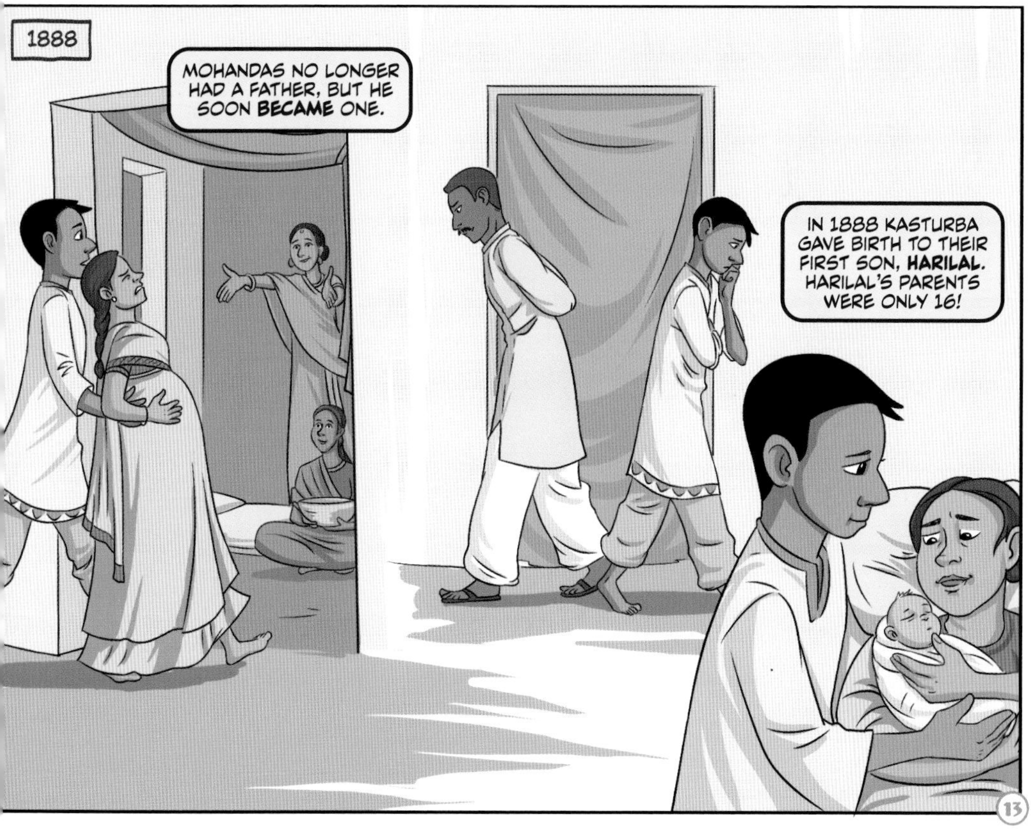
1888
MOHANDAS NO LONGER HAD A FATHER, BUT HE SOON BECAME ONE.
IN 1888 KASTURBA GAVE BIRTH TO THEIR FIRST SON, HARILAL. HARILAL'S PARENTS WERE ONLY 16!

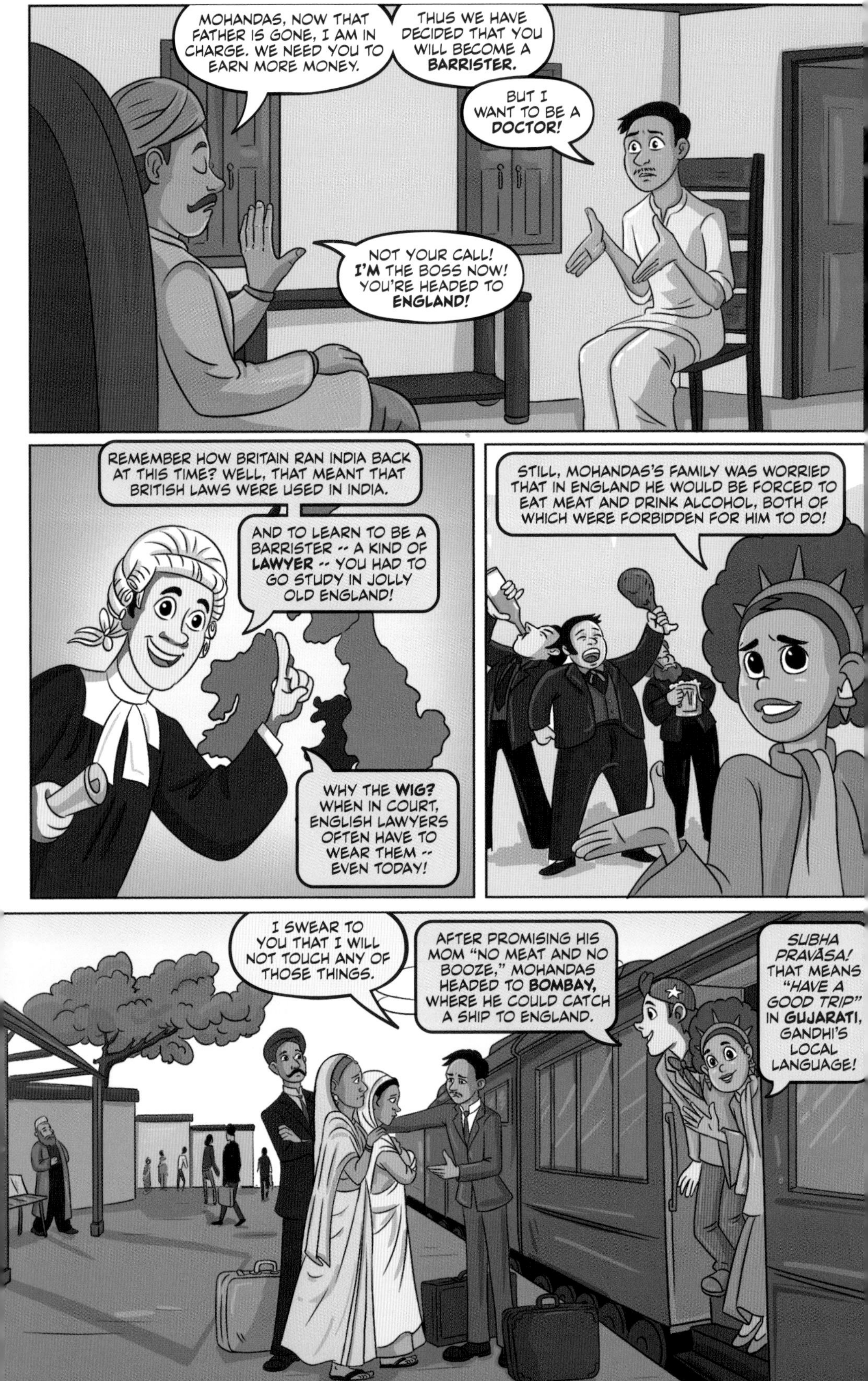
MOHANDAS, NOW THAT FATHER IS GONE, I AM IN CHARGE. WE NEED YOU TO EARN MORE MONEY.
THUS WE HAVE DECIDED THAT YOU WILL BECOME A BARRISTER.
BUT I WANT TO BE A DOCTOR!
NOT YOUR CALL! I'M THE BOSS NOW! YOU'RE HEADED TO ENGLAND!
REMEMBER HOW BRITAIN RAN INDIA BACK AT THIS TIME? WELL, THAT MEANT THAT BRITISH LAWS WERE USED IN INDIA.
AND TO LEARN TO BE A BARRISTER -- A KIND OF LAWYER -- YOU HAD TO GO STUDY IN JOLLY OLD ENGLAND!
WHY THE WIG? WHEN IN COURT, ENGLISH LAWYERS OFTEN HAVE TO WEAR THEM -- EVEN TODAY!
STILL, MOHANDAS'S FAMILY WAS WORRIED THAT IN ENGLAND HE WOULD BE FORCED TO EAT MEAT AND DRINK ALCOHOL, BOTH OF WHICH WERE FORBIDDEN FOR HIM TO DO!
I SWEAR TO YOU THAT I WILL NOT TOUCH ANY OF THOSE THINGS.
AFTER PROMISING HIS MOM "NO MEAT AND NO BOOZE," MOHANDAS HEADED TO BOMBAY, WHERE HE COULD CATCH A SHIP TO ENGLAND.
SUBHA PRAVĀSA! THAT MEANS "HAVE A GOOD TRIP" IN GUJARATI, GANDHI'S LOCAL LANGUAGE!

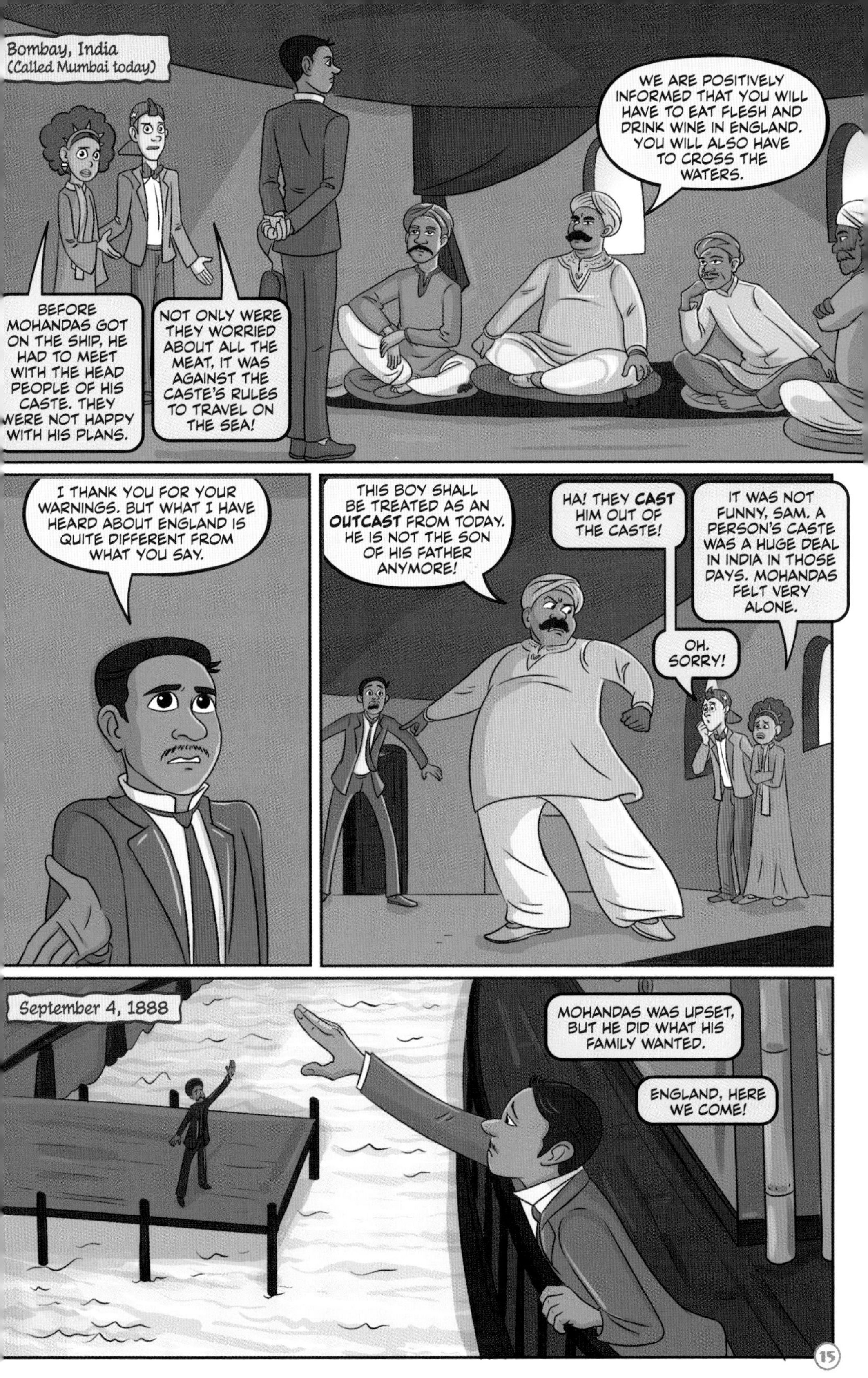
Bombay, India
(Called Mumbai today)
WE ARE POSITIVELY INFORMED THAT YOU WILL HAVE TO EAT FLESH AND DRINK WINE IN ENGLAND. YOU WILL ALSO HAVE TO CROSS THE WATERS.
BEFORE MOHANDAS GOT ON THE SHIP, HE HAD TO MEET WITH THE HEAD PEOPLE OF HIS CASTE. THEY WERE NOT HAPPY WITH HIS PLANS.
NOT ONLY WERE THEY WORRIED ABOUT ALL THE MEAT, IT WAS AGAINST THE CASTE'S RULES TO TRAVEL ON THE SEA!
I THANK YOU FOR YOUR WARNINGS. BUT WHAT I HAVE HEARD ABOUT ENGLAND IS QUITE DIFFERENT FROM WHAT YOU SAY.
THIS BOY SHALL BE TREATED AS AN **OUTCAST** FROM TODAY. HE IS NOT THE SON OF HIS FATHER ANYMORE!
HA! THEY **CAST** HIM OUT OF THE CASTE!
IT WAS NOT FUNNY, SAM. A PERSON'S CASTE WAS A HUGE DEAL IN INDIA IN THOSE DAYS. MOHANDAS FELT VERY ALONE.
OH. SORRY!
September 4, 1888
MOHANDAS WAS UPSET, BUT HE DID WHAT HIS FAMILY WANTED.
ENGLAND, HERE WE COME!

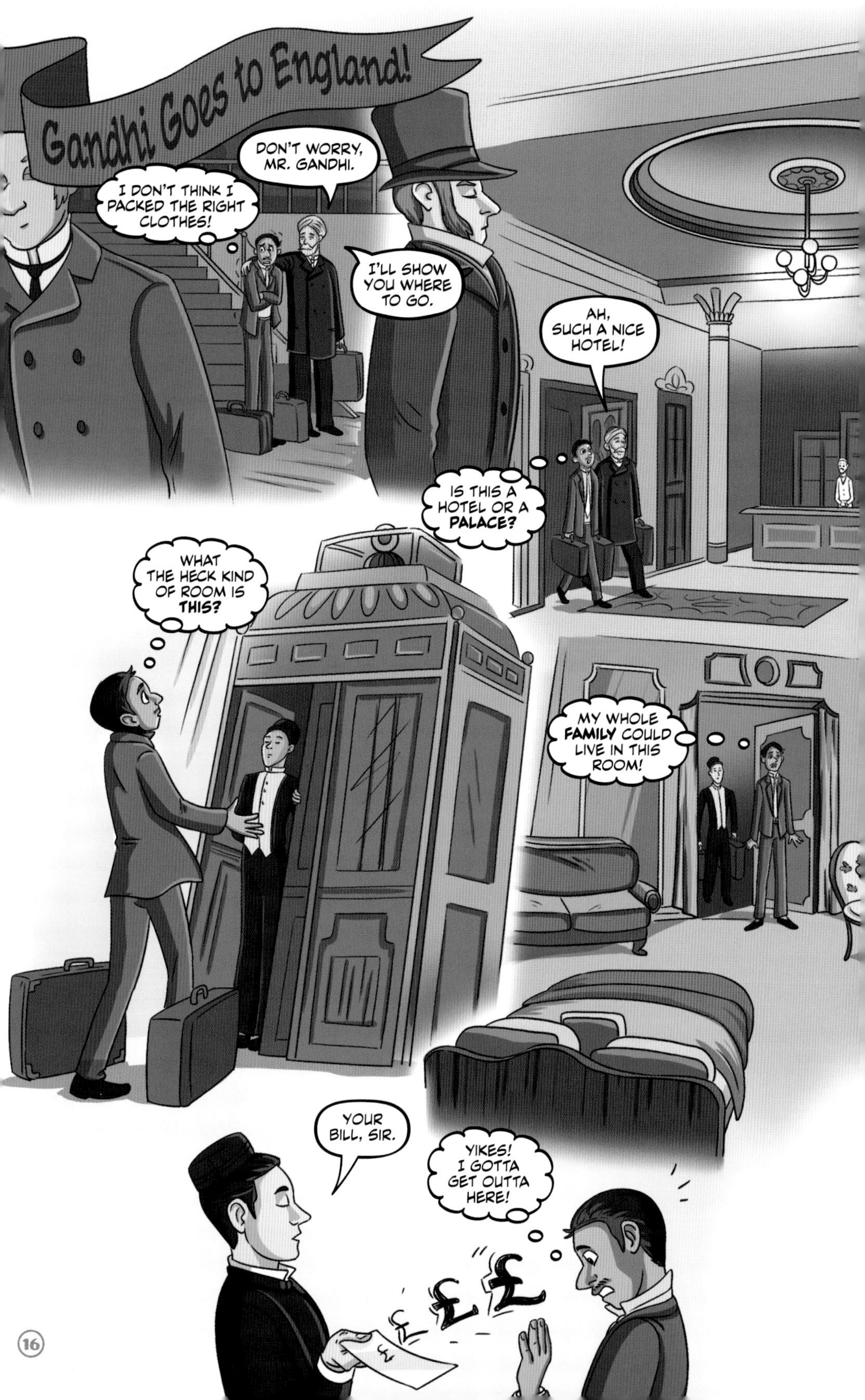
Gandhi Goes to England!
I DON'T THINK I PACKED THE RIGHT CLOTHES!
DON'T WORRY, MR. GANDHI.
I'LL SHOW YOU WHERE TO GO.
AH, SUCH A NICE HOTEL!
IS THIS A HOTEL OR A PALACE?
WHAT THE HECK KIND OF ROOM IS THIS?
MY WHOLE FAMILY COULD LIVE IN THIS ROOM!
YOUR BILL, SIR.
YIKES! I GOTTA GET OUTTA HERE!

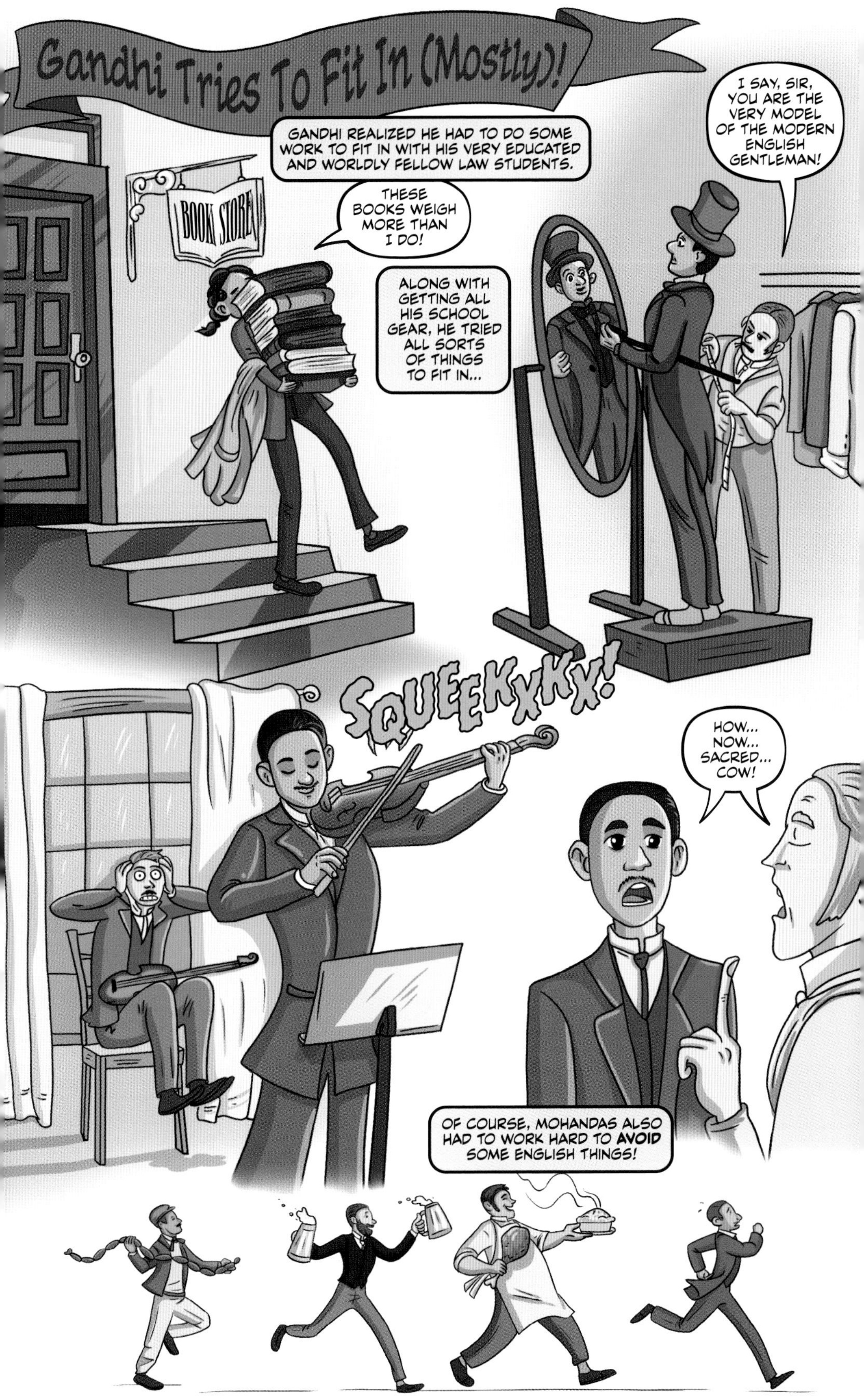

Gandhi Tries To Fit In (Mostly)!
GANDHI REALIZED HE HAD TO DO SOME WORK TO FIT IN WITH HIS VERY EDUCATED AND WORLDLY FELLOW LAW STUDENTS.
BOOK STORE
THESE BOOKS WEIGH MORE THAN I DO!
ALONG WITH GETTING ALL HIS SCHOOL GEAR, HE TRIED ALL SORTS OF THINGS TO FIT IN...
I SAY, SIR, YOU ARE THE VERY MODEL OF THE MODERN ENGLISH GENTLEMAN!
SQUEEKXKX!
HOW... NOW... SACRED... COW!
OF COURSE, MOHANDAS ALSO HAD TO WORK HARD TO **AVOID** SOME ENGLISH THINGS!

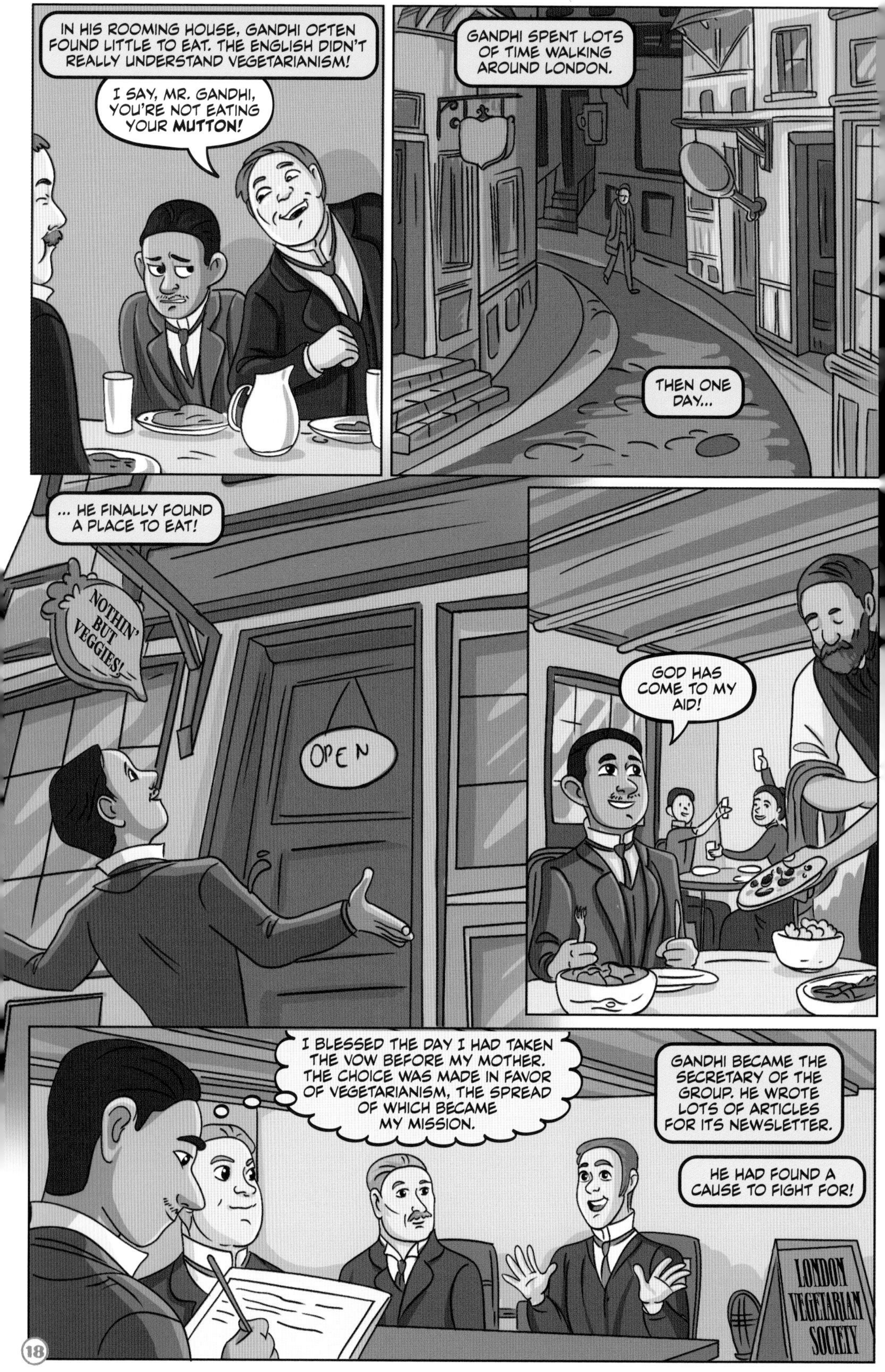
IN HIS ROOMING HOUSE, GANDHI OFTEN FOUND LITTLE TO EAT. THE ENGLISH DIDN'T REALLY UNDERSTAND VEGETARIANISM!
I SAY, MR. GANDHI, YOU'RE NOT EATING YOUR **MUTTON**!
GANDHI SPENT LOTS OF TIME WALKING AROUND LONDON.
THEN ONE DAY...
... HE FINALLY FOUND A PLACE TO EAT!
NOTHIN' BUT VEGGIES!
OPEN
GOD HAS COME TO MY AID!
I BLESSED THE DAY I HAD TAKEN THE VOW BEFORE MY MOTHER. THE CHOICE WAS MADE IN FAVOR OF VEGETARIANISM, THE SPREAD OF WHICH BECAME MY MISSION.
GANDHI BECAME THE SECRETARY OF THE GROUP. HE WROTE LOTS OF ARTICLES FOR ITS NEWSLETTER.
HE HAD FOUND A CAUSE TO FIGHT FOR!
LONDON VEGETARIAN SOCIETY

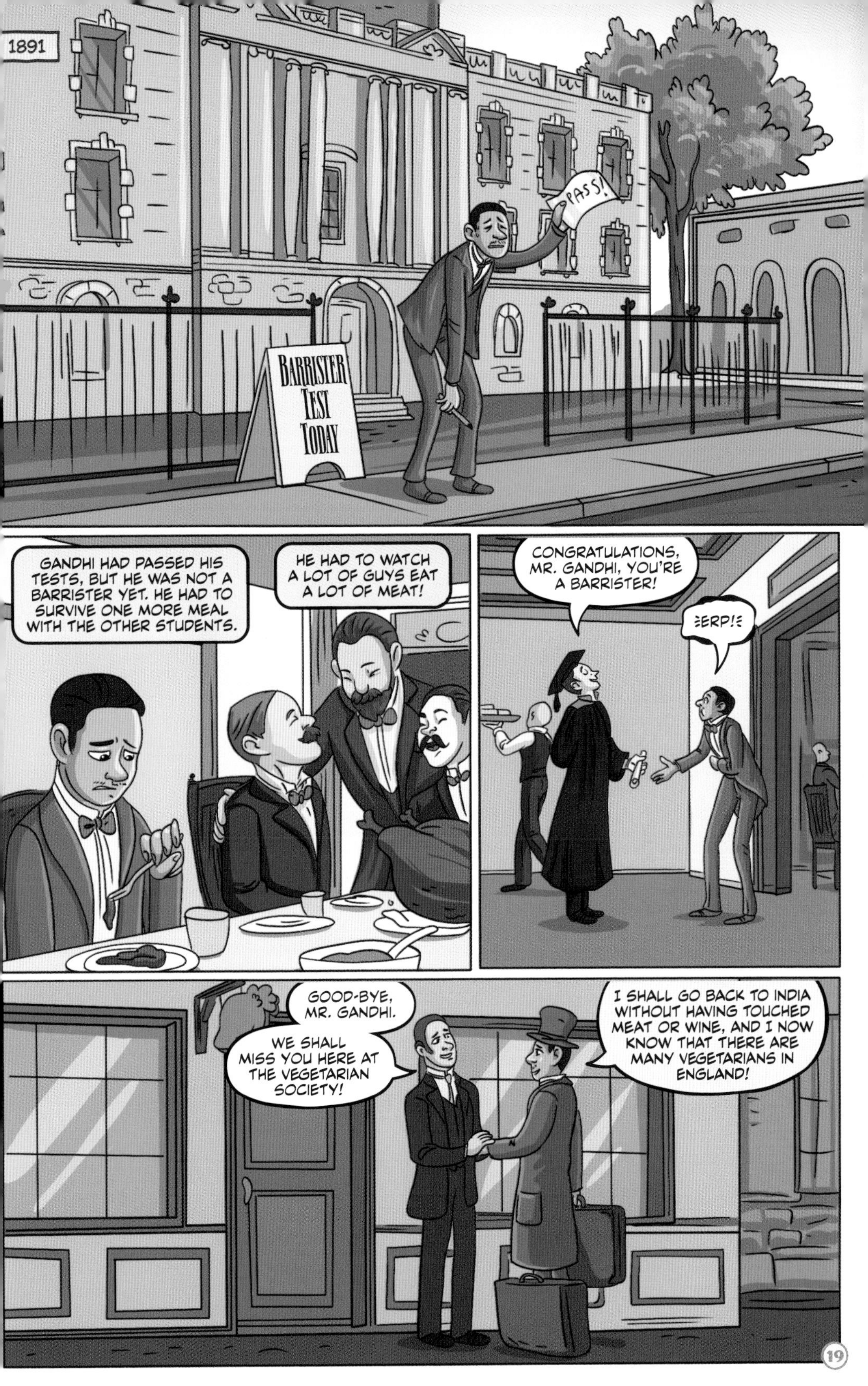
1891
PASS!
BARRISTER TEST TODAY
GANDHI HAD PASSED HIS TESTS, BUT HE WAS NOT A BARRISTER YET. HE HAD TO SURVIVE ONE MORE MEAL WITH THE OTHER STUDENTS.
HE HAD TO WATCH A LOT OF GUYS EAT A LOT OF MEAT!
CONGRATULATIONS, MR. GANDHI, YOU'RE A BARRISTER!
ERP!
GOOD-BYE, MR. GANDHI.
WE SHALL MISS YOU HERE AT THE VEGETARIAN SOCIETY!
I SHALL GO BACK TO INDIA WITHOUT HAVING TOUCHED MEAT OR WINE, AND I NOW KNOW THAT THERE ARE MANY VEGETARIANS IN ENGLAND!

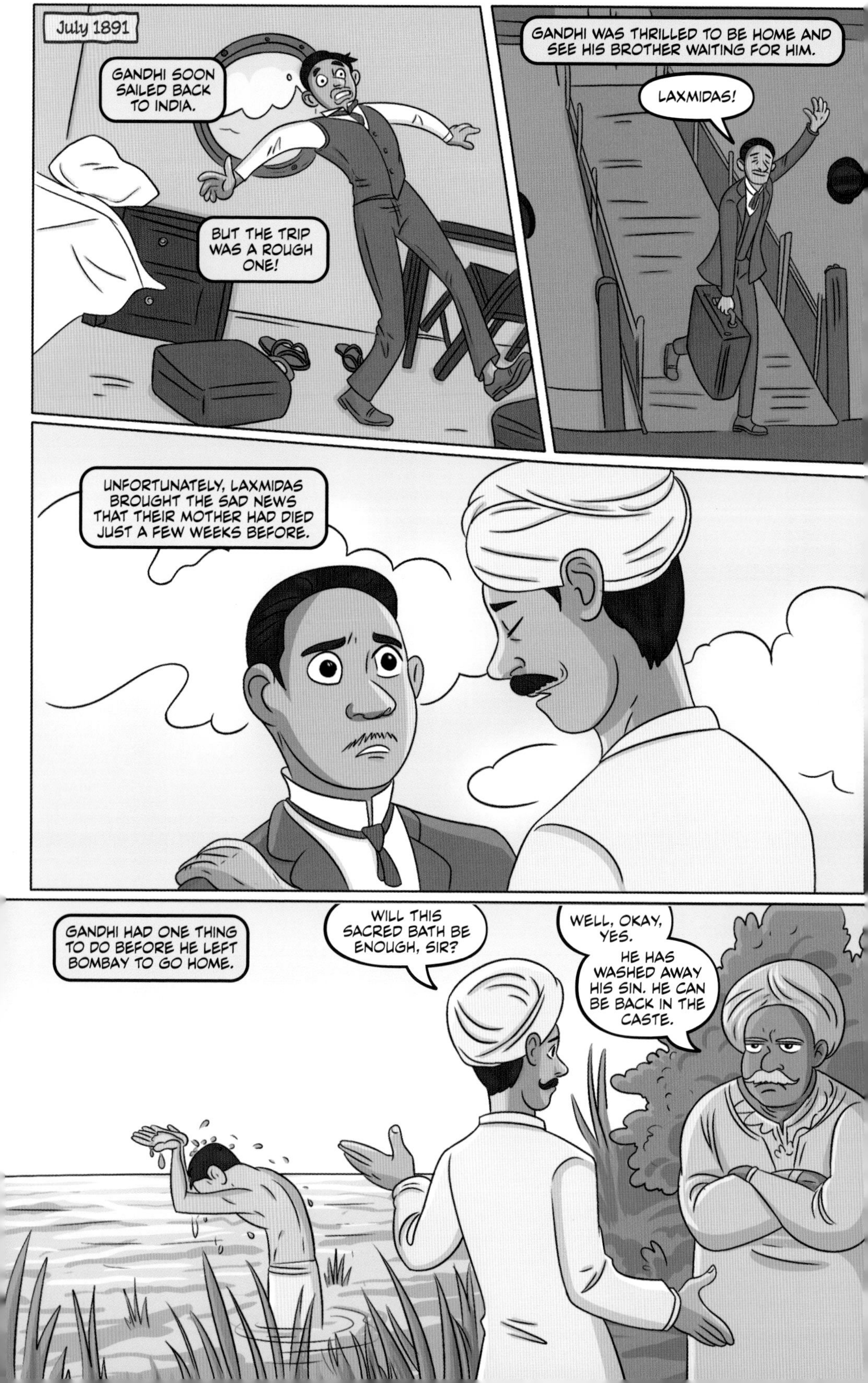
July 1891
GANDHI SOON SAILED BACK TO INDIA.
BUT THE TRIP WAS A ROUGH ONE!
GANDHI WAS THRILLED TO BE HOME AND SEE HIS BROTHER WAITING FOR HIM.
LAXMIDAS!
UNFORTUNATELY, LAXMIDAS BROUGHT THE SAD NEWS THAT THEIR MOTHER HAD DIED JUST A FEW WEEKS BEFORE.
GANDHI HAD ONE THING TO DO BEFORE HE LEFT BOMBAY TO GO HOME.
WILL THIS SACRED BATH BE ENOUGH, SIR?
WELL, OKAY, YES.
HE HAS WASHED AWAY HIS SIN. HE CAN BE BACK IN THE CASTE.

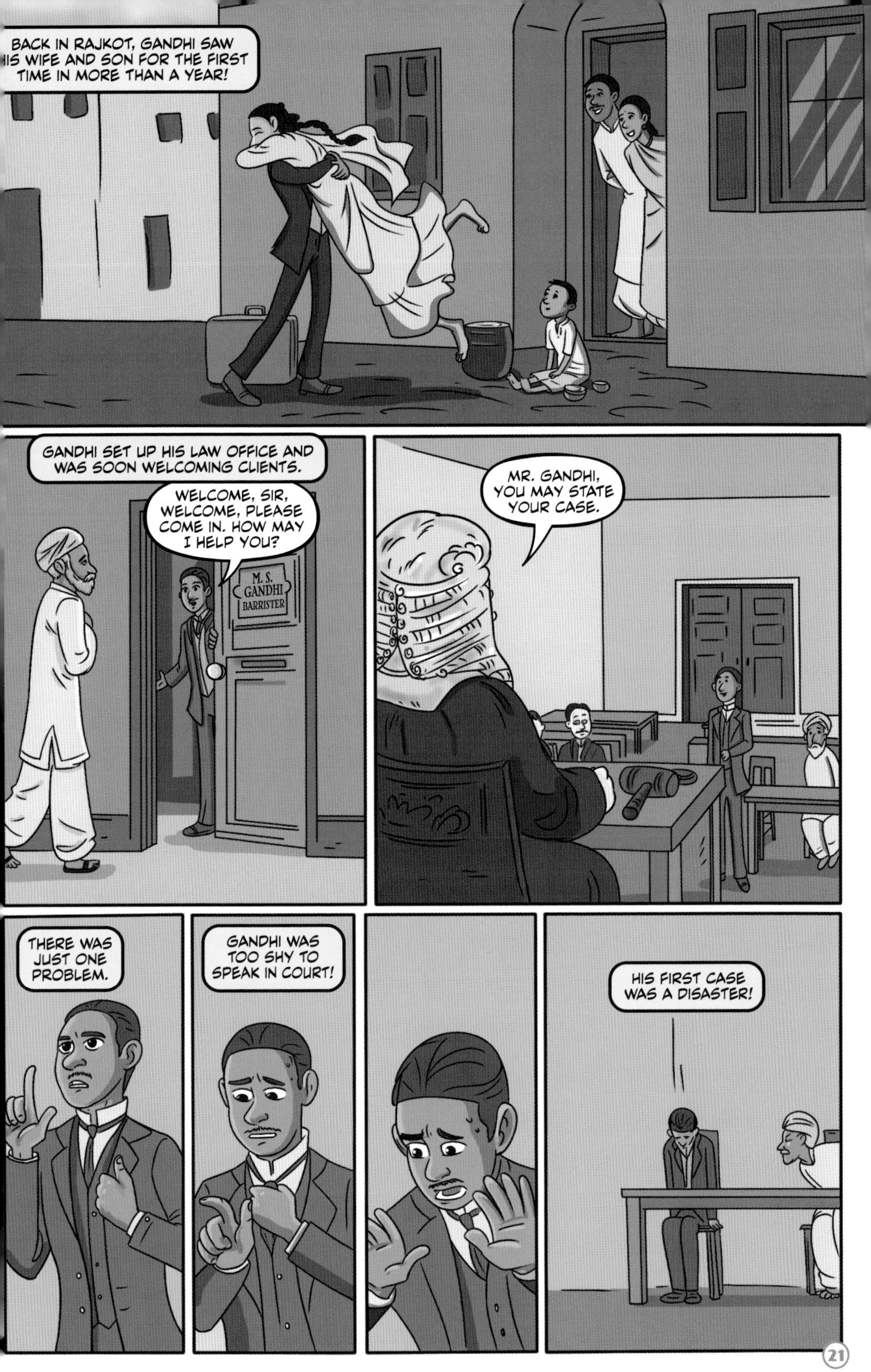

BACK IN RAJKOT, GANDHI SAW HIS WIFE AND SON FOR THE FIRST TIME IN MORE THAN A YEAR!
GANDHI SET UP HIS LAW OFFICE AND WAS SOON WELCOMING CLIENTS.
WELCOME, SIR, WELCOME, PLEASE COME IN. HOW MAY I HELP YOU?
M. S. GANDHI BARRISTER
MR. GANDHI, YOU MAY STATE YOUR CASE.
THERE WAS JUST ONE PROBLEM.
GANDHI WAS TOO SHY TO SPEAK IN COURT!
HIS FIRST CASE WAS A DISASTER!

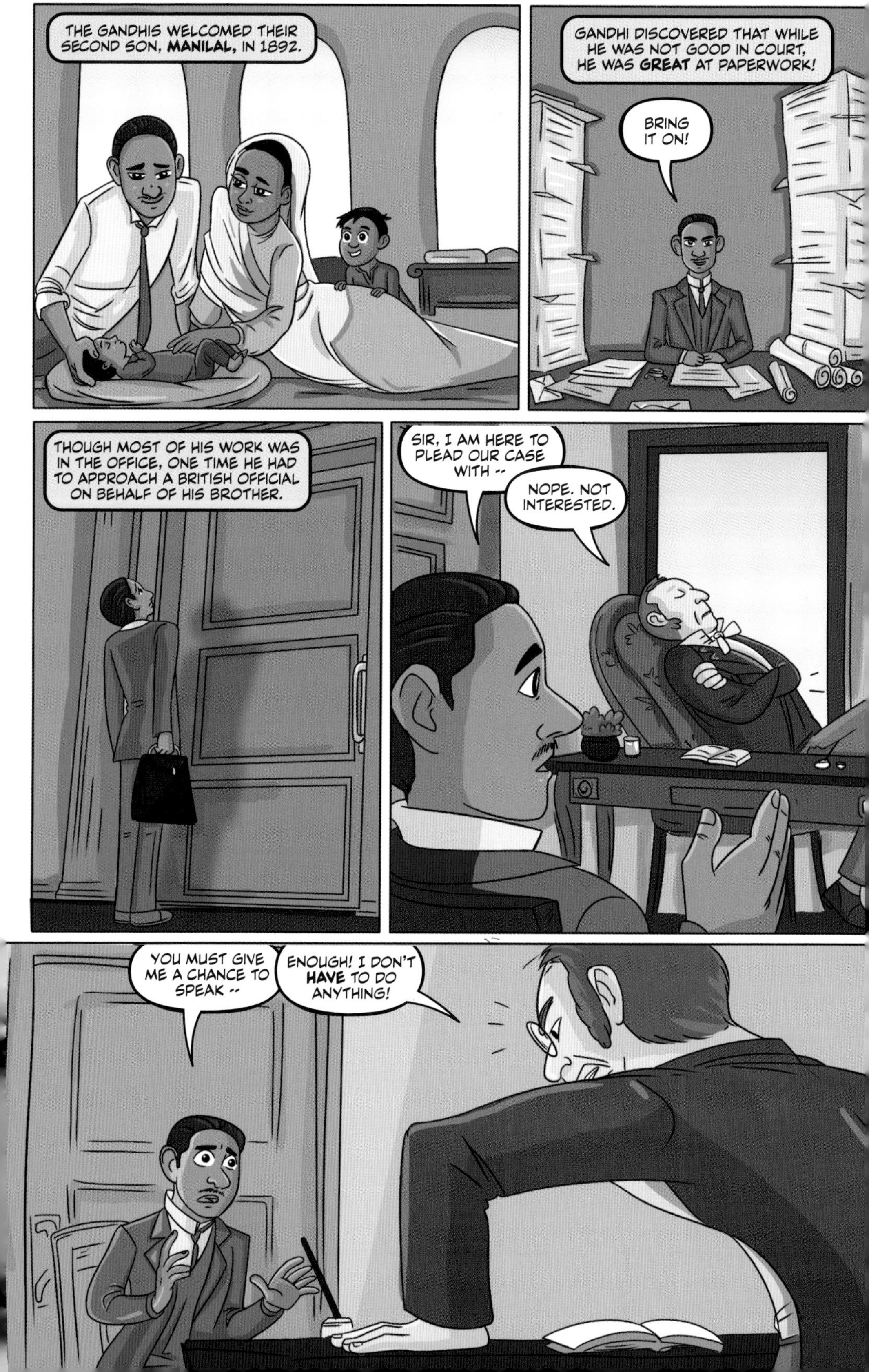

THE GANDHIS WELCOMED THEIR SECOND SON, **MANILAL,** IN 1892.
GANDHI DISCOVERED THAT WHILE HE WAS NOT GOOD IN COURT, HE WAS **GREAT** AT PAPERWORK!
BRING IT ON!
THOUGH MOST OF HIS WORK WAS IN THE OFFICE, ONE TIME HE HAD TO APPROACH A BRITISH OFFICIAL ON BEHALF OF HIS BROTHER.
SIR, I AM HERE TO PLEAD OUR CASE WITH --
NOPE. NOT INTERESTED.
YOU MUST GIVE ME A CHANCE TO SPEAK --
ENOUGH! I DON'T **HAVE** TO DO ANYTHING!

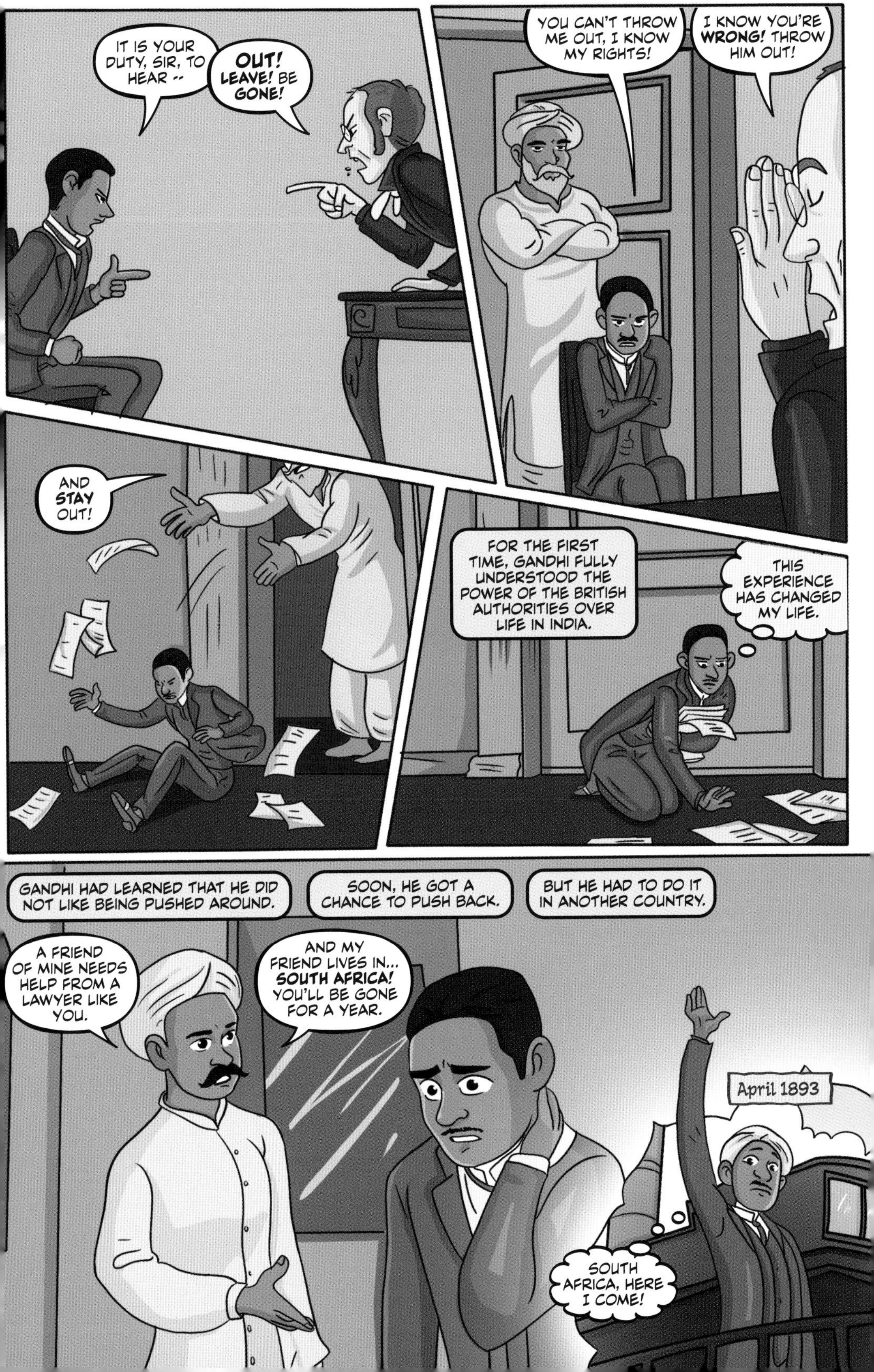
IT IS YOUR DUTY, SIR, TO HEAR --
OUT! LEAVE! BE GONE!
YOU CAN'T THROW ME OUT, I KNOW MY RIGHTS!
I KNOW YOU'RE WRONG! THROW HIM OUT!
AND STAY OUT!
FOR THE FIRST TIME, GANDHI FULLY UNDERSTOOD THE POWER OF THE BRITISH AUTHORITIES OVER LIFE IN INDIA.
THIS EXPERIENCE HAS CHANGED MY LIFE.
GANDHI HAD LEARNED THAT HE DID NOT LIKE BEING PUSHED AROUND.
SOON, HE GOT A CHANCE TO PUSH BACK.
BUT HE HAD TO DO IT IN ANOTHER COUNTRY.
A FRIEND OF MINE NEEDS HELP FROM A LAWYER LIKE YOU.
AND MY FRIEND LIVES IN... SOUTH AFRICA! YOU'LL BE GONE FOR A YEAR.
April 1893
SOUTH AFRICA, HERE I COME!

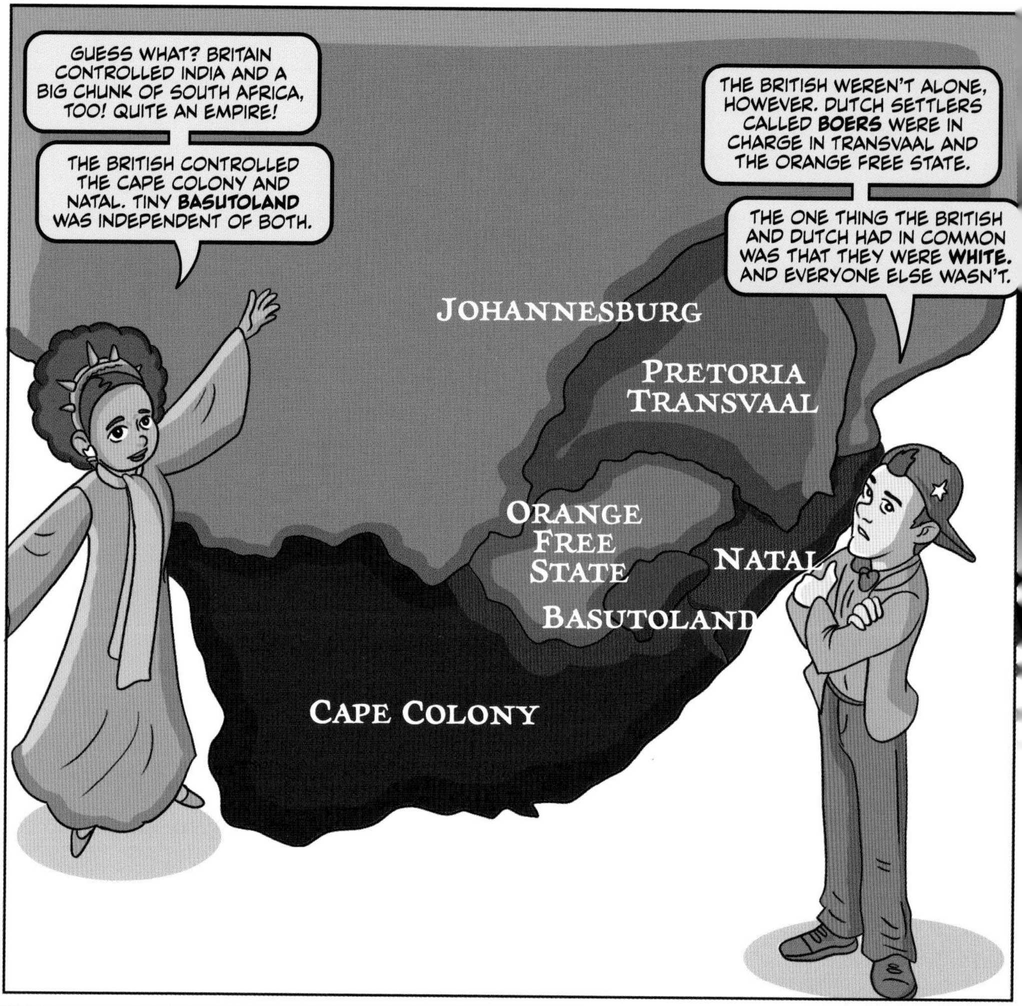
GUESS WHAT? BRITAIN CONTROLLED INDIA AND A BIG CHUNK OF SOUTH AFRICA, TOO! QUITE AN EMPIRE!
THE BRITISH CONTROLLED THE CAPE COLONY AND NATAL. TINY **BASUTOLAND** WAS INDEPENDENT OF BOTH.
THE BRITISH WEREN'T ALONE, HOWEVER. DUTCH SETTLERS CALLED **BOERS** WERE IN CHARGE IN TRANSVAAL AND THE ORANGE FREE STATE.
THE ONE THING THE BRITISH AND DUTCH HAD IN COMMON WAS THAT THEY WERE **WHITE**. AND EVERYONE ELSE WASN'T.
JOHANNESBURG
PRETORIA
TRANSVAAL
ORANGE FREE STATE
NATAL
BASUTOLAND
CAPE COLONY

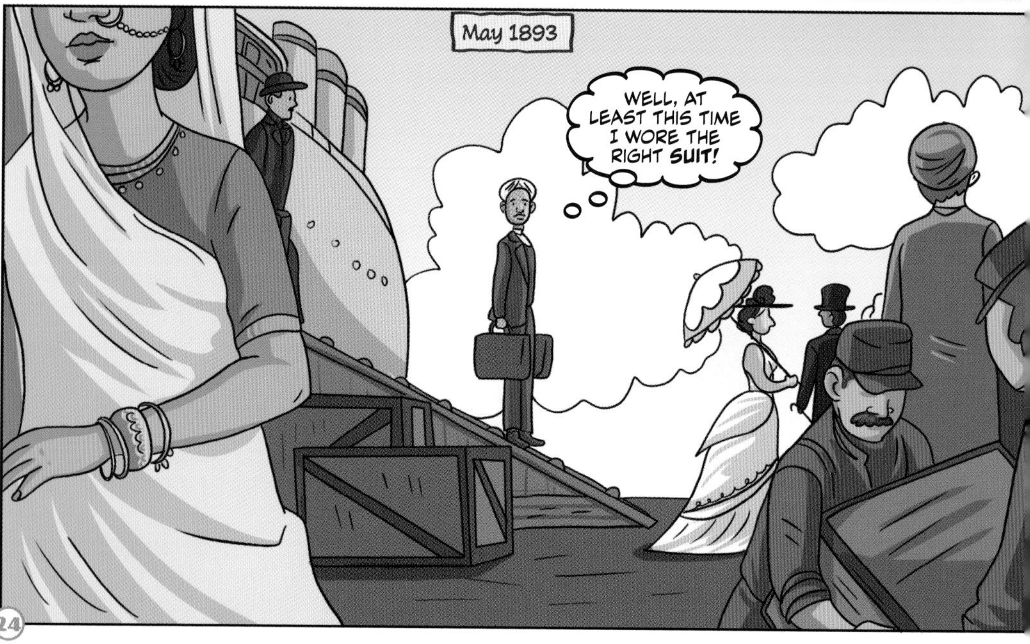
May 1893
WELL, AT LEAST THIS TIME I WORE THE RIGHT **SUIT!**

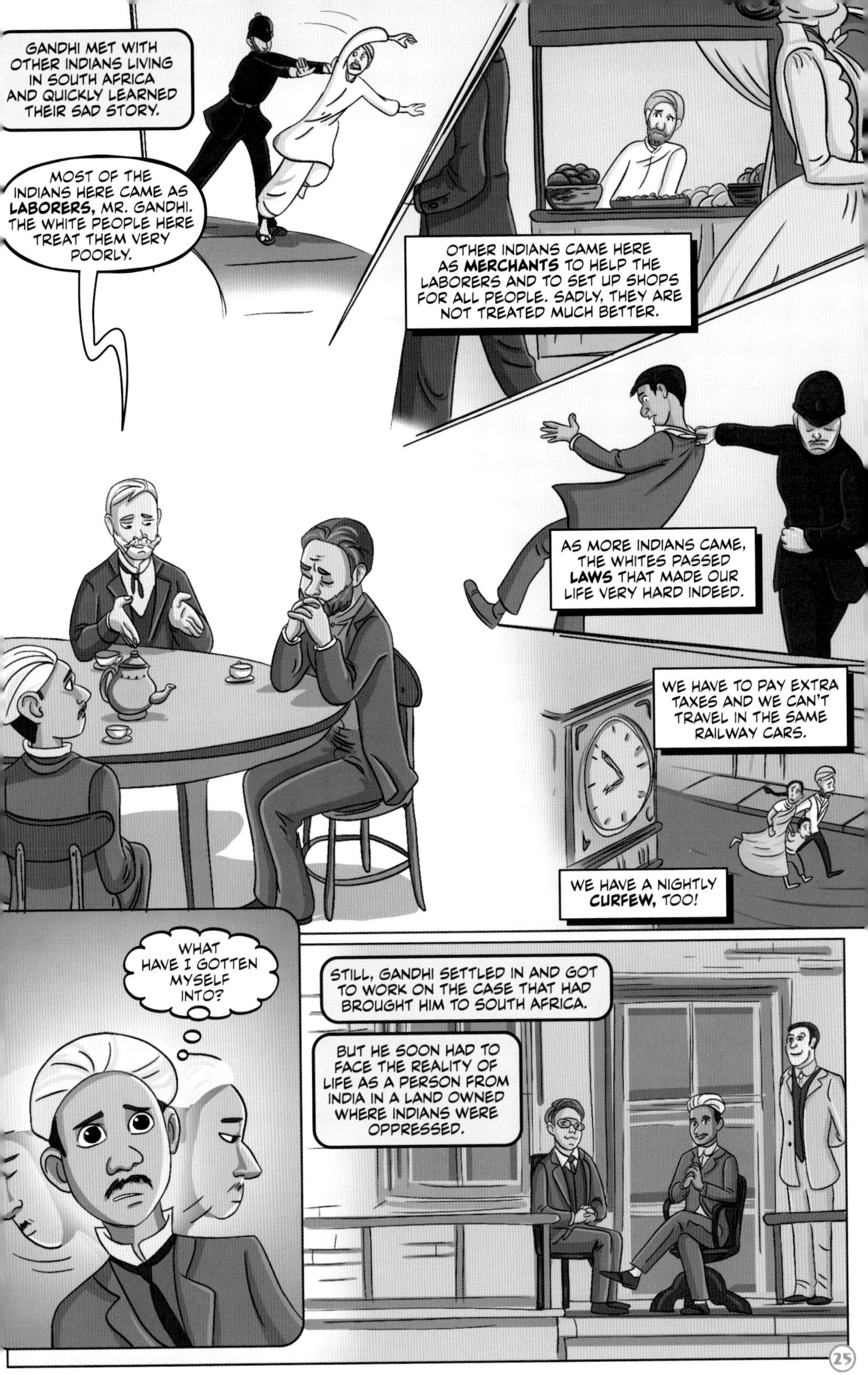
GANDHI MET WITH OTHER INDIANS LIVING IN SOUTH AFRICA AND QUICKLY LEARNED THEIR SAD STORY.
MOST OF THE INDIANS HERE CAME AS **LABORERS,** MR. GANDHI. THE WHITE PEOPLE HERE TREAT THEM VERY POORLY.
OTHER INDIANS CAME HERE AS **MERCHANTS** TO HELP THE LABORERS AND TO SET UP SHOPS FOR ALL PEOPLE. SADLY, THEY ARE NOT TREATED MUCH BETTER.
AS MORE INDIANS CAME, THE WHITES PASSED **LAWS** THAT MADE OUR LIFE VERY HARD INDEED.
WE HAVE TO PAY EXTRA TAXES AND WE CAN'T TRAVEL IN THE SAME RAILWAY CARS.
WE HAVE A NIGHTLY **CURFEW,** TOO!
WHAT HAVE I GOTTEN MYSELF INTO?
STILL, GANDHI SETTLED IN AND GOT TO WORK ON THE CASE THAT HAD BROUGHT HIM TO SOUTH AFRICA.
BUT HE SOON HAD TO FACE THE REALITY OF LIFE AS A PERSON FROM INDIA IN A LAND OWNED WHERE INDIANS WERE OPPRESSED.

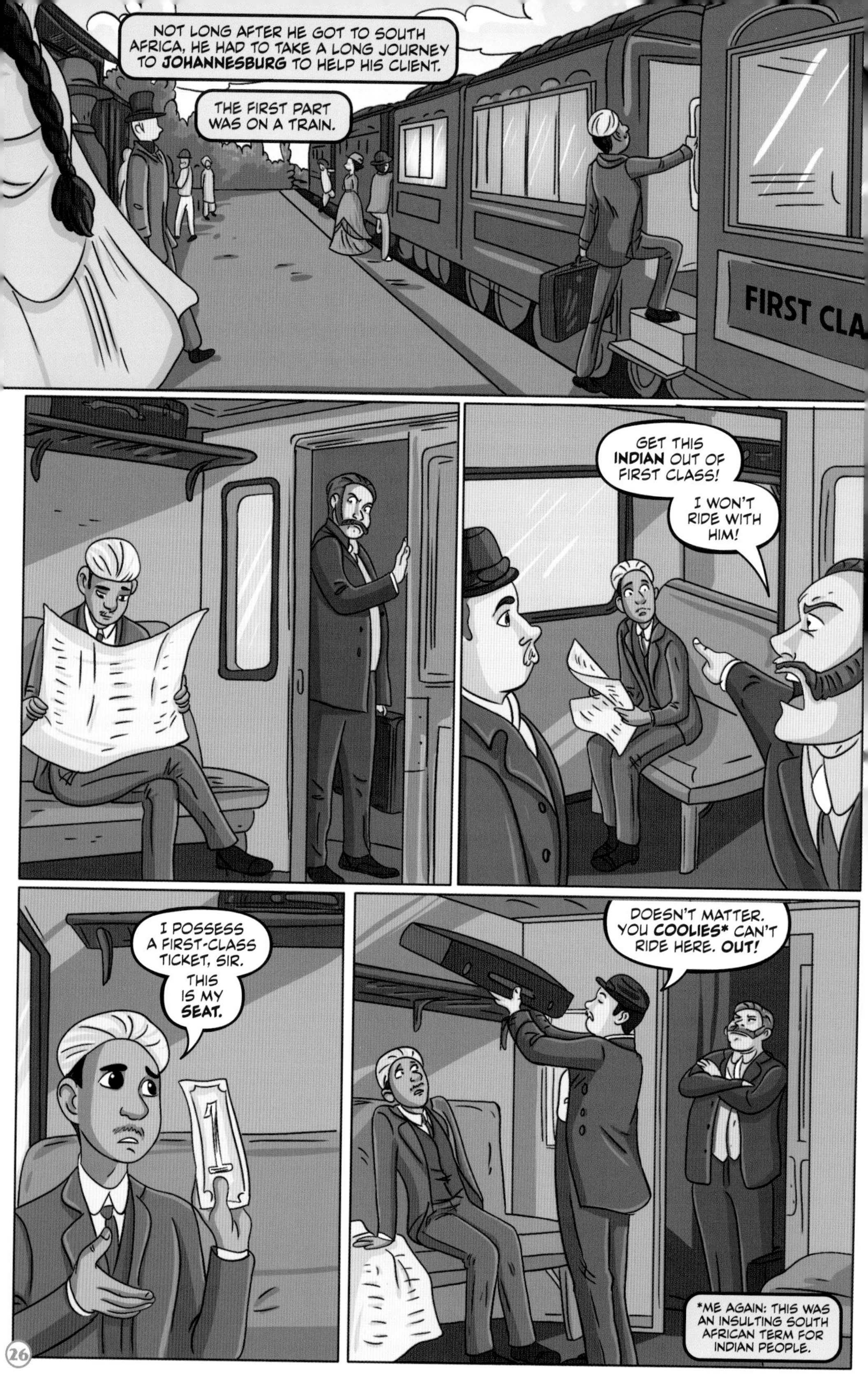
NOT LONG AFTER HE GOT TO SOUTH AFRICA, HE HAD TO TAKE A LONG JOURNEY TO **JOHANNESBURG** TO HELP HIS CLIENT.
THE FIRST PART WAS ON A TRAIN.
FIRST CLA
GET THIS **INDIAN** OUT OF FIRST CLASS!
I WON'T RIDE WITH HIM!
I POSSESS A FIRST-CLASS TICKET, SIR.
THIS IS MY **SEAT.**
1
DOESN'T MATTER. YOU **COOLIES*** CAN'T RIDE HERE. **OUT!**
*ME AGAIN: THIS WAS AN INSULTING SOUTH AFRICAN TERM FOR INDIAN PEOPLE.

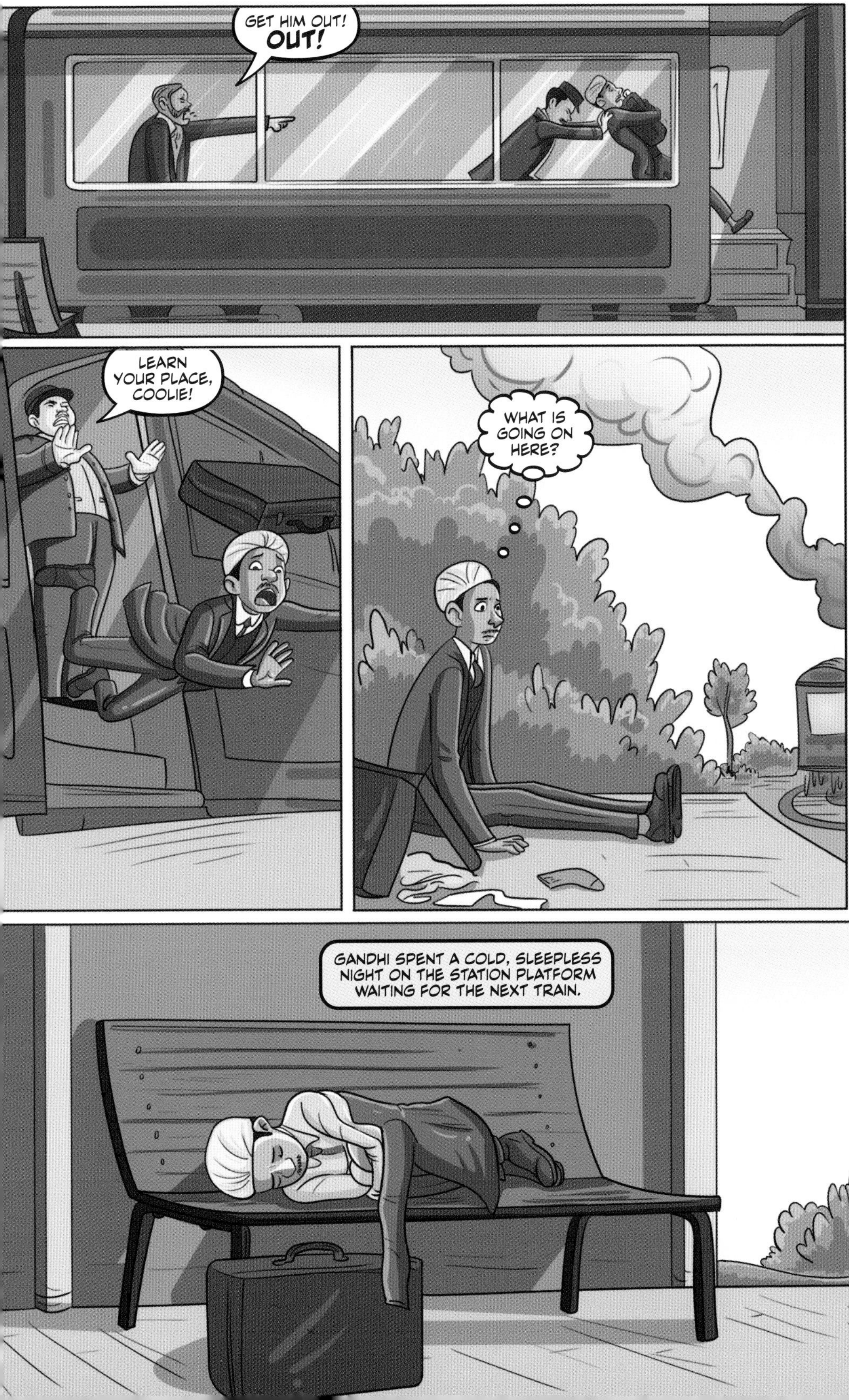
GET HIM OUT! OUT!
LEARN YOUR PLACE, COOLIE!
WHAT IS GOING ON HERE?
GANDHI SPENT A COLD, SLEEPLESS NIGHT ON THE STATION PLATFORM WAITING FOR THE NEXT TRAIN.

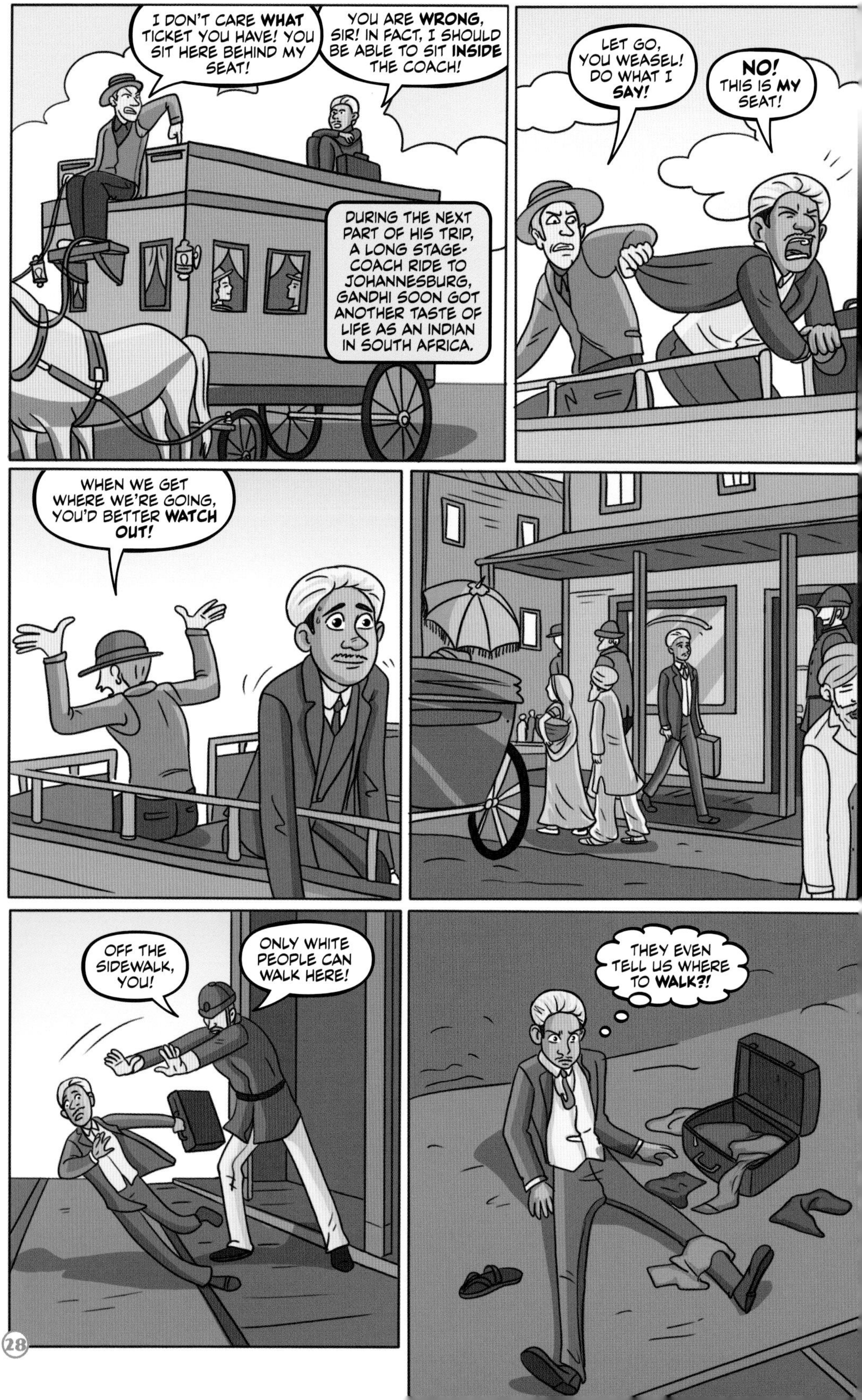
I DON'T CARE WHAT TICKET YOU HAVE! YOU SIT HERE BEHIND MY SEAT!
YOU ARE WRONG, SIR! IN FACT, I SHOULD BE ABLE TO SIT INSIDE THE COACH!
DURING THE NEXT PART OF HIS TRIP, A LONG STAGE-COACH RIDE TO JOHANNESBURG, GANDHI SOON GOT ANOTHER TASTE OF LIFE AS AN INDIAN IN SOUTH AFRICA.
LET GO, YOU WEASEL! DO WHAT I SAY!
NO! THIS IS MY SEAT!
WHEN WE GET WHERE WE'RE GOING, YOU'D BETTER WATCH OUT!
OFF THE SIDEWALK, YOU!
ONLY WHITE PEOPLE CAN WALK HERE!
THEY EVEN TELL US WHERE TO WALK?!

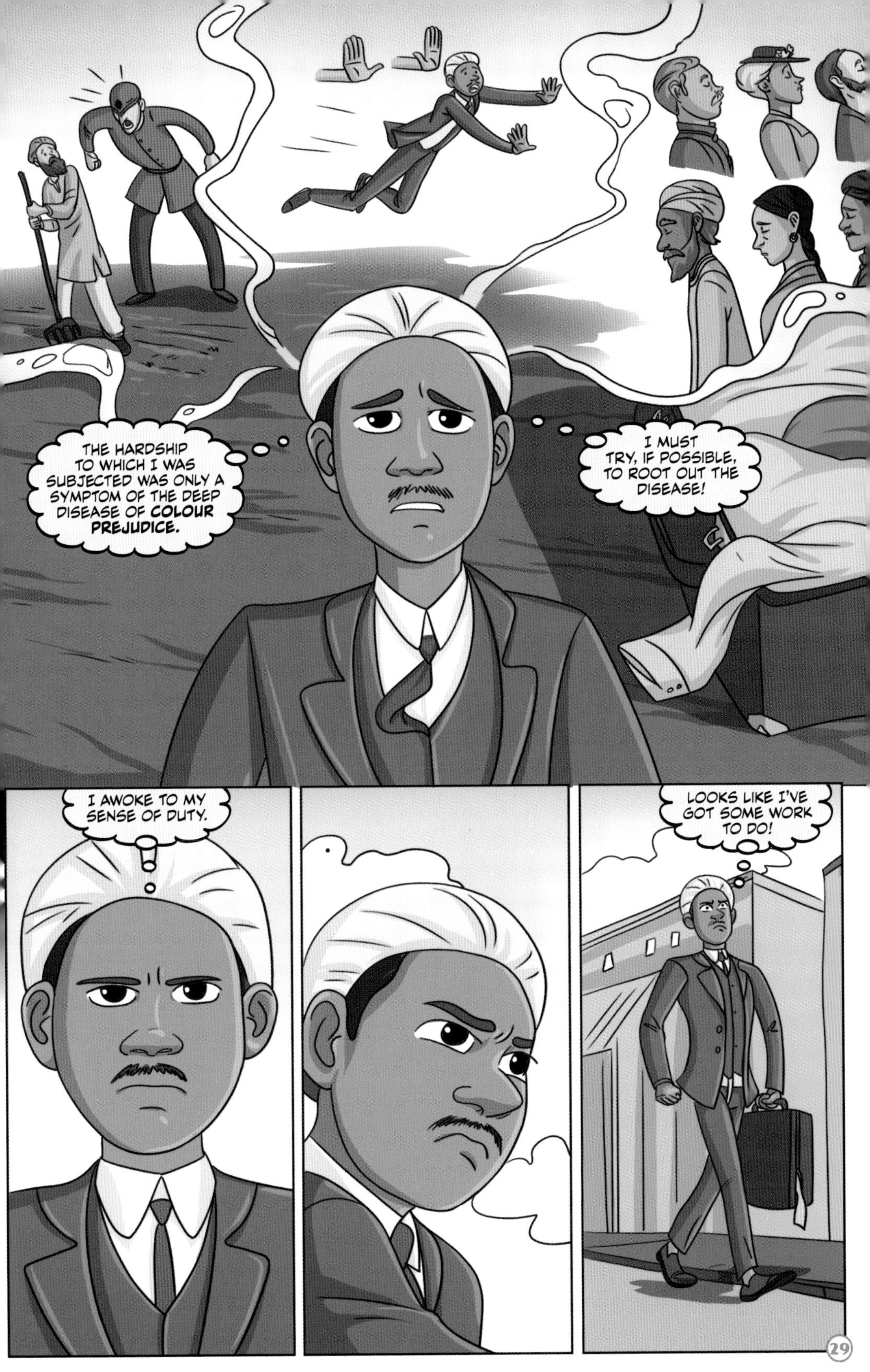
THE HARDSHIP TO WHICH I WAS SUBJECTED WAS ONLY A SYMPTOM OF THE DEEP DISEASE OF **COLOUR PREJUDICE.**
I MUST TRY, IF POSSIBLE, TO ROOT OUT THE DISEASE!
I AWOKE TO MY SENSE OF DUTY.
LOOKS LIKE I'VE GOT SOME WORK TO DO!

THE FIRST WORK HE DID WAS TO WIN HIS **BIG CASE**. THAT WAS WHAT HE HAD BEEN SENT TO SOUTH AFRICA TO DO IN THE FIRST PLACE.

NICE GOING, MR. GANDHI! YOU'RE ONE AND OH!

THOUGH HE COULD HAVE GONE BACK TO INDIA, HE STAYED AND, OVER THE NEXT FEW YEARS, BECAME A LEADING VOICE AND LEADER IN THE FIGHT FOR INDIAN RIGHTS IN SOUTH AFRICA.

And why are the Indians treated so badly? They are British subjects. Is this fair play?

NOW THEY WANT TO TAKE AWAY OUR RIGHT TO **VOTE?**

WE CANNOT STAND FOR THIS!

ONE AT A TIME, ONE AT A TIME! I WILL TAKE ALL THESE PETITIONS TO THE GOVERNMENT.

TOGETHER, WE CAN MAKE THINGS CHANGE!

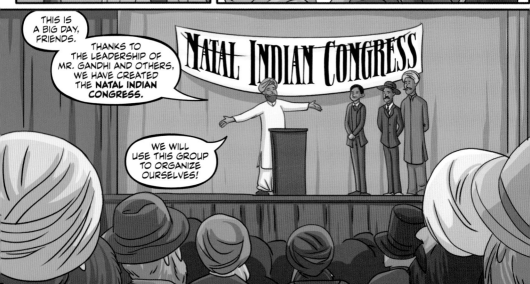

THIS IS A BIG DAY, FRIENDS.

THANKS TO THE LEADERSHIP OF MR. GANDHI AND OTHERS, WE HAVE CREATED THE **NATAL INDIAN CONGRESS**.

NATAL INDIAN CONGRESS

WE WILL USE THIS GROUP TO ORGANIZE OURSELVES!

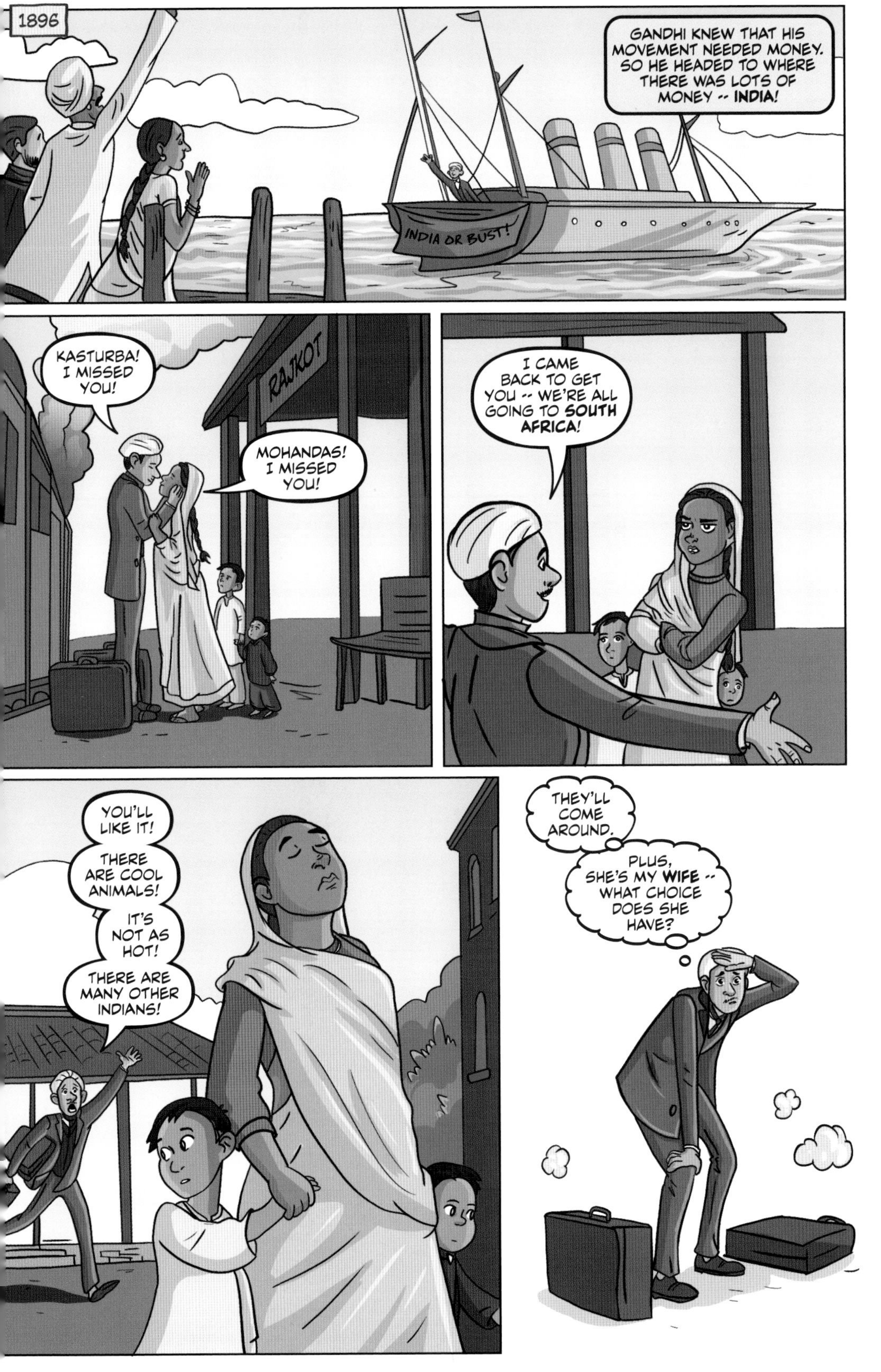
1896
GANDHI KNEW THAT HIS MOVEMENT NEEDED MONEY. SO HE HEADED TO WHERE THERE WAS LOTS OF MONEY -- **INDIA!**
INDIA OR BUST!
KASTURBA! I MISSED YOU!
RAJKOT
MOHANDAS! I MISSED YOU!
I CAME BACK TO GET YOU -- WE'RE ALL GOING TO **SOUTH AFRICA!**
YOU'LL LIKE IT!
THERE ARE COOL ANIMALS!
IT'S NOT AS HOT!
THERE ARE MANY OTHER INDIANS!
THEY'LL COME AROUND.
PLUS, SHE'S MY **WIFE** -- WHAT CHOICE DOES SHE HAVE?

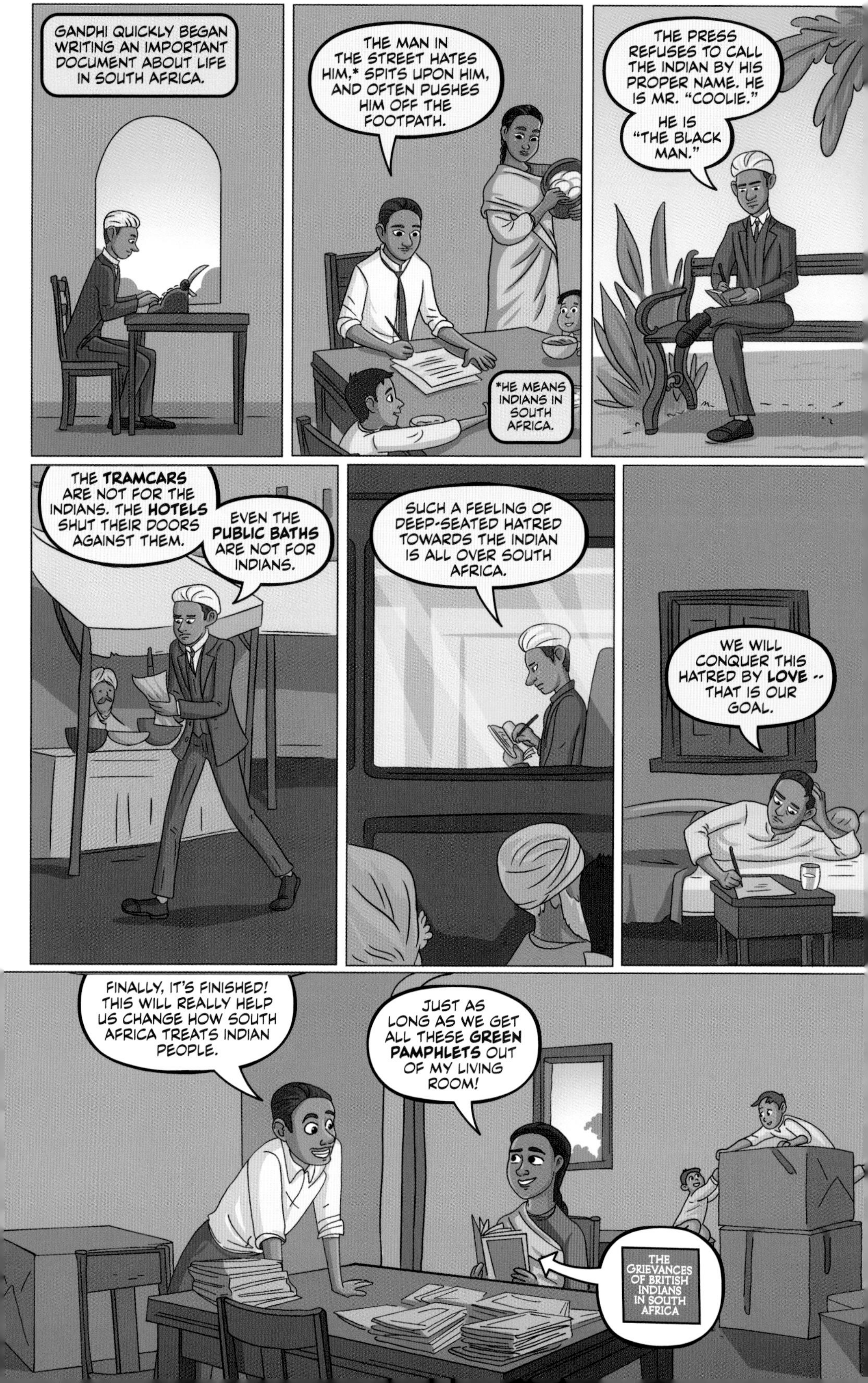

GANDHI QUICKLY BEGAN WRITING AN IMPORTANT DOCUMENT ABOUT LIFE IN SOUTH AFRICA.
THE MAN IN THE STREET HATES HIM,* SPITS UPON HIM, AND OFTEN PUSHES HIM OFF THE FOOTPATH.
*HE MEANS INDIANS IN SOUTH AFRICA.
THE PRESS REFUSES TO CALL THE INDIAN BY HIS PROPER NAME. HE IS MR. "COOLIE."
HE IS "THE BLACK MAN."
THE **TRAMCARS** ARE NOT FOR THE INDIANS. THE **HOTELS** SHUT THEIR DOORS AGAINST THEM.
EVEN THE **PUBLIC BATHS** ARE NOT FOR INDIANS.
SUCH A FEELING OF DEEP-SEATED HATRED TOWARDS THE INDIAN IS ALL OVER SOUTH AFRICA.
WE WILL CONQUER THIS HATRED BY **LOVE** -- THAT IS OUR GOAL.
FINALLY, IT'S FINISHED! THIS WILL REALLY HELP US CHANGE HOW SOUTH AFRICA TREATS INDIAN PEOPLE.
JUST AS LONG AS WE GET ALL THESE **GREEN PAMPHLETS** OUT OF MY LIVING ROOM!
THE GRIEVANCES OF BRITISH INDIANS IN SOUTH AFRICA

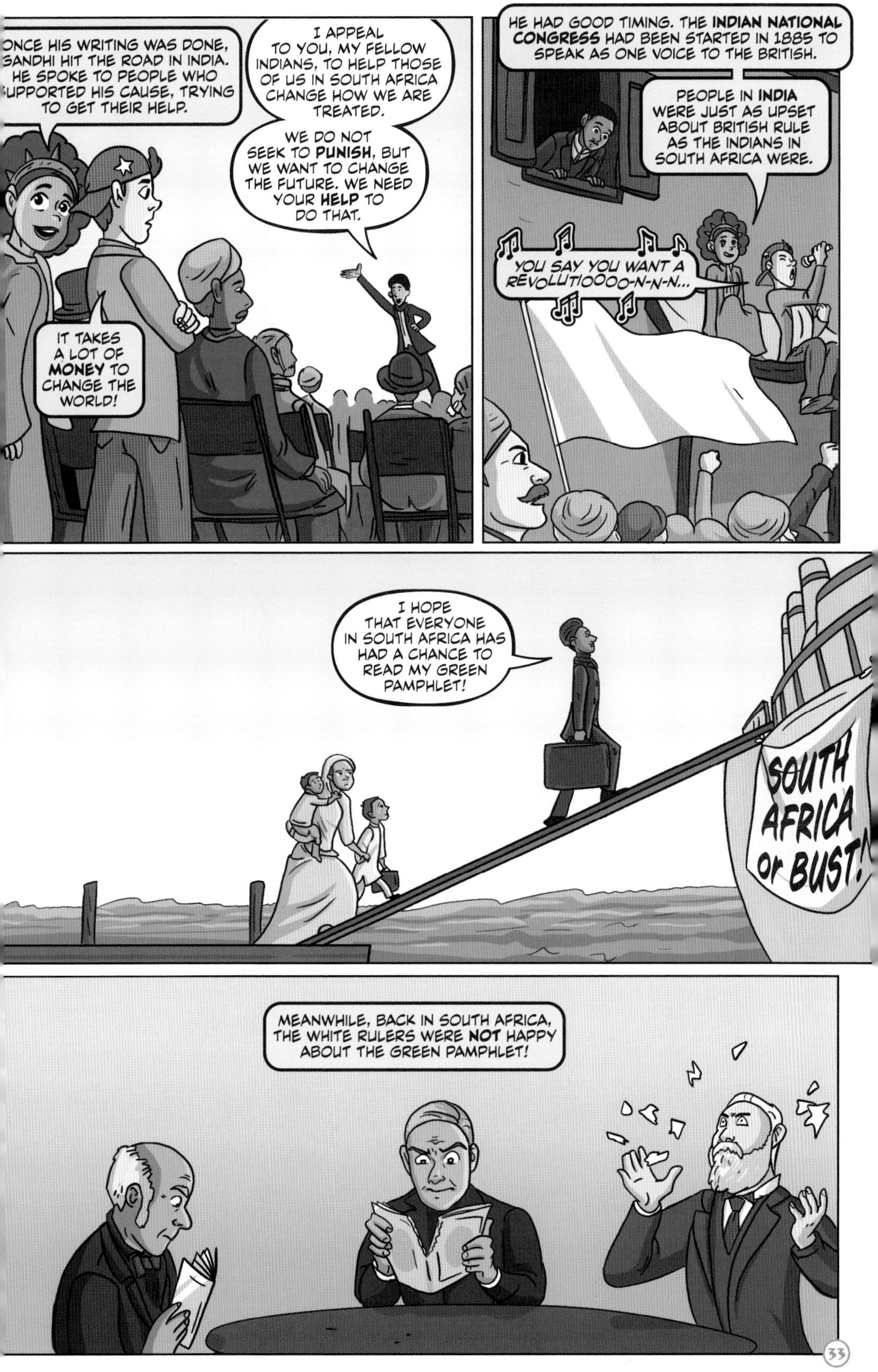

ONCE HIS WRITING WAS DONE, GANDHI HIT THE ROAD IN INDIA. HE SPOKE TO PEOPLE WHO SUPPORTED HIS CAUSE, TRYING TO GET THEIR HELP.
I APPEAL TO YOU, MY FELLOW INDIANS, TO HELP THOSE OF US IN SOUTH AFRICA CHANGE HOW WE ARE TREATED.
WE DO NOT SEEK TO **PUNISH**, BUT WE WANT TO CHANGE THE FUTURE. WE NEED YOUR **HELP** TO DO THAT.
IT TAKES A LOT OF **MONEY** TO CHANGE THE WORLD!
HE HAD GOOD TIMING. THE **INDIAN NATIONAL CONGRESS** HAD BEEN STARTED IN 1885 TO SPEAK AS ONE VOICE TO THE BRITISH.
PEOPLE IN **INDIA** WERE JUST AS UPSET ABOUT BRITISH RULE AS THE INDIANS IN SOUTH AFRICA WERE.
YOU SAY YOU WANT A REVOLUTIOOOO-N-N-N...
I HOPE THAT EVERYONE IN SOUTH AFRICA HAS HAD A CHANCE TO READ MY GREEN PAMPHLET!
SOUTH AFRICA or BUST!
MEANWHILE, BACK IN SOUTH AFRICA, THE WHITE RULERS WERE **NOT** HAPPY ABOUT THE GREEN PAMPHLET!

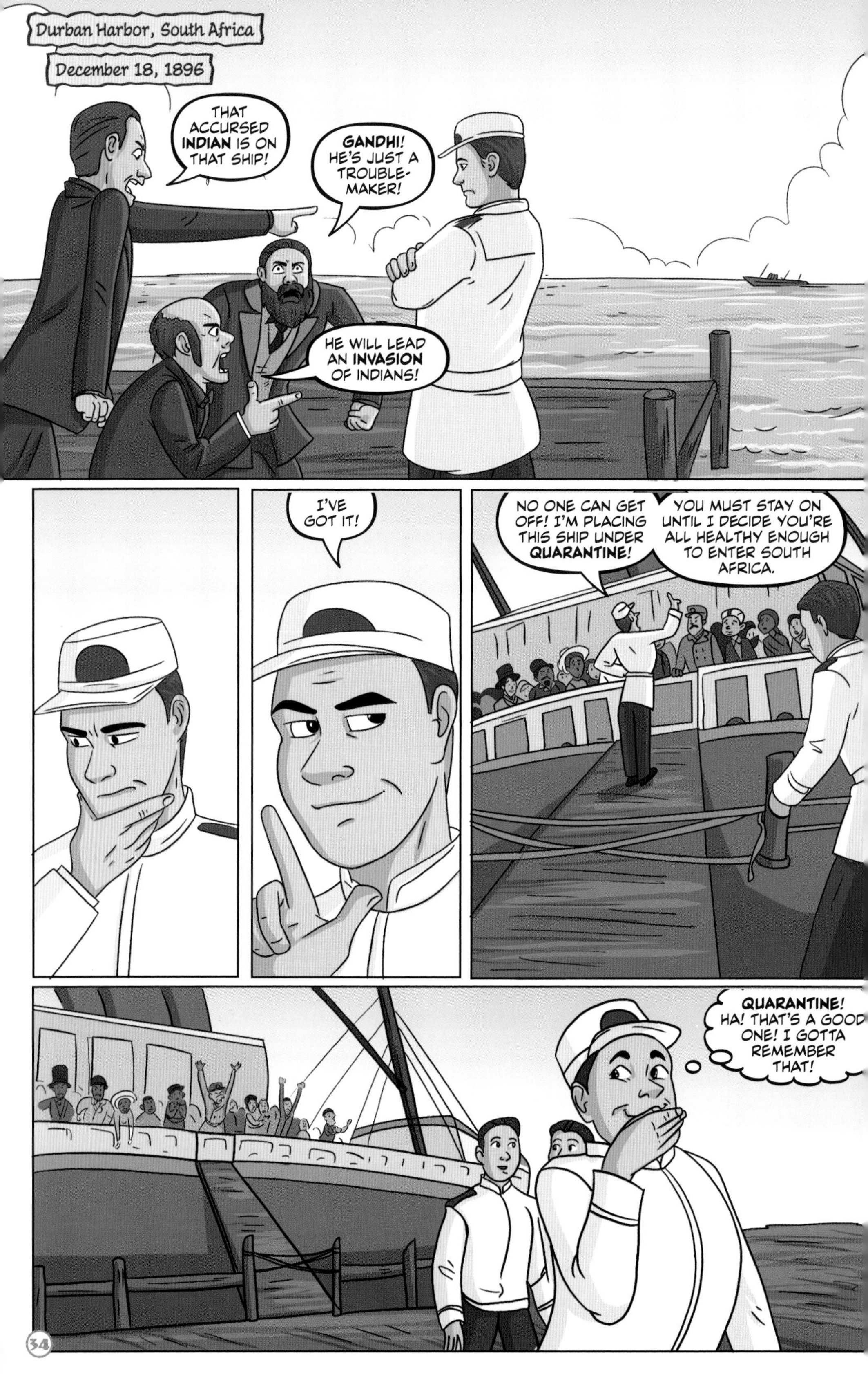
Durban Harbor, South Africa
December 18, 1896
THAT ACCURSED INDIAN IS ON THAT SHIP!
GANDHI! HE'S JUST A TROUBLE-MAKER!
HE WILL LEAD AN INVASION OF INDIANS!
I'VE GOT IT!
NO ONE CAN GET OFF! I'M PLACING THIS SHIP UNDER QUARANTINE!
YOU MUST STAY ON UNTIL I DECIDE YOU'RE ALL HEALTHY ENOUGH TO ENTER SOUTH AFRICA.
QUARANTINE! HA! THAT'S A GOOD ONE! I GOTTA REMEMBER THAT!

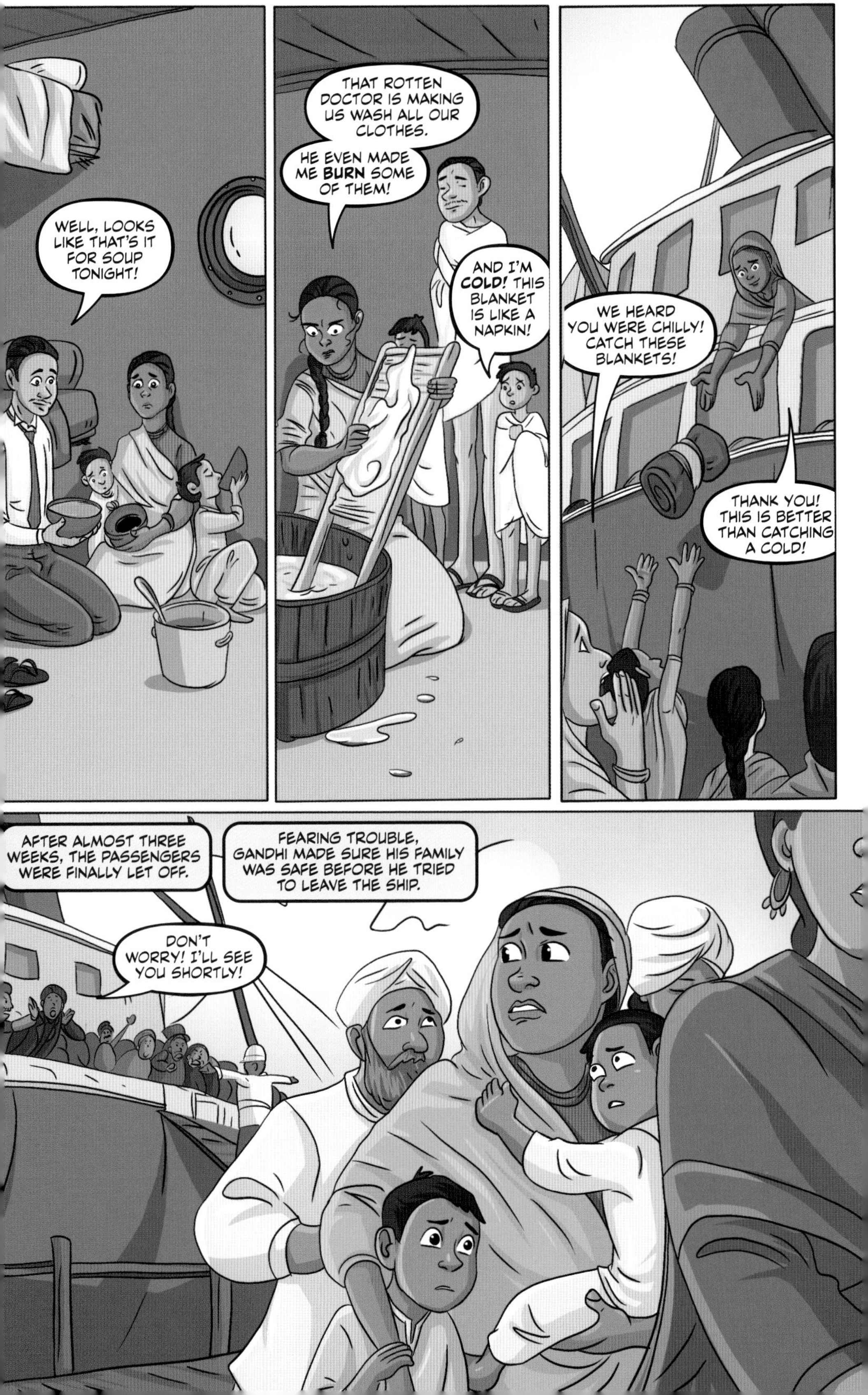
WELL, LOOKS LIKE THAT'S IT FOR SOUP TONIGHT!
THAT ROTTEN DOCTOR IS MAKING US WASH ALL OUR CLOTHES.
HE EVEN MADE ME BURN SOME OF THEM!
AND I'M COLD! THIS BLANKET IS LIKE A NAPKIN!
WE HEARD YOU WERE CHILLY! CATCH THESE BLANKETS!
THANK YOU! THIS IS BETTER THAN CATCHING A COLD!
AFTER ALMOST THREE WEEKS, THE PASSENGERS WERE FINALLY LET OFF.
FEARING TROUBLE, GANDHI MADE SURE HIS FAMILY WAS SAFE BEFORE HE TRIED TO LEAVE THE SHIP.
DON'T WORRY! I'LL SEE YOU SHORTLY!

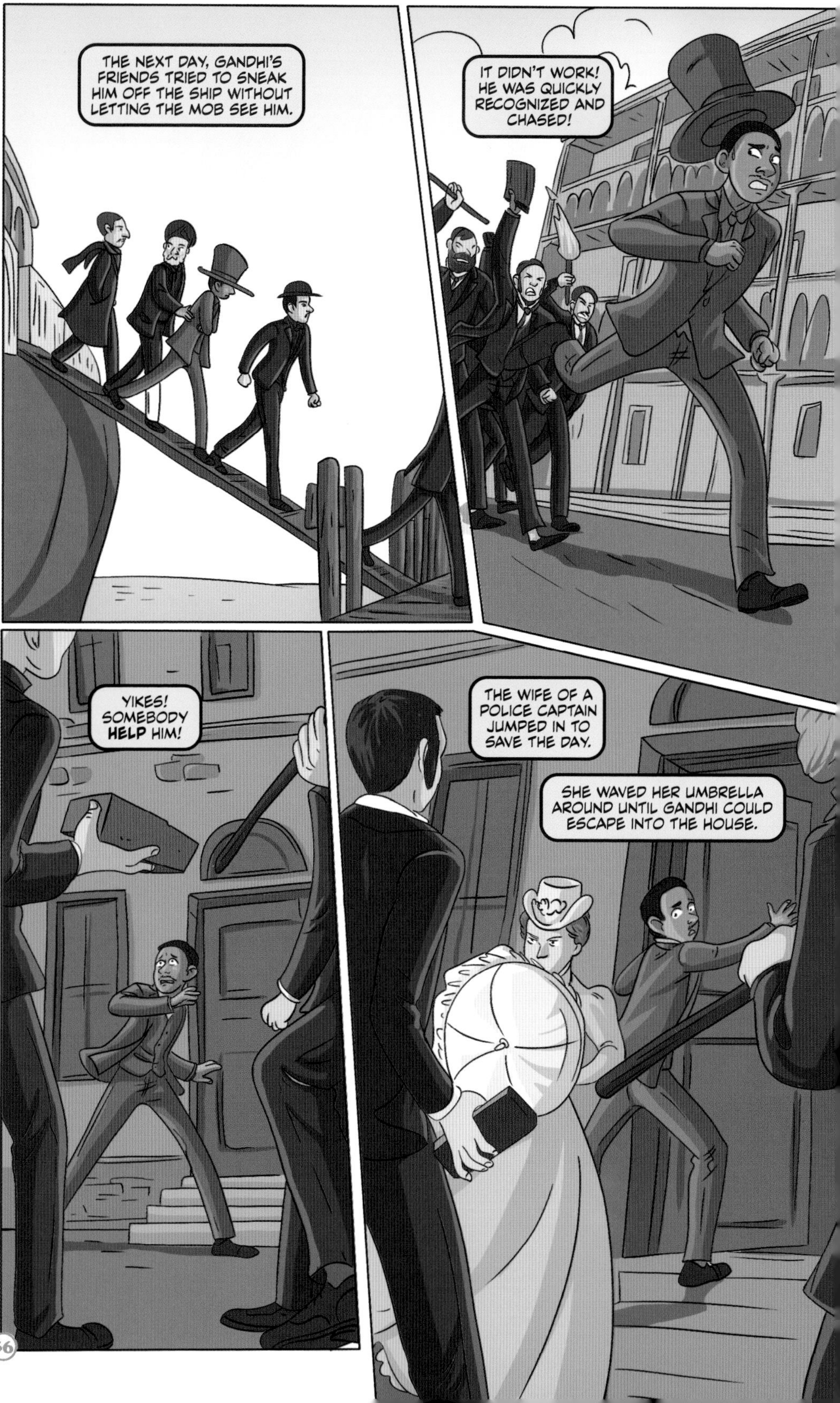
THE NEXT DAY, GANDHI'S FRIENDS TRIED TO SNEAK HIM OFF THE SHIP WITHOUT LETTING THE MOB SEE HIM.
IT DIDN'T WORK! HE WAS QUICKLY RECOGNIZED AND CHASED!
YIKES! SOMEBODY **HELP** HIM!
THE WIFE OF A POLICE CAPTAIN JUMPED IN TO SAVE THE DAY.
SHE WAVED HER UMBRELLA AROUND UNTIL GANDHI COULD ESCAPE INTO THE HOUSE.

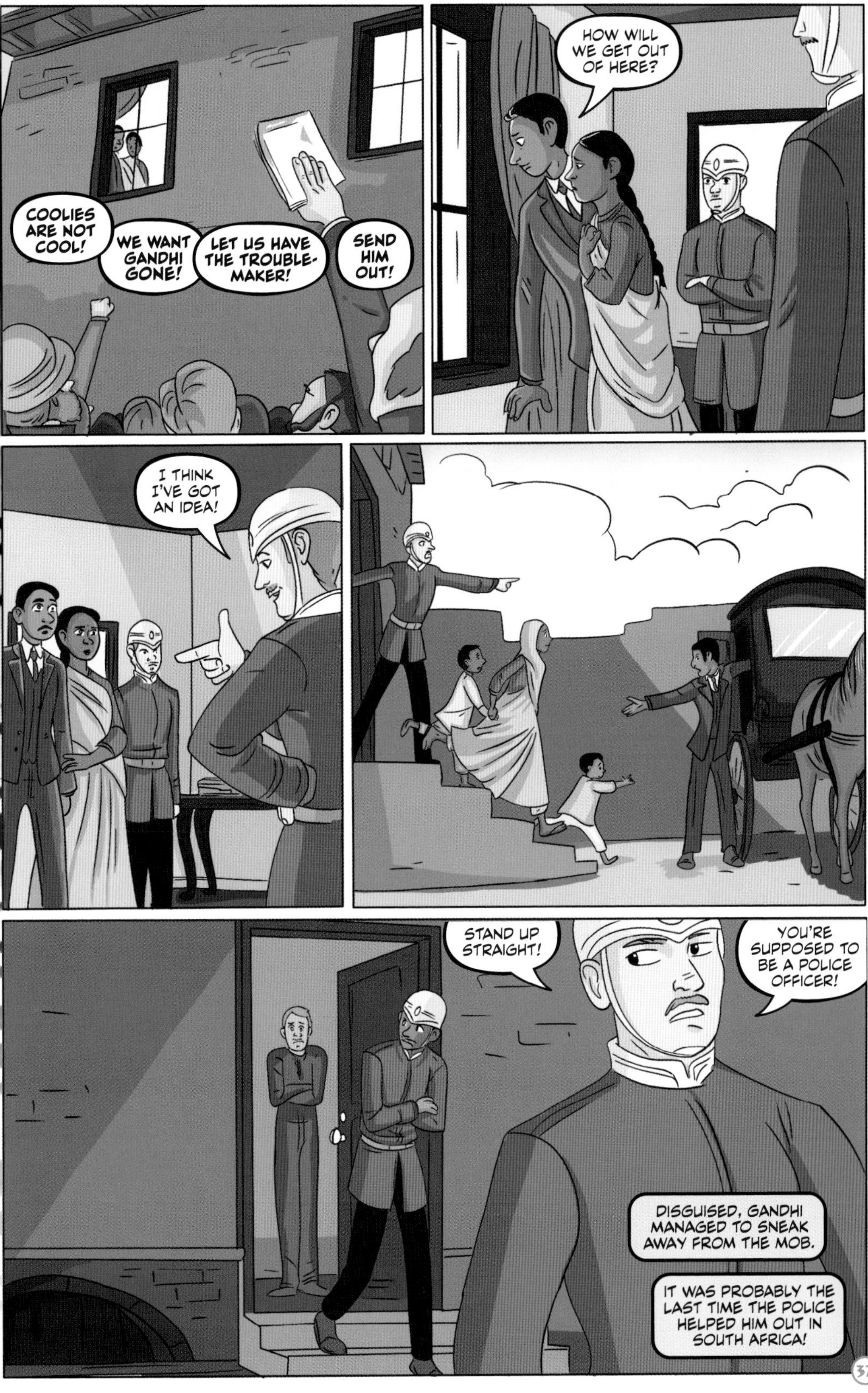
COOLIES ARE NOT COOL!
WE WANT GANDHI GONE!
LET US HAVE THE TROUBLE-MAKER!
SEND HIM OUT!
HOW WILL WE GET OUT OF HERE?
I THINK I'VE GOT AN IDEA!
STAND UP STRAIGHT!
YOU'RE SUPPOSED TO BE A POLICE OFFICER!
DISGUISED, GANDHI MANAGED TO SNEAK AWAY FROM THE MOB.
IT WAS PROBABLY THE LAST TIME THE POLICE HELPED HIM OUT IN SOUTH AFRICA!

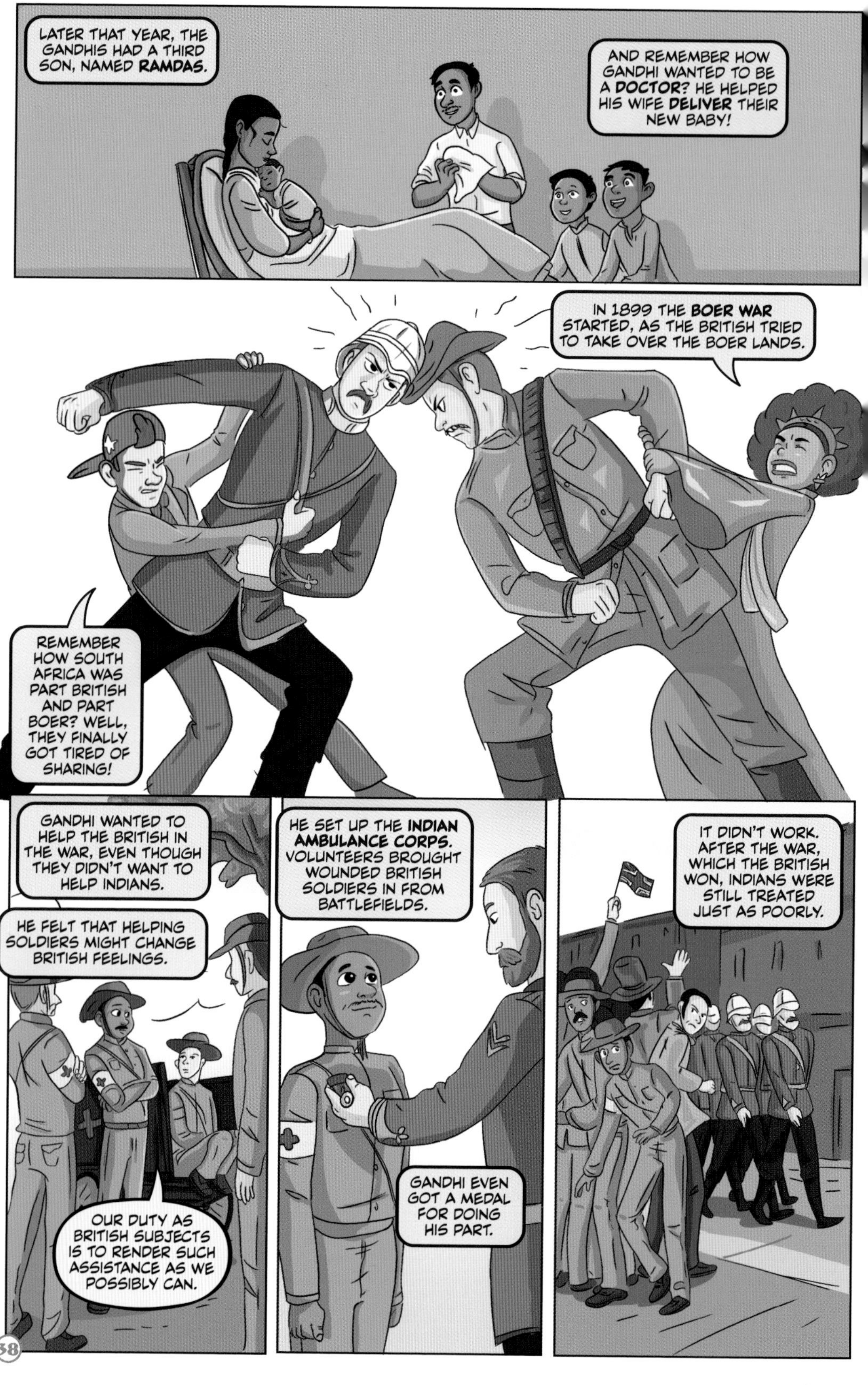
LATER THAT YEAR, THE GANDHIS HAD A THIRD SON, NAMED **RAMDAS**.
AND REMEMBER HOW GANDHI WANTED TO BE A **DOCTOR**? HE HELPED HIS WIFE **DELIVER** THEIR NEW BABY!
IN 1899 THE **BOER WAR** STARTED, AS THE BRITISH TRIED TO TAKE OVER THE BOER LANDS.
REMEMBER HOW SOUTH AFRICA WAS PART BRITISH AND PART BOER? WELL, THEY FINALLY GOT TIRED OF SHARING!
GANDHI WANTED TO HELP THE BRITISH IN THE WAR, EVEN THOUGH THEY DIDN'T WANT TO HELP INDIANS.
HE FELT THAT HELPING SOLDIERS MIGHT CHANGE BRITISH FEELINGS.
OUR DUTY AS BRITISH SUBJECTS IS TO RENDER SUCH ASSISTANCE AS WE POSSIBLY CAN.
HE SET UP THE **INDIAN AMBULANCE CORPS.** VOLUNTEERS BROUGHT WOUNDED BRITISH SOLDIERS IN FROM BATTLEFIELDS.
GANDHI EVEN GOT A MEDAL FOR DOING HIS PART.
IT DIDN'T WORK. AFTER THE WAR, WHICH THE BRITISH WON, INDIANS WERE STILL TREATED JUST AS POORLY.

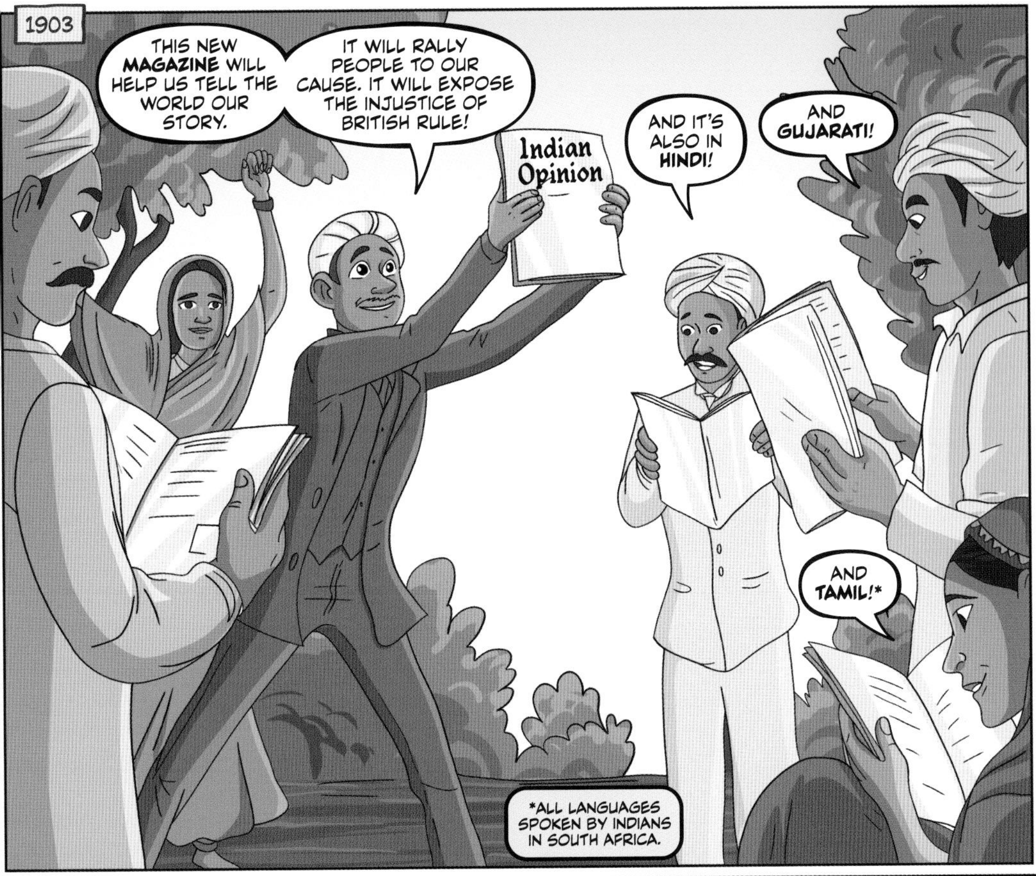
1903
THIS NEW MAGAZINE WILL HELP US TELL THE WORLD OUR STORY.
IT WILL RALLY PEOPLE TO OUR CAUSE. IT WILL EXPOSE THE INJUSTICE OF BRITISH RULE!
Indian Opinion
AND IT'S ALSO IN HINDI!
AND GUJARATI!
AND TAMIL!*
*ALL LANGUAGES SPOKEN BY INDIANS IN SOUTH AFRICA.

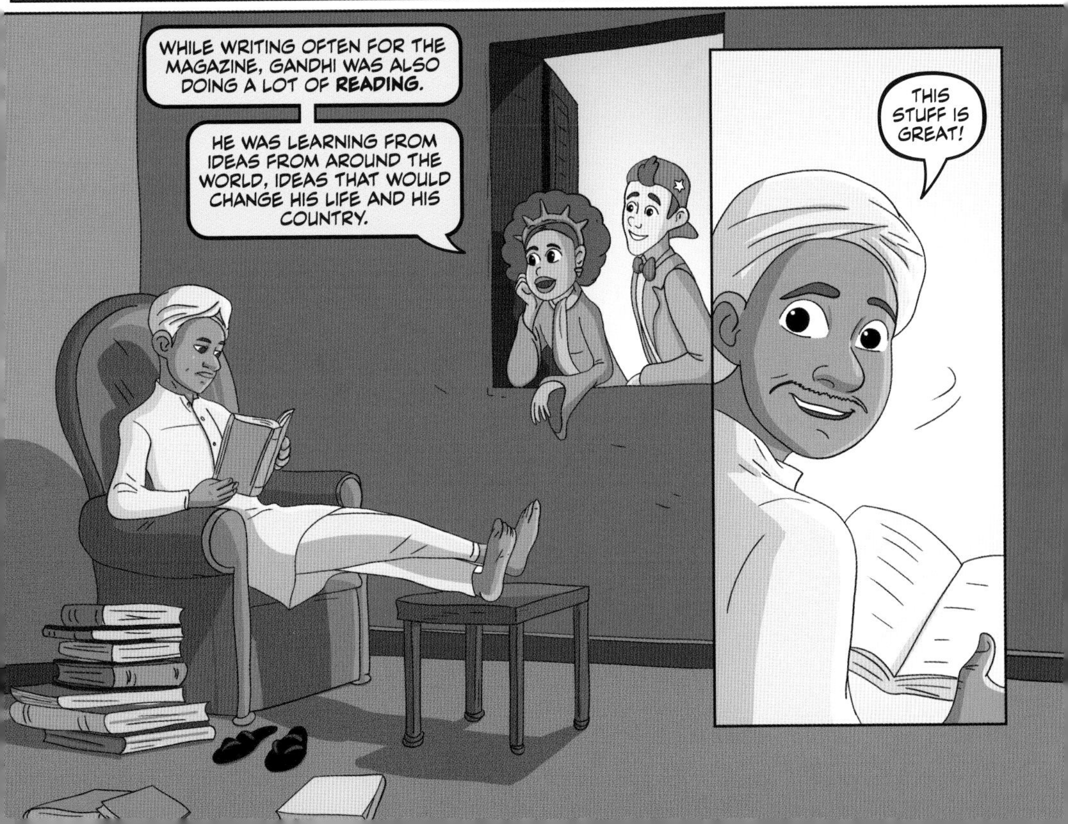
WHILE WRITING OFTEN FOR THE MAGAZINE, GANDHI WAS ALSO DOING A LOT OF READING.
HE WAS LEARNING FROM IDEAS FROM AROUND THE WORLD, IDEAS THAT WOULD CHANGE HIS LIFE AND HIS COUNTRY.
THIS STUFF IS GREAT!

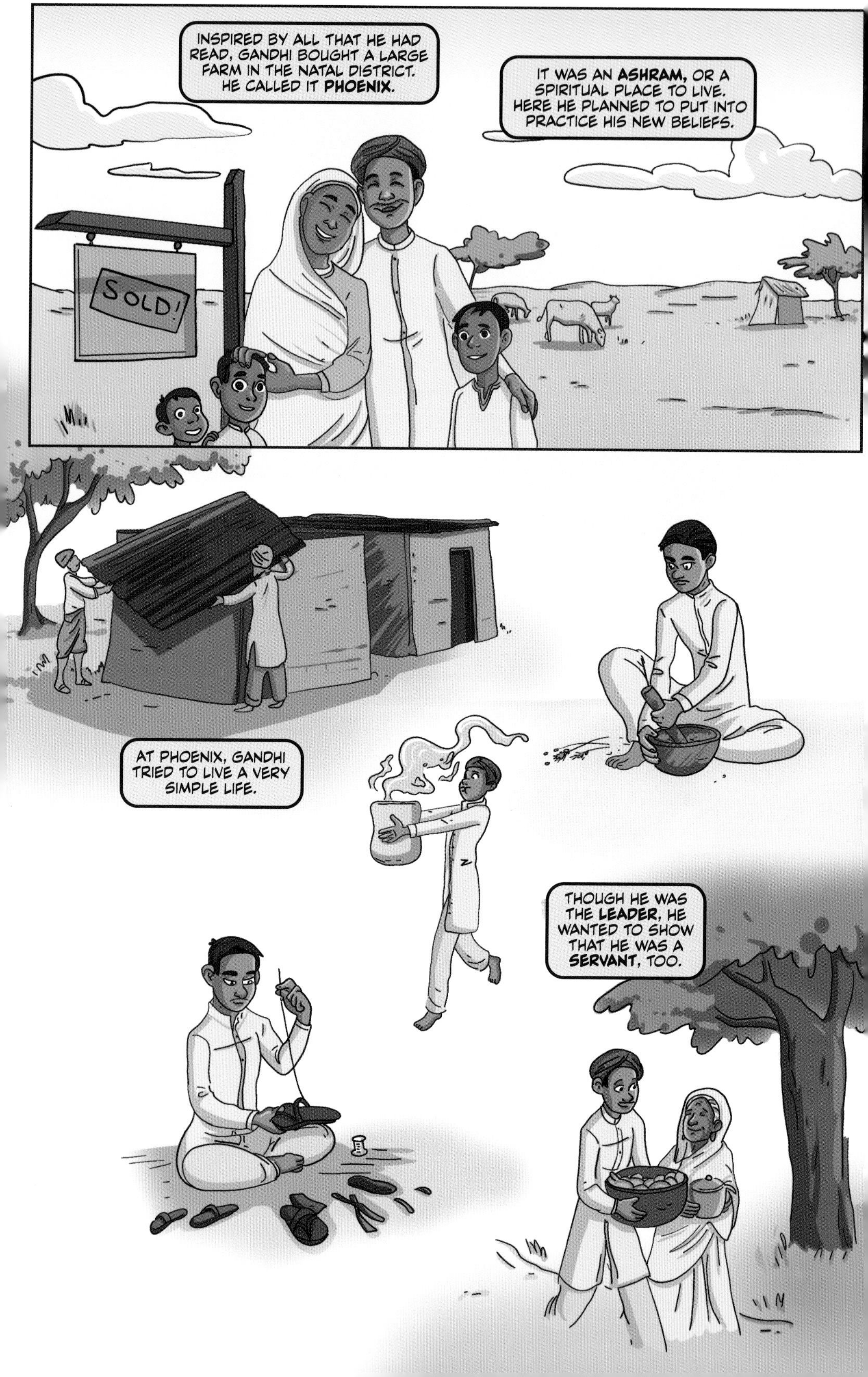
INSPIRED BY ALL THAT HE HAD READ, GANDHI BOUGHT A LARGE FARM IN THE NATAL DISTRICT. HE CALLED IT **PHOENIX.**
IT WAS AN **ASHRAM,** OR A SPIRITUAL PLACE TO LIVE. HERE HE PLANNED TO PUT INTO PRACTICE HIS NEW BELIEFS.
SOLD!
AT PHOENIX, GANDHI TRIED TO LIVE A VERY SIMPLE LIFE.
THOUGH HE WAS THE **LEADER,** HE WANTED TO SHOW THAT HE WAS A **SERVANT,** TOO.

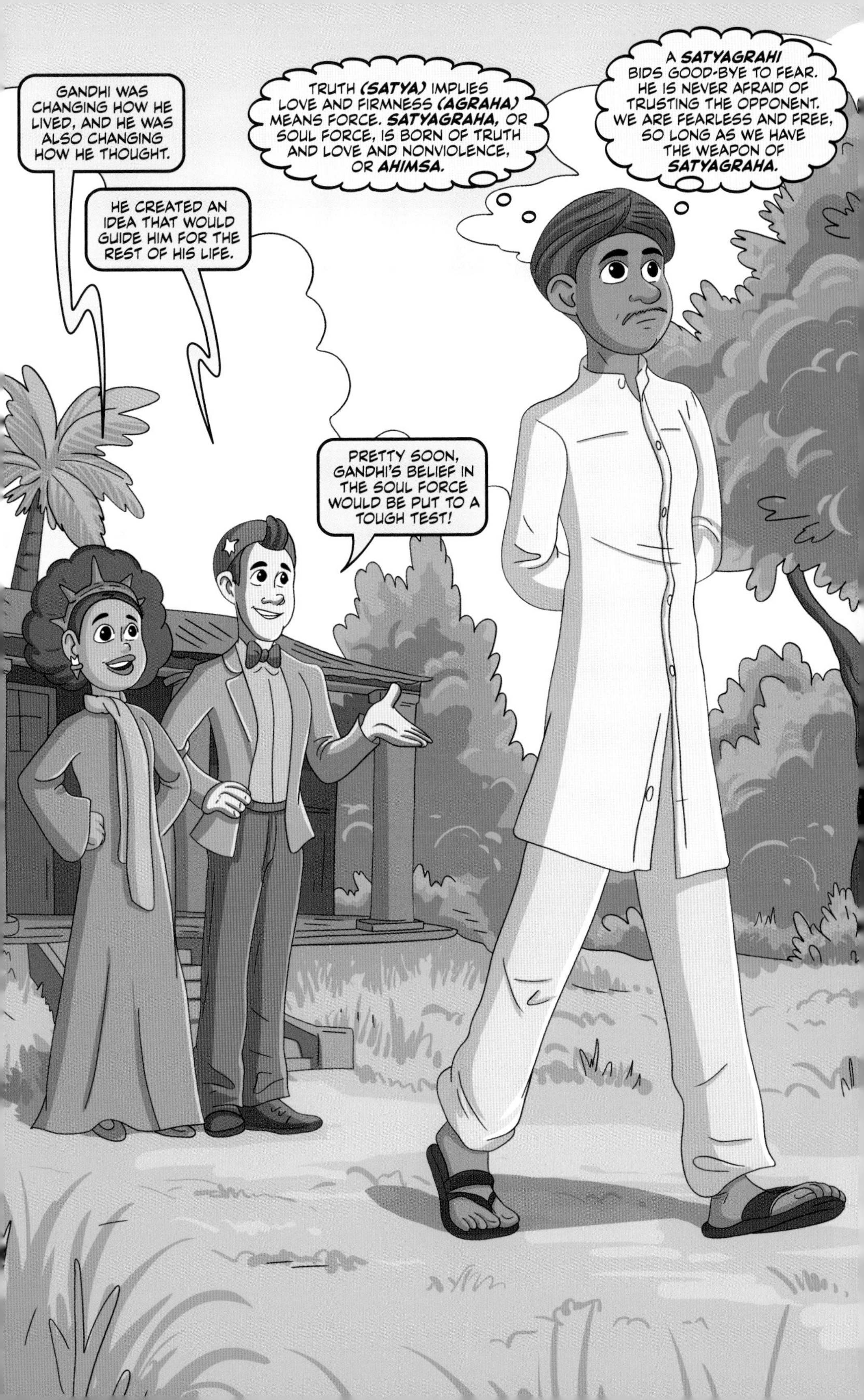
GANDHI WAS CHANGING HOW HE LIVED, AND HE WAS ALSO CHANGING HOW HE THOUGHT.
HE CREATED AN IDEA THAT WOULD GUIDE HIM FOR THE REST OF HIS LIFE.
TRUTH (SATYA) IMPLIES LOVE AND FIRMNESS (AGRAHA) MEANS FORCE. SATYAGRAHA, OR SOUL FORCE, IS BORN OF TRUTH AND LOVE AND NONVIOLENCE, OR AHIMSA.
A SATYAGRAHI BIDS GOOD-BYE TO FEAR. HE IS NEVER AFRAID OF TRUSTING THE OPPONENT. WE ARE FEARLESS AND FREE, SO LONG AS WE HAVE THE WEAPON OF SATYAGRAHA.
PRETTY SOON, GANDHI'S BELIEF IN THE SOUL FORCE WOULD BE PUT TO A TOUGH TEST!

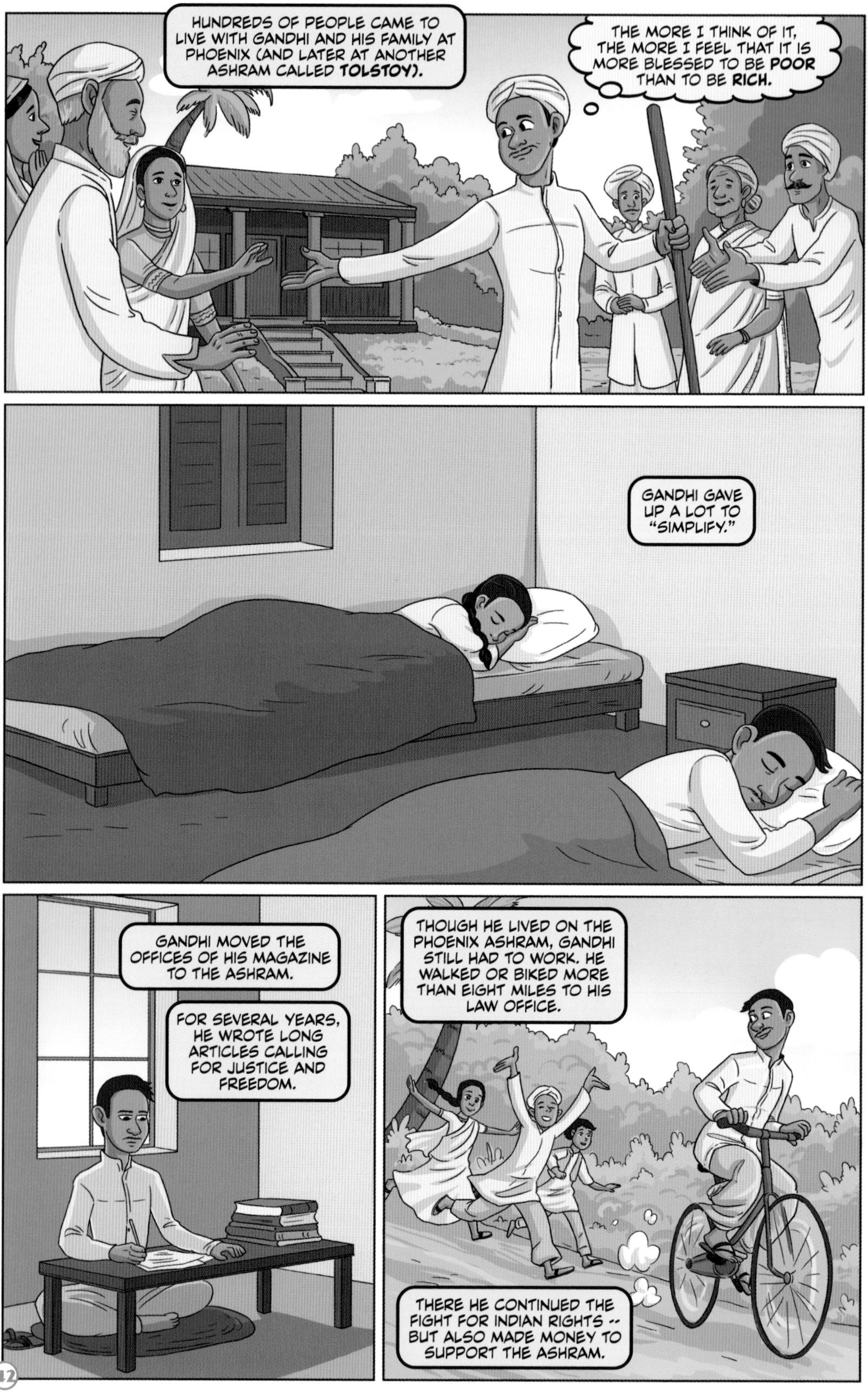

HUNDREDS OF PEOPLE CAME TO LIVE WITH GANDHI AND HIS FAMILY AT PHOENIX (AND LATER AT ANOTHER ASHRAM CALLED **TOLSTOY**).
THE MORE I THINK OF IT, THE MORE I FEEL THAT IT IS MORE BLESSED TO BE **POOR** THAN TO BE **RICH.**
GANDHI GAVE UP A LOT TO "SIMPLIFY."
GANDHI MOVED THE OFFICES OF HIS MAGAZINE TO THE ASHRAM.
FOR SEVERAL YEARS, HE WROTE LONG ARTICLES CALLING FOR JUSTICE AND FREEDOM.
THOUGH HE LIVED ON THE PHOENIX ASHRAM, GANDHI STILL HAD TO WORK. HE WALKED OR BIKED MORE THAN EIGHT MILES TO HIS LAW OFFICE.
THERE HE CONTINUED THE FIGHT FOR INDIAN RIGHTS -- BUT ALSO MADE MONEY TO SUPPORT THE ASHRAM.

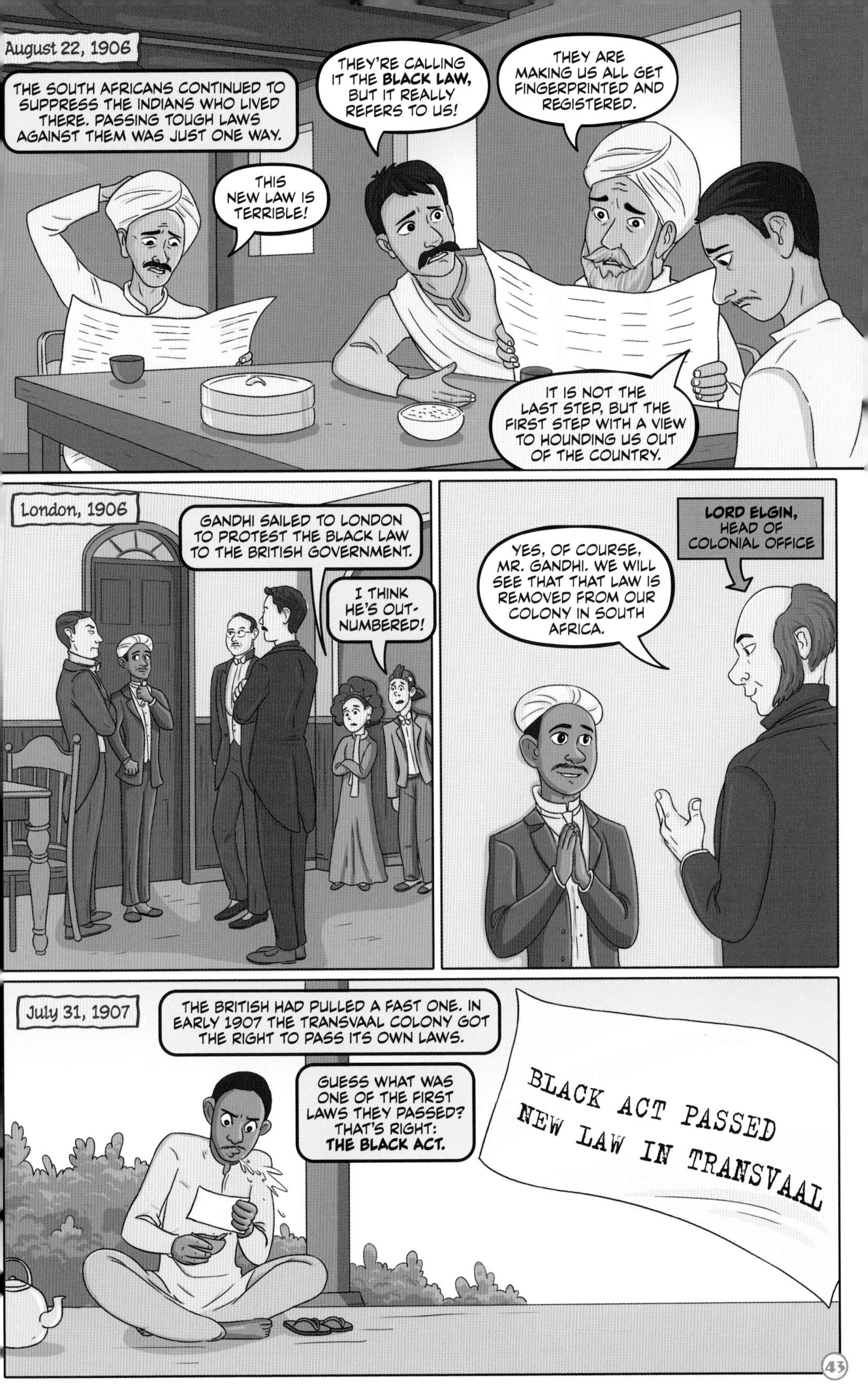
August 22, 1906
THE SOUTH AFRICANS CONTINUED TO SUPPRESS THE INDIANS WHO LIVED THERE. PASSING TOUGH LAWS AGAINST THEM WAS JUST ONE WAY.
THEY'RE CALLING IT THE **BLACK LAW,** BUT IT REALLY REFERS TO US!
THEY ARE MAKING US ALL GET FINGERPRINTED AND REGISTERED.
THIS NEW LAW IS TERRIBLE!
IT IS NOT THE LAST STEP, BUT THE FIRST STEP WITH A VIEW TO HOUNDING US OUT OF THE COUNTRY.
London, 1906
GANDHI SAILED TO LONDON TO PROTEST THE BLACK LAW TO THE BRITISH GOVERNMENT.
I THINK HE'S OUT-NUMBERED!
LORD ELGIN, HEAD OF COLONIAL OFFICE
YES, OF COURSE, MR. GANDHI. WE WILL SEE THAT THAT LAW IS REMOVED FROM OUR COLONY IN SOUTH AFRICA.
July 31, 1907
THE BRITISH HAD PULLED A FAST ONE. IN EARLY 1907 THE TRANSVAAL COLONY GOT THE RIGHT TO PASS ITS OWN LAWS.
GUESS WHAT WAS ONE OF THE FIRST LAWS THEY PASSED? THAT'S RIGHT: **THE BLACK ACT.**
BLACK ACT PASSED
NEW LAW IN TRANSVAAL

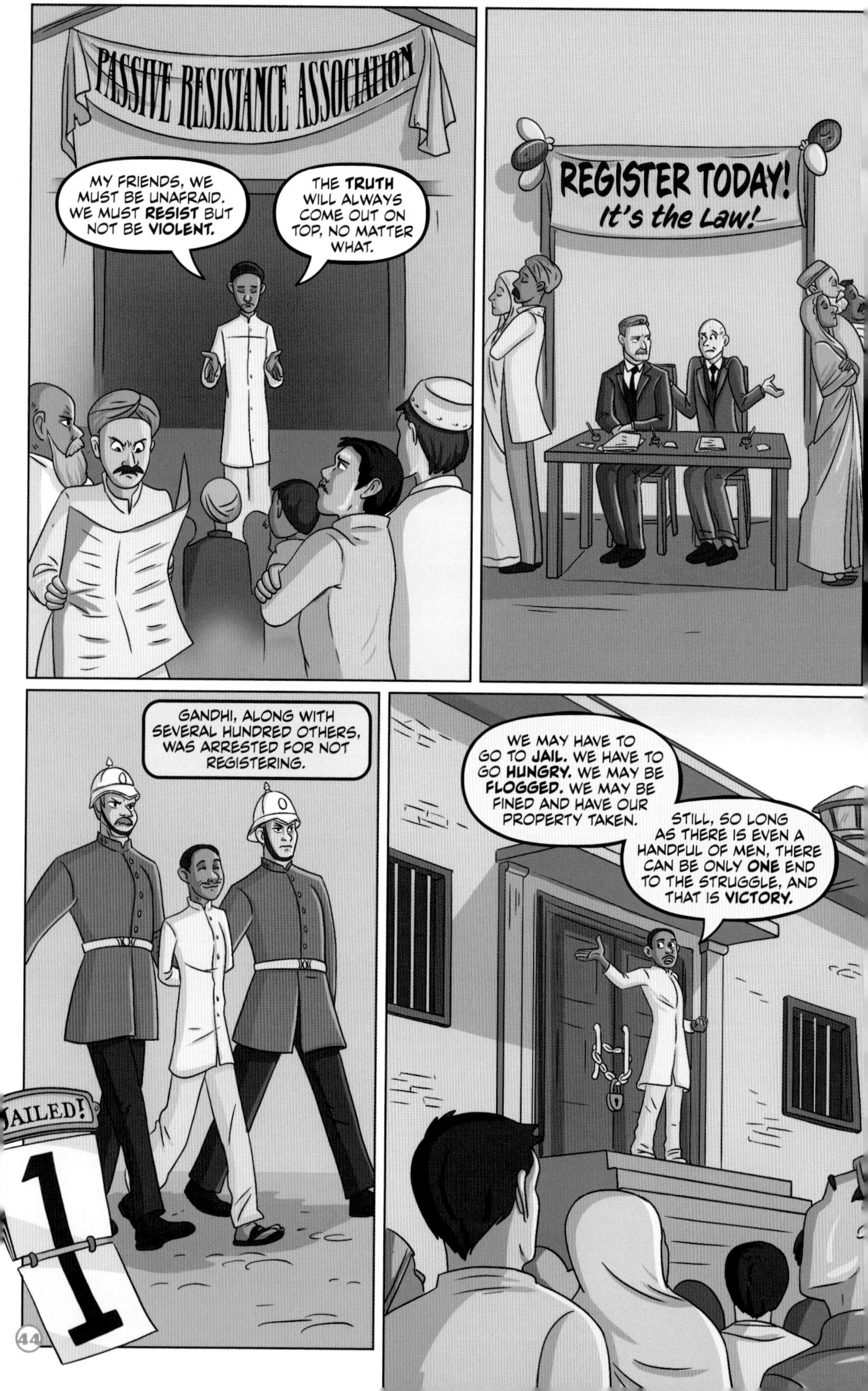
PASSIVE RESISTANCE ASSOCIATION
MY FRIENDS, WE MUST BE UNAFRAID. WE MUST **RESIST** BUT NOT BE **VIOLENT.**
THE **TRUTH** WILL ALWAYS COME OUT ON TOP, NO MATTER WHAT.
REGISTER TODAY! It's the Law!
GANDHI, ALONG WITH SEVERAL HUNDRED OTHERS, WAS ARRESTED FOR NOT REGISTERING.
WE MAY HAVE TO GO TO **JAIL.** WE HAVE TO GO **HUNGRY.** WE MAY BE **FLOGGED.** WE MAY BE FINED AND HAVE OUR PROPERTY TAKEN.
STILL, SO LONG AS THERE IS EVEN A HANDFUL OF MEN, THERE CAN BE ONLY **ONE** END TO THE STRUGGLE, AND THAT IS **VICTORY.**

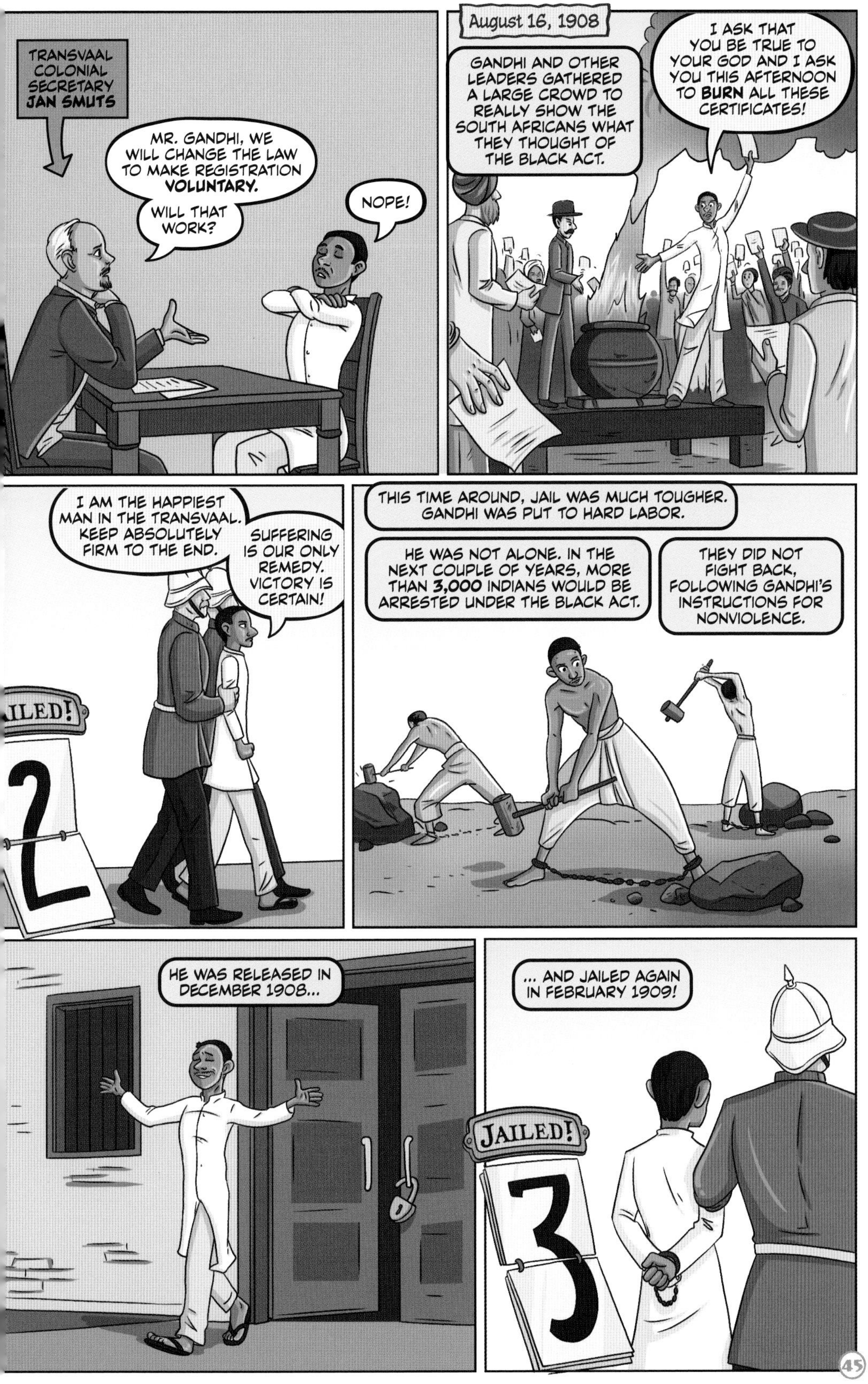
TRANSVAAL COLONIAL SECRETARY JAN SMUTS
MR. GANDHI, WE WILL CHANGE THE LAW TO MAKE REGISTRATION VOLUNTARY.
WILL THAT WORK?
NOPE!
August 16, 1908
GANDHI AND OTHER LEADERS GATHERED A LARGE CROWD TO REALLY SHOW THE SOUTH AFRICANS WHAT THEY THOUGHT OF THE BLACK ACT.
I ASK THAT YOU BE TRUE TO YOUR GOD AND I ASK YOU THIS AFTERNOON TO BURN ALL THESE CERTIFICATES!
I AM THE HAPPIEST MAN IN THE TRANSVAAL. KEEP ABSOLUTELY FIRM TO THE END.
SUFFERING IS OUR ONLY REMEDY. VICTORY IS CERTAIN!
AILED!
2
THIS TIME AROUND, JAIL WAS MUCH TOUGHER. GANDHI WAS PUT TO HARD LABOR.
HE WAS NOT ALONE. IN THE NEXT COUPLE OF YEARS, MORE THAN 3,000 INDIANS WOULD BE ARRESTED UNDER THE BLACK ACT.
THEY DID NOT FIGHT BACK, FOLLOWING GANDHI'S INSTRUCTIONS FOR NONVIOLENCE.
HE WAS RELEASED IN DECEMBER 1908...
... AND JAILED AGAIN IN FEBRUARY 1909!
JAILED!
3

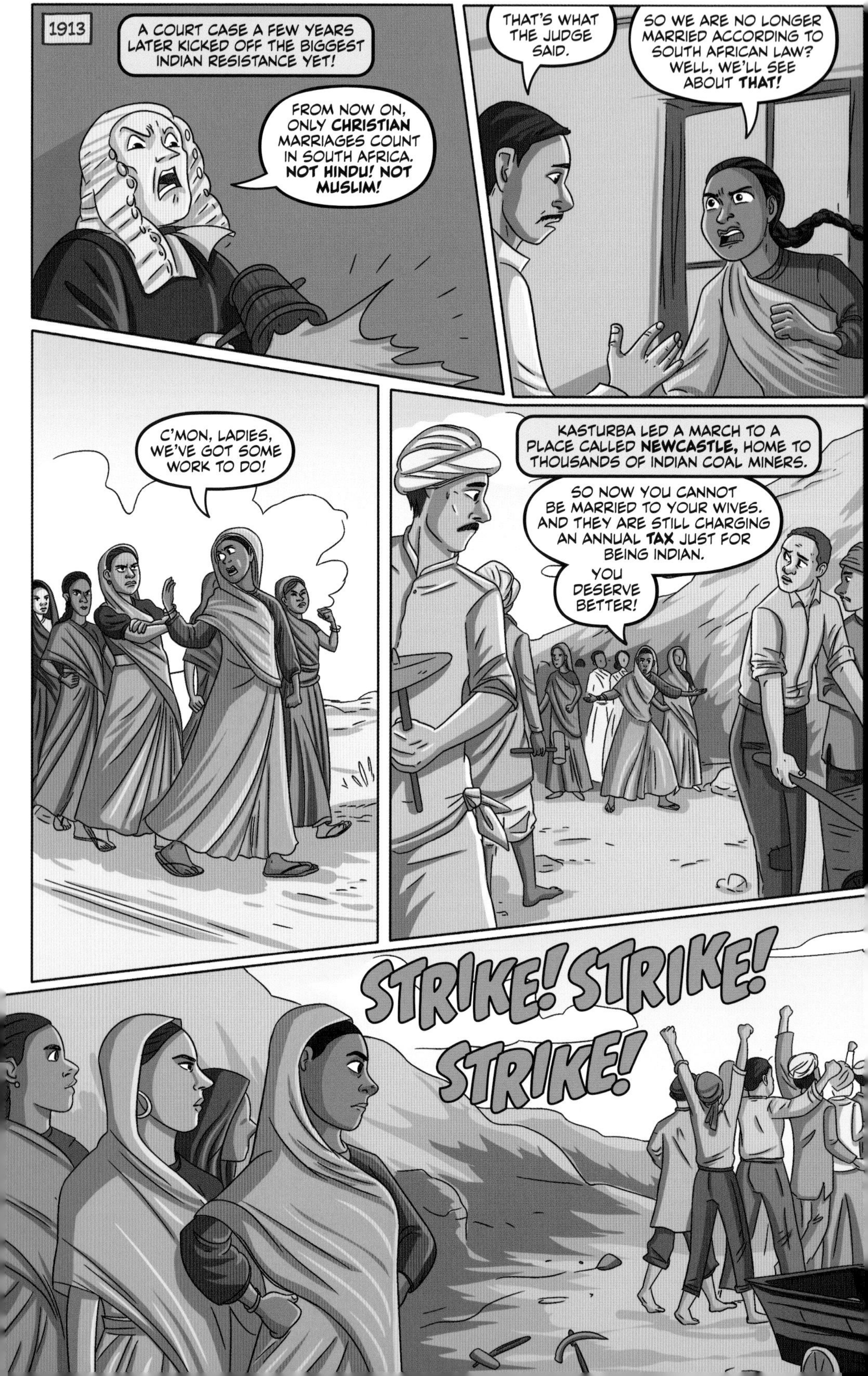
1913
A COURT CASE A FEW YEARS LATER KICKED OFF THE BIGGEST INDIAN RESISTANCE YET!
FROM NOW ON, ONLY **CHRISTIAN** MARRIAGES COUNT IN SOUTH AFRICA. **NOT HINDU! NOT MUSLIM!**
THAT'S WHAT THE JUDGE SAID.
SO WE ARE NO LONGER MARRIED ACCORDING TO SOUTH AFRICAN LAW? WELL, WE'LL SEE ABOUT **THAT!**
C'MON, LADIES, WE'VE GOT SOME WORK TO DO!
KASTURBA LED A MARCH TO A PLACE CALLED **NEWCASTLE,** HOME TO THOUSANDS OF INDIAN COAL MINERS.
SO NOW YOU CANNOT BE MARRIED TO YOUR WIVES. AND THEY ARE STILL CHARGING AN ANNUAL **TAX** JUST FOR BEING INDIAN.
YOU DESERVE BETTER!
STRIKE! STRIKE!
STRIKE!

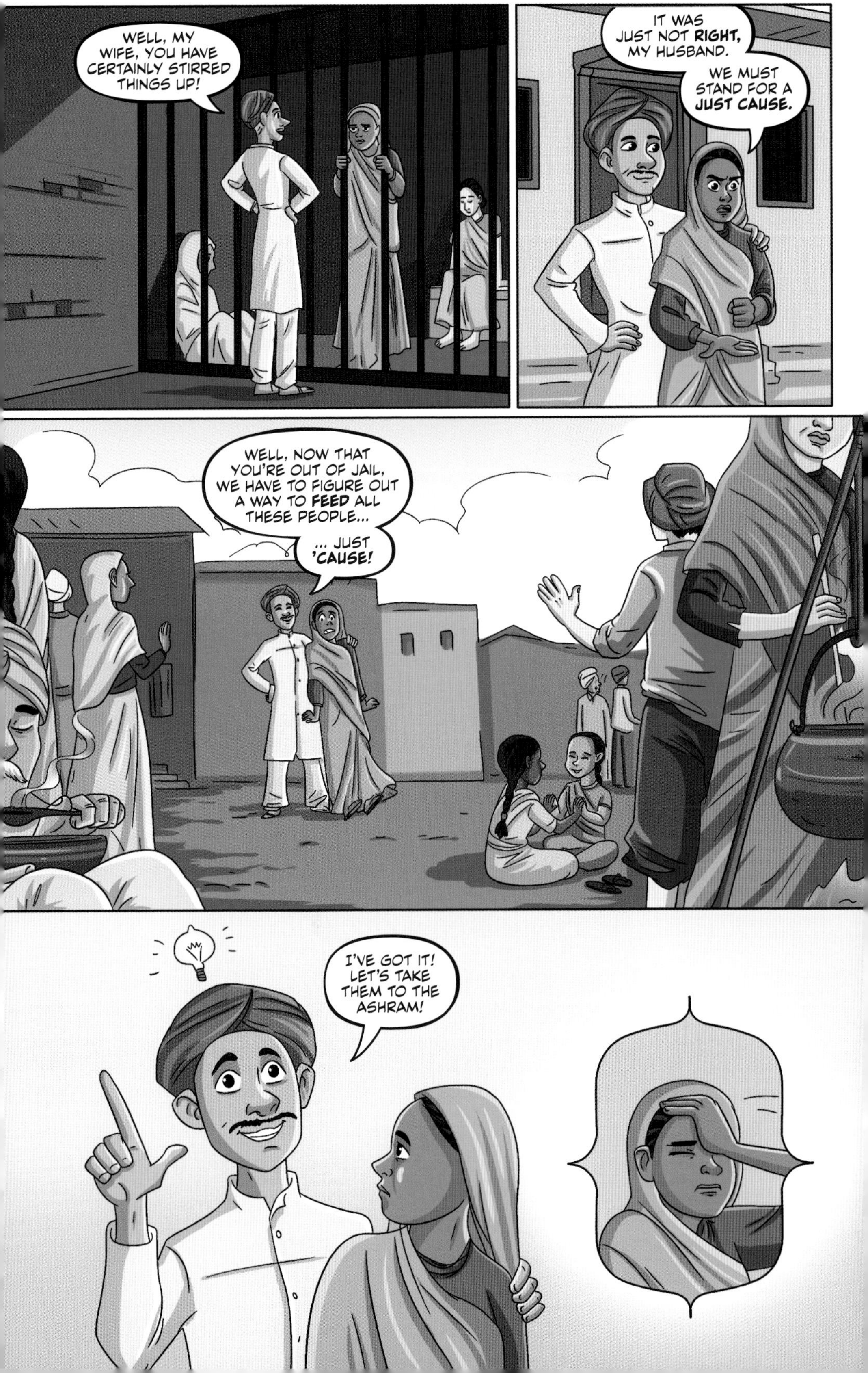
WELL, MY WIFE, YOU HAVE CERTAINLY STIRRED THINGS UP!
IT WAS JUST NOT RIGHT, MY HUSBAND.
WE MUST STAND FOR A JUST CAUSE.
WELL, NOW THAT YOU'RE OUT OF JAIL, WE HAVE TO FIGURE OUT A WAY TO FEED ALL THESE PEOPLE...
... JUST 'CAUSE!
I'VE GOT IT! LET'S TAKE THEM TO THE ASHRAM!

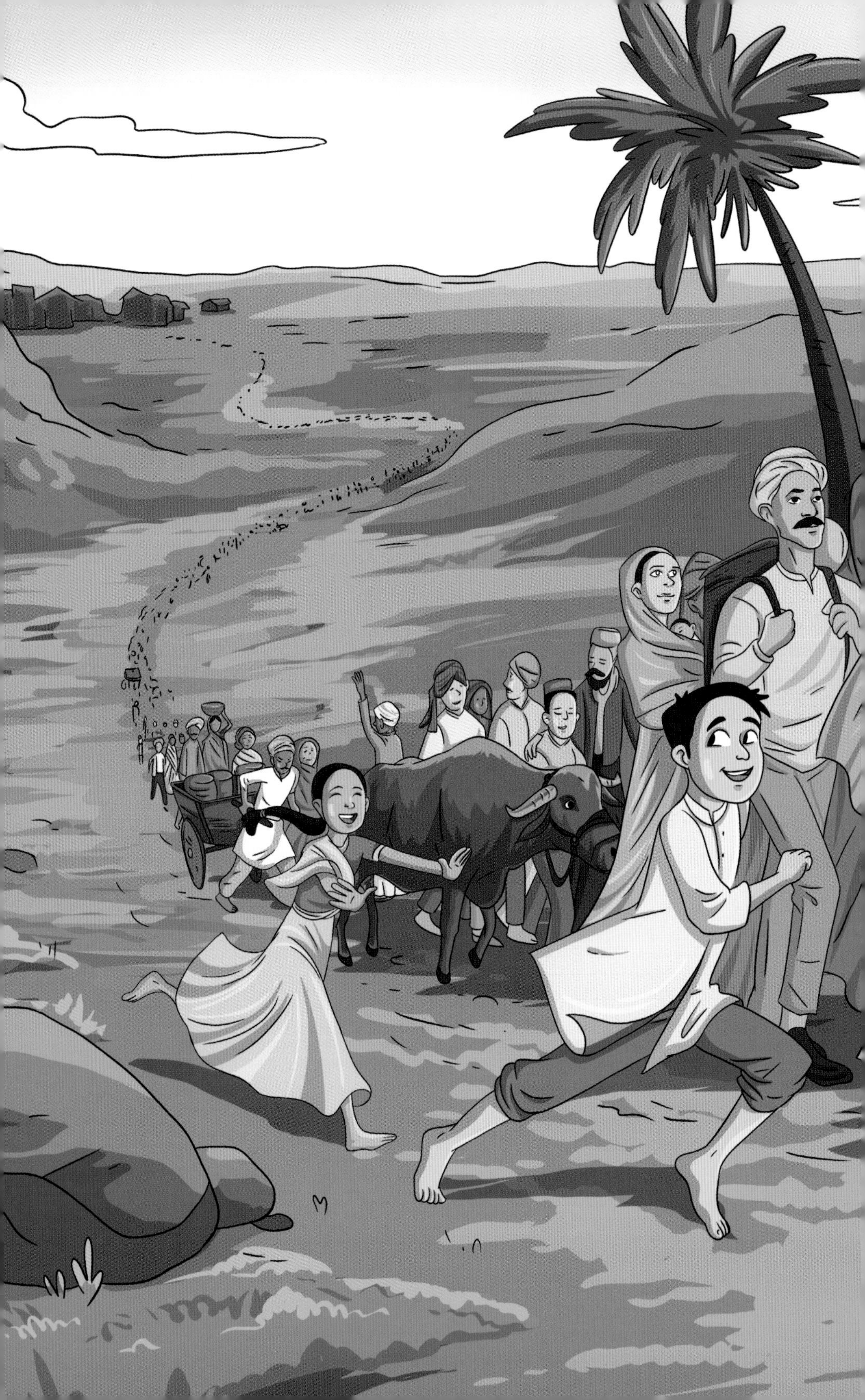

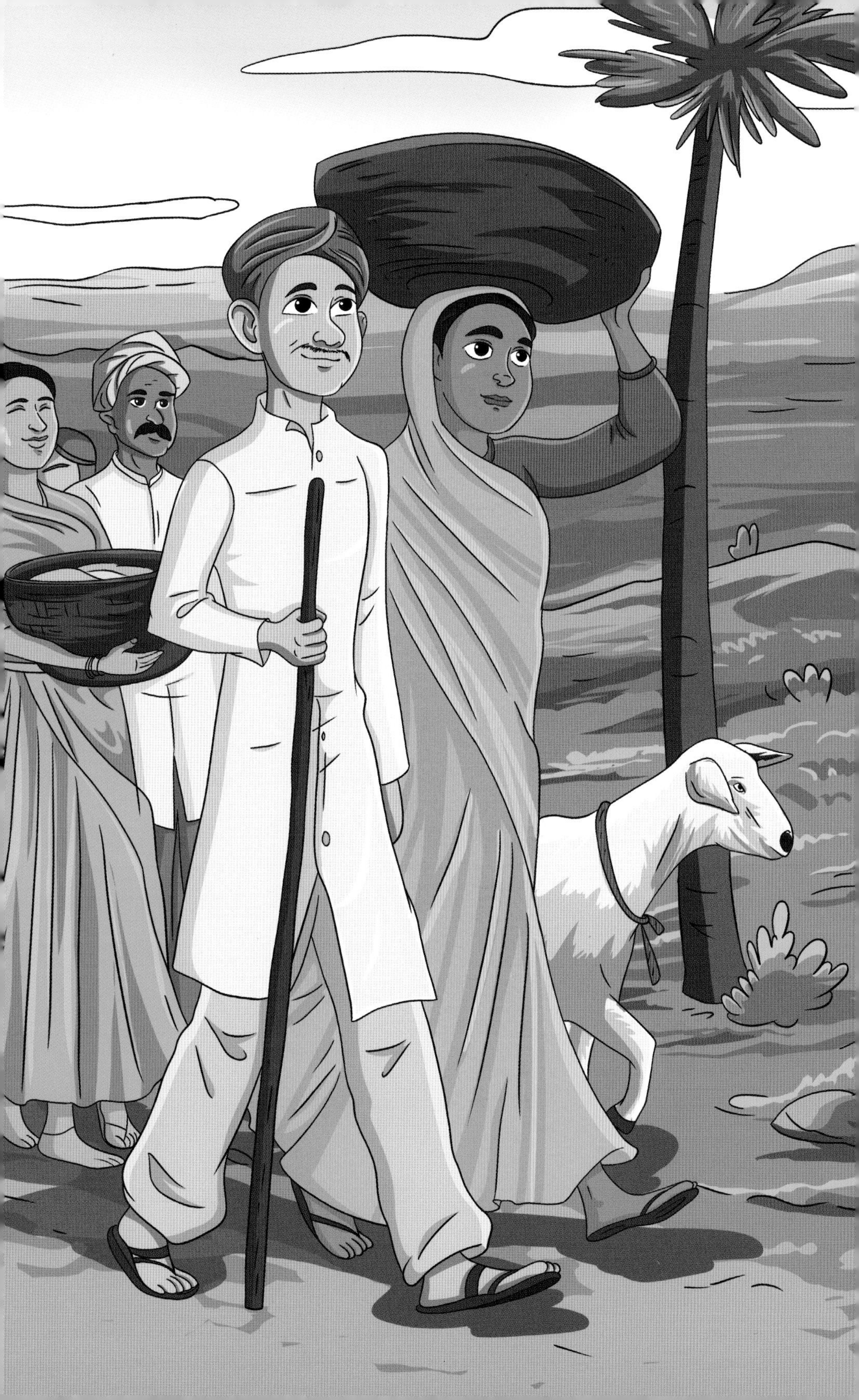

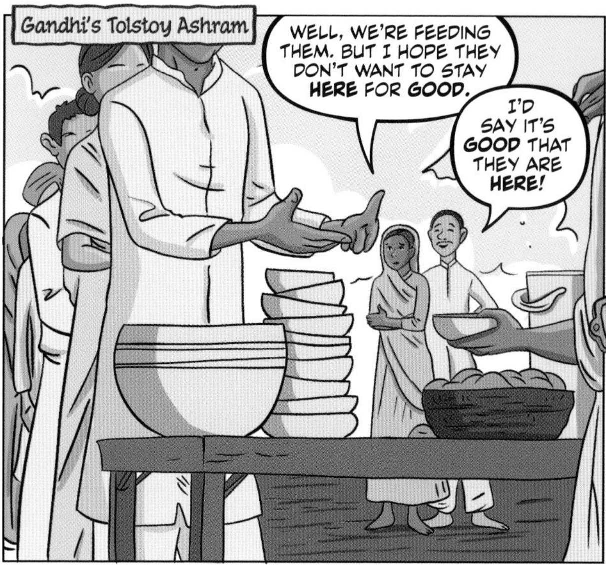
Gandhi's Tolstoy Ashram
WELL, WE'RE FEEDING THEM. BUT I HOPE THEY DON'T WANT TO STAY HERE FOR GOOD.
I'D SAY IT'S GOOD THAT THEY ARE HERE!

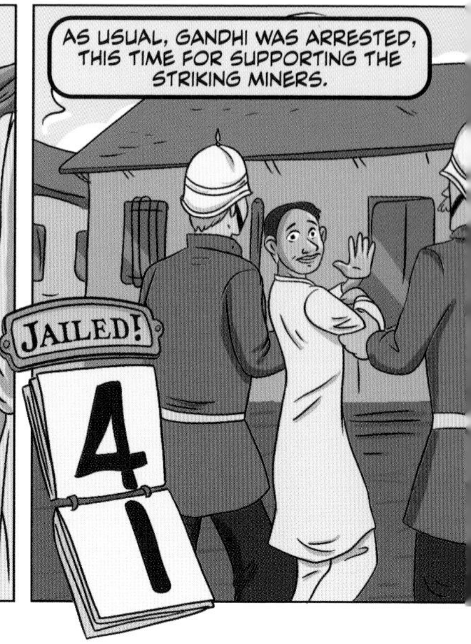
AS USUAL, GANDHI WAS ARRESTED, THIS TIME FOR SUPPORTING THE STRIKING MINERS.
JAILED!
41

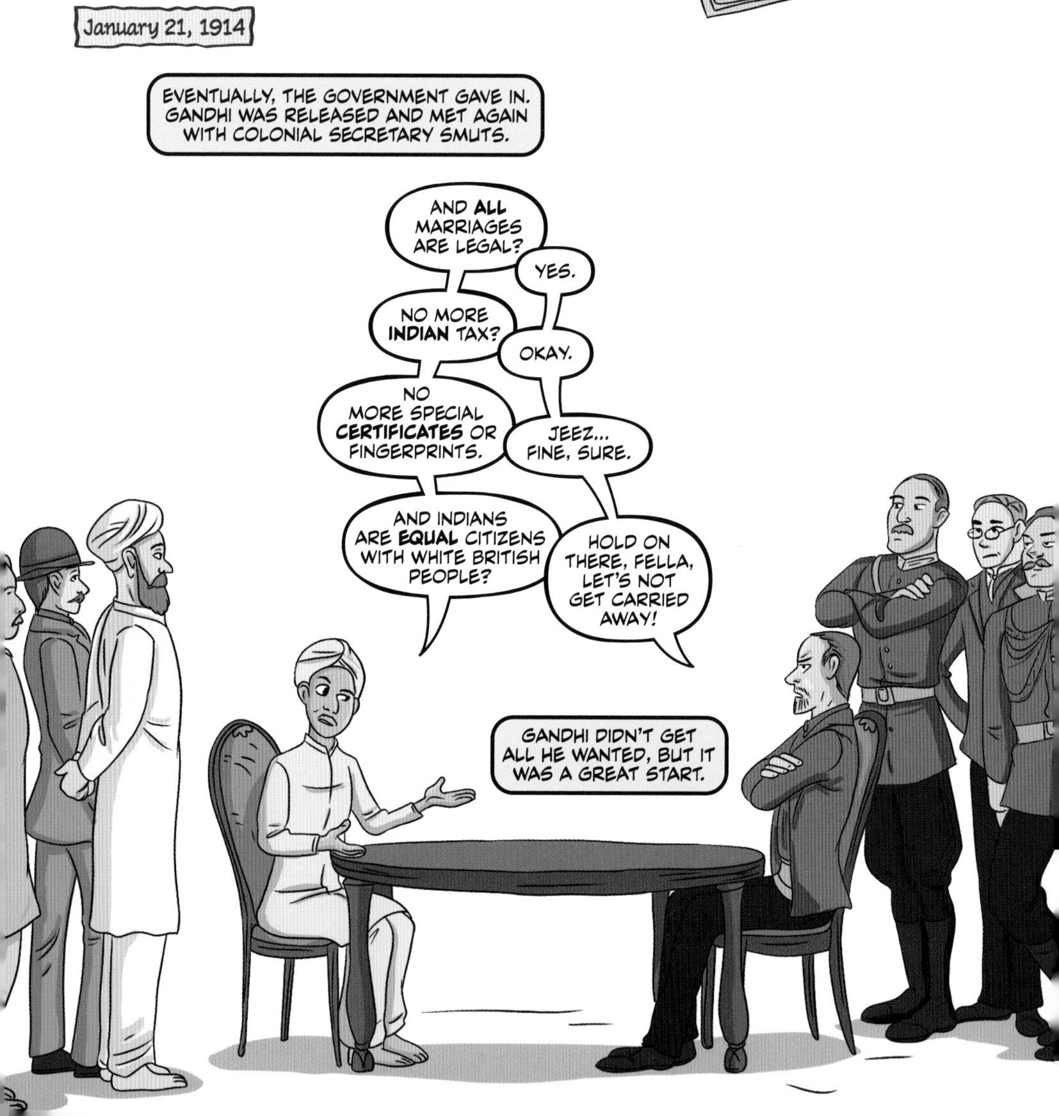
January 21, 1914
EVENTUALLY, THE GOVERNMENT GAVE IN. GANDHI WAS RELEASED AND MET AGAIN WITH COLONIAL SECRETARY SMUTS.
AND ALL MARRIAGES ARE LEGAL?
YES.
NO MORE INDIAN TAX?
OKAY.
NO MORE SPECIAL CERTIFICATES OR FINGERPRINTS.
JEEZ... FINE, SURE.
AND INDIANS ARE EQUAL CITIZENS WITH WHITE BRITISH PEOPLE?
HOLD ON THERE, FELLA, LET'S NOT GET CARRIED AWAY!
GANDHI DIDN'T GET ALL HE WANTED, BUT IT WAS A GREAT START.

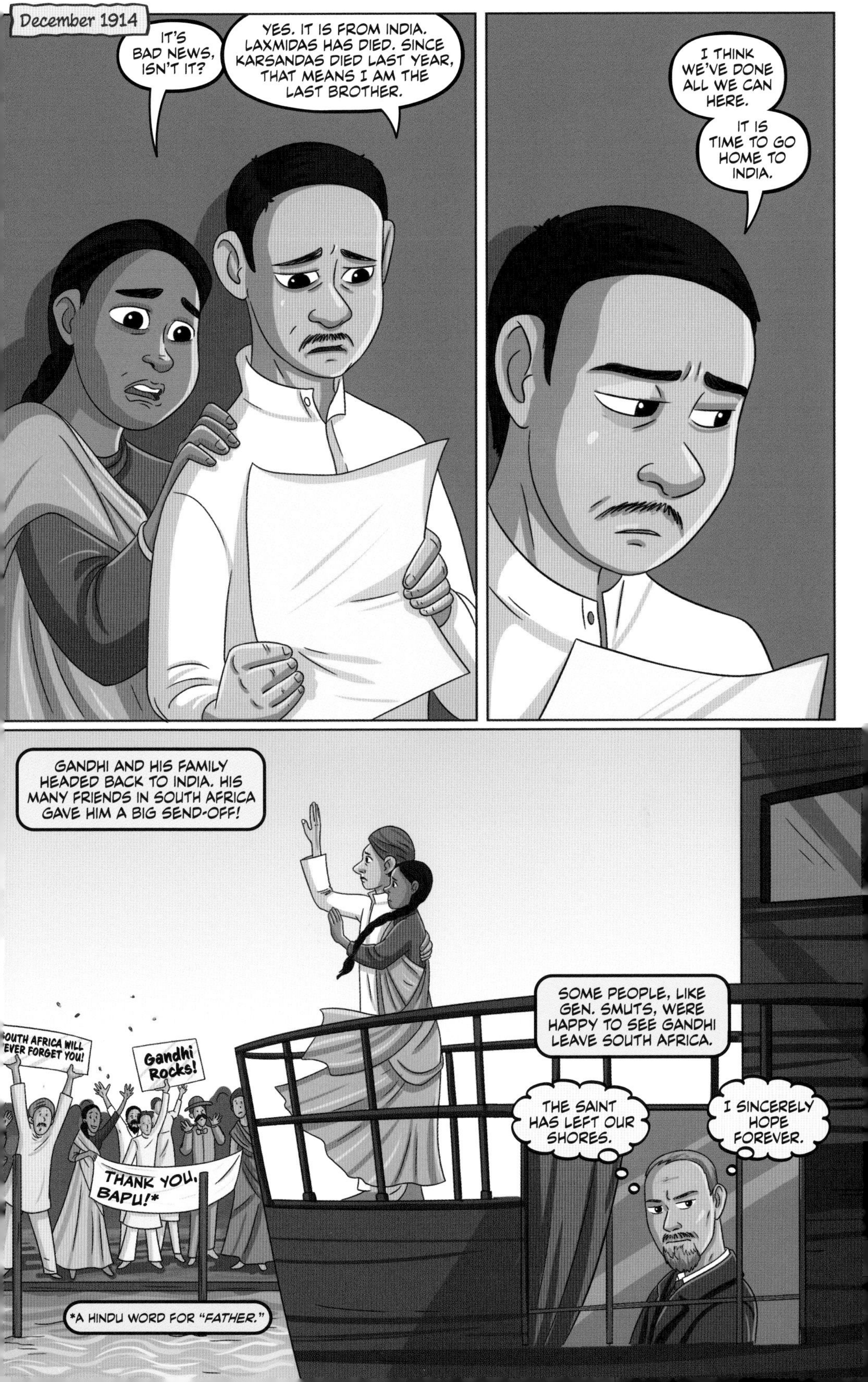
December 1914
IT'S BAD NEWS, ISN'T IT?
YES. IT IS FROM INDIA. LAXMIDAS HAS DIED. SINCE KARSANDAS DIED LAST YEAR, THAT MEANS I AM THE LAST BROTHER.
I THINK WE'VE DONE ALL WE CAN HERE.
IT IS TIME TO GO HOME TO INDIA.
GANDHI AND HIS FAMILY HEADED BACK TO INDIA. HIS MANY FRIENDS IN SOUTH AFRICA GAVE HIM A BIG SEND-OFF!
OUTH AFRICA WILL
EVER FORGET YOU!
Gandhi Rocks!
THANK YOU, BAPU!*
SOME PEOPLE, LIKE GEN. SMUTS, WERE HAPPY TO SEE GANDHI LEAVE SOUTH AFRICA.
THE SAINT HAS LEFT OUR SHORES.
I SINCERELY HOPE FOREVER.
*A HINDU WORD FOR "FATHER."

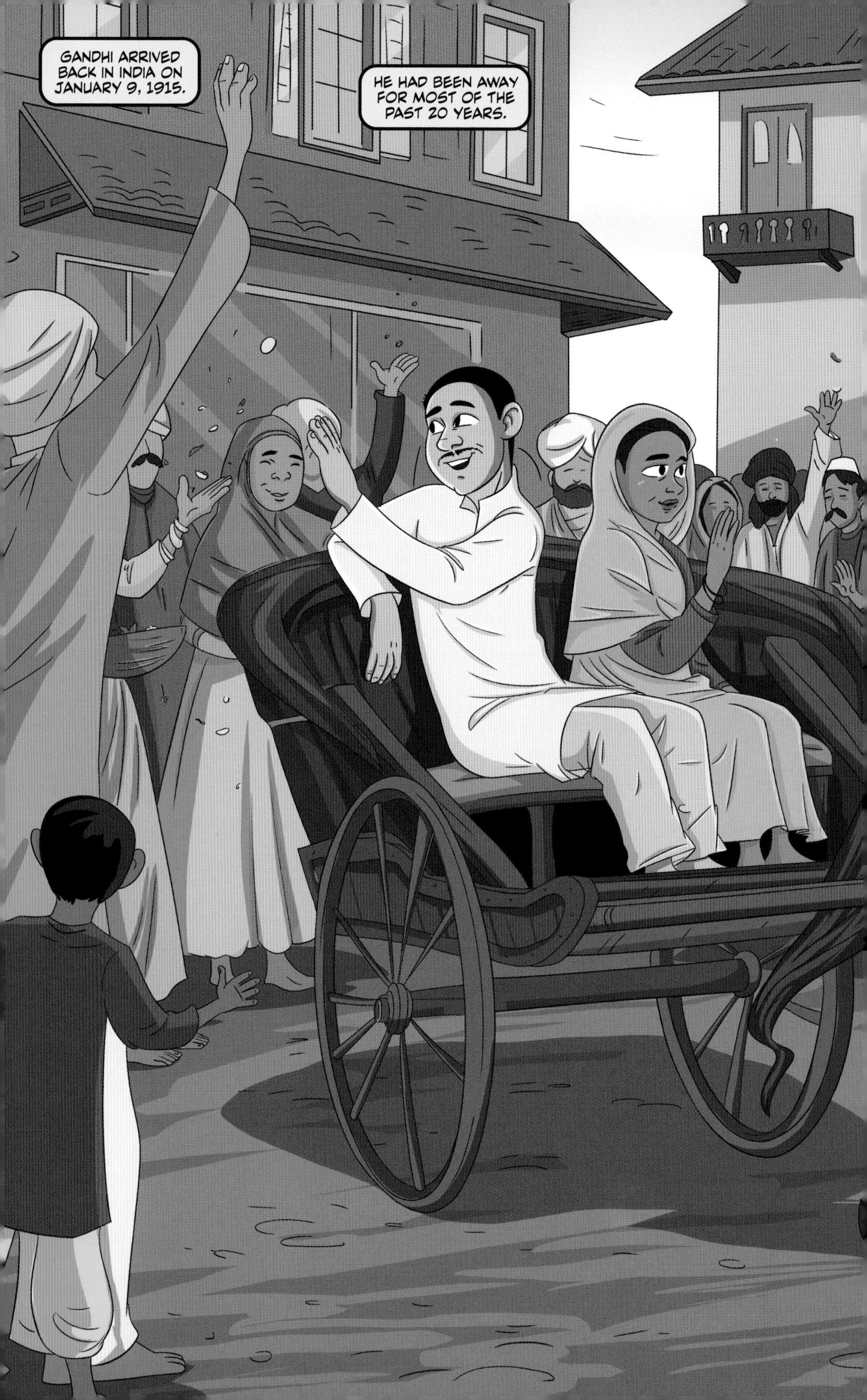
GANDHI ARRIVED BACK IN INDIA ON JANUARY 9, 1915.
HE HAD BEEN AWAY FOR MOST OF THE PAST 20 YEARS.

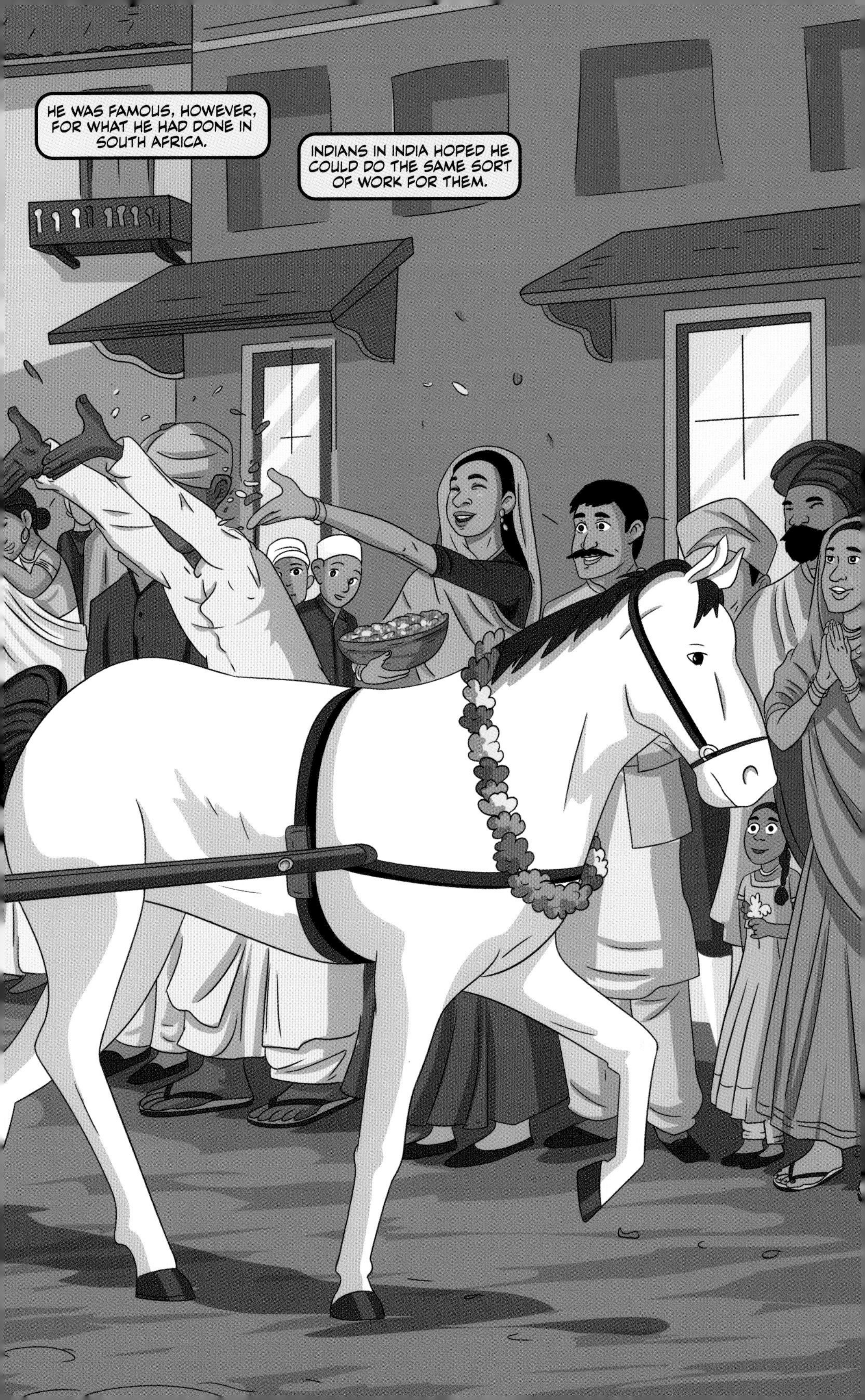
HE WAS FAMOUS, HOWEVER, FOR WHAT HE HAD DONE IN SOUTH AFRICA.
INDIANS IN INDIA HOPED HE COULD DO THE SAME SORT OF WORK FOR THEM.

MOHAN, IT IS SO NICE TO BE HOME AGAIN!

WELL, DON'T GET TOO COMFORTABLE.

I HAVE A LOT OF PEOPLE TO SEE, AND LOTS TO DO!

NO REST FOR THE WEARY!

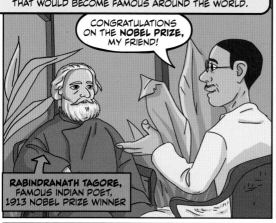

ALL SORTS OF FAMOUS PEOPLE IN INDIA WANTED TO MEET WITH GANDHI. ONE OF THEM GAVE HIM AN HONORARY TITLE THAT WOULD BECOME FAMOUS AROUND THE WORLD.

CONGRATULATIONS ON THE **NOBEL PRIZE,** MY FRIEND!

RABINDRANATH TAGORE, FAMOUS INDIAN POET, 1913 NOBEL PRIZE WINNER

NO, BAPU, OUR THANKS TO YOU FOR ALL YOU HAVE DONE.

YOU HAVE EARNED THE TITLE OF **MAHATMA** -- WHICH MEANS "GREAT SOUL" -- FOR YOUR LEADERSHIP AND LOVE.

AS HE HAD IN SOUTH AFRICA, GANDHI SOON SET UP AN ASHRAM WHERE HE AND OTHERS COULD LIVE A SIMPLE LIFE.

HE NAMED IT FOR HIS IDEA OF SOUL FORCE: **SATYAGRAHA!**

BUT BAPU, WE ARE **DALIT,** WE ARE **UNTOUCHABLE.**

HERE AT SATYAGRAHA ASHRAM, ALL ARE EQUAL... THERE ARE NO **CASTES** HERE.

GANDHI WANTED TO REDISCOVER THE COUNTRY HE HAD BEEN AWAY FROM FOR SO LONG.

HE SPENT MONTHS TRAVELING BY TRAIN TO SEE DISTANT VILLAGES.

THOUGH HE COULD AFFORD TO RIDE IN FIRST CLASS, HE ALWAYS TOOK A THIRD-CLASS SEAT.

54

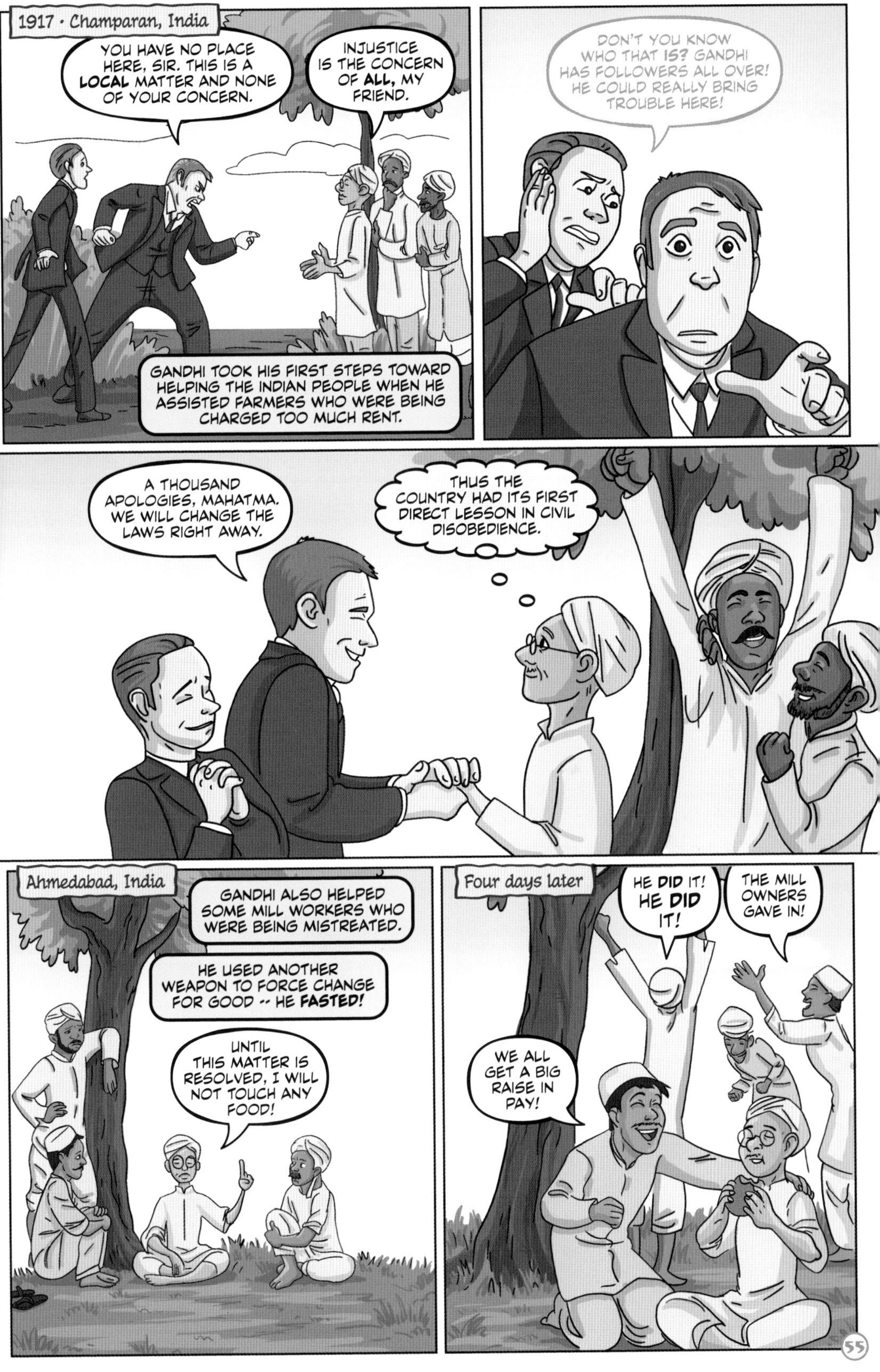
1917 • Champaran, India
YOU HAVE NO PLACE HERE, SIR. THIS IS A LOCAL MATTER AND NONE OF YOUR CONCERN.
INJUSTICE IS THE CONCERN OF ALL, MY FRIEND.
GANDHI TOOK HIS FIRST STEPS TOWARD HELPING THE INDIAN PEOPLE WHEN HE ASSISTED FARMERS WHO WERE BEING CHARGED TOO MUCH RENT.
DON'T YOU KNOW WHO THAT IS? GANDHI HAS FOLLOWERS ALL OVER! HE COULD REALLY BRING TROUBLE HERE!
A THOUSAND APOLOGIES, MAHATMA. WE WILL CHANGE THE LAWS RIGHT AWAY.
THUS THE COUNTRY HAD ITS FIRST DIRECT LESSON IN CIVIL DISOBEDIENCE.
Ahmedabad, India
GANDHI ALSO HELPED SOME MILL WORKERS WHO WERE BEING MISTREATED.
HE USED ANOTHER WEAPON TO FORCE CHANGE FOR GOOD -- HE FASTED!
UNTIL THIS MATTER IS RESOLVED, I WILL NOT TOUCH ANY FOOD!
Four days later
HE DID IT! HE DID IT!
THE MILL OWNERS GAVE IN!
WE ALL GET A BIG RAISE IN PAY!

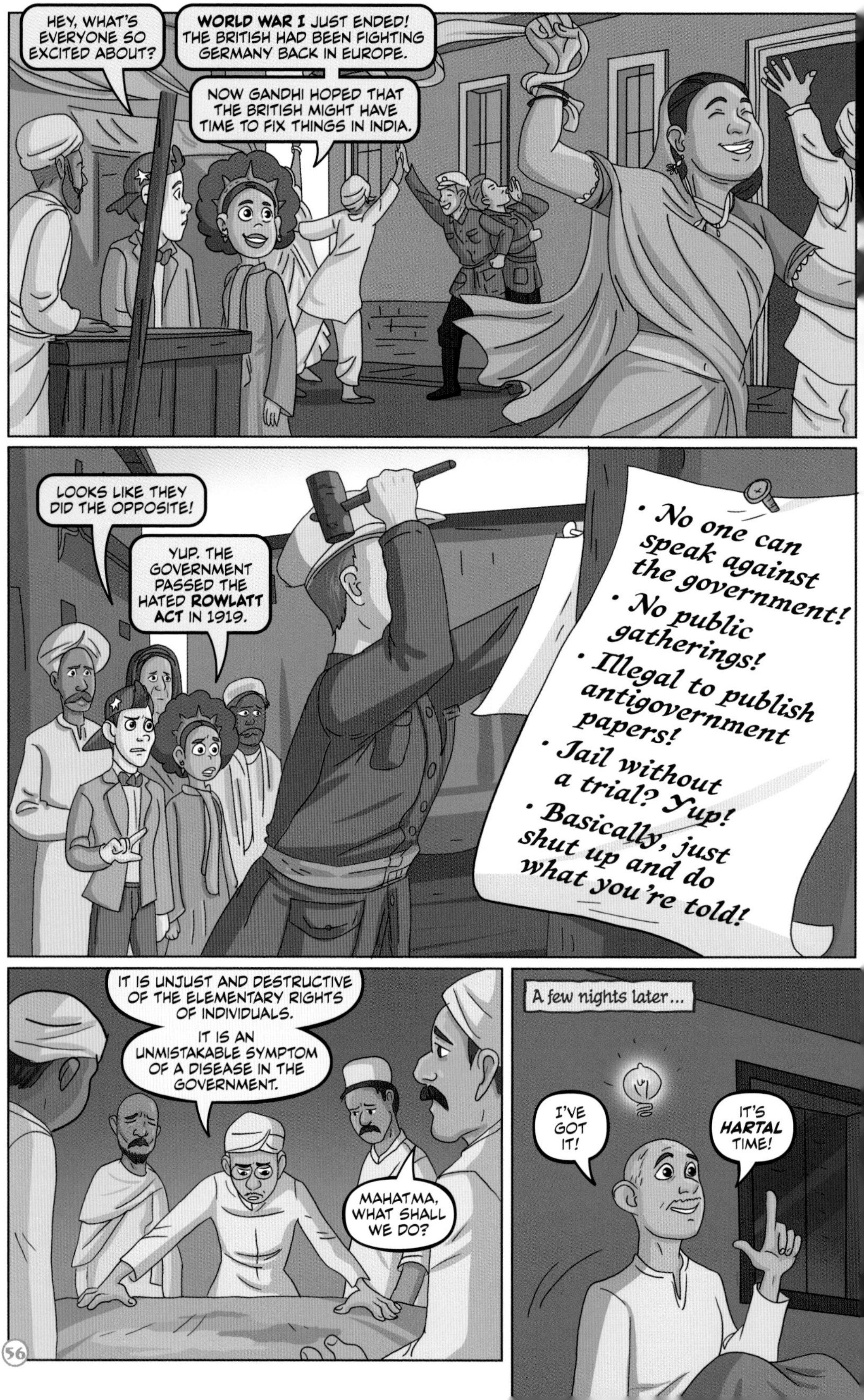
HEY, WHAT'S EVERYONE SO EXCITED ABOUT?
WORLD WAR I JUST ENDED! THE BRITISH HAD BEEN FIGHTING GERMANY BACK IN EUROPE.
NOW GANDHI HOPED THAT THE BRITISH MIGHT HAVE TIME TO FIX THINGS IN INDIA.
LOOKS LIKE THEY DID THE OPPOSITE!
YUP. THE GOVERNMENT PASSED THE HATED ROWLATT ACT IN 1919.
• No one can speak against the government!
• No public gatherings!
• Illegal to publish antigovernment papers!
• Jail without a trial? Yup!
• Basically, just shut up and do what you're told!
IT IS UNJUST AND DESTRUCTIVE OF THE ELEMENTARY RIGHTS OF INDIVIDUALS.
IT IS AN UNMISTAKABLE SYMPTOM OF A DISEASE IN THE GOVERNMENT.
MAHATMA, WHAT SHALL WE DO?
A few nights later...
I'VE GOT IT!
IT'S HARTAL TIME!

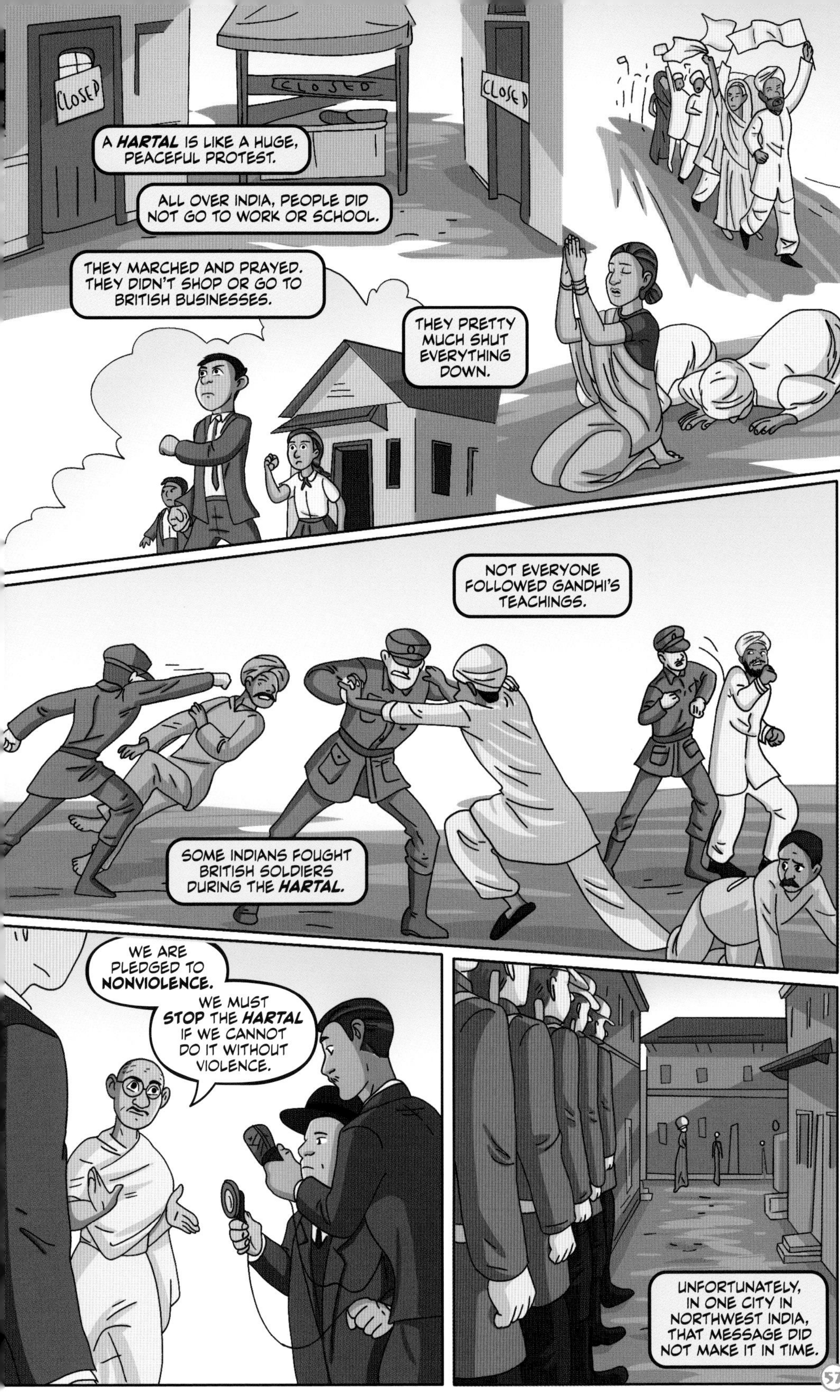
CLOSED
CLOSED
CLOSED
A **HARTAL** IS LIKE A HUGE, PEACEFUL PROTEST.
ALL OVER INDIA, PEOPLE DID NOT GO TO WORK OR SCHOOL.
THEY MARCHED AND PRAYED. THEY DIDN'T SHOP OR GO TO BRITISH BUSINESSES.
THEY PRETTY MUCH SHUT EVERYTHING DOWN.
NOT EVERYONE FOLLOWED GANDHI'S TEACHINGS.
SOME INDIANS FOUGHT BRITISH SOLDIERS DURING THE ***HARTAL.***
WE ARE PLEDGED TO **NONVIOLENCE.**
WE MUST **STOP** THE ***HARTAL*** IF WE CANNOT DO IT WITHOUT VIOLENCE.
UNFORTUNATELY, IN ONE CITY IN NORTHWEST INDIA, THAT MESSAGE DID NOT MAKE IT IN TIME.

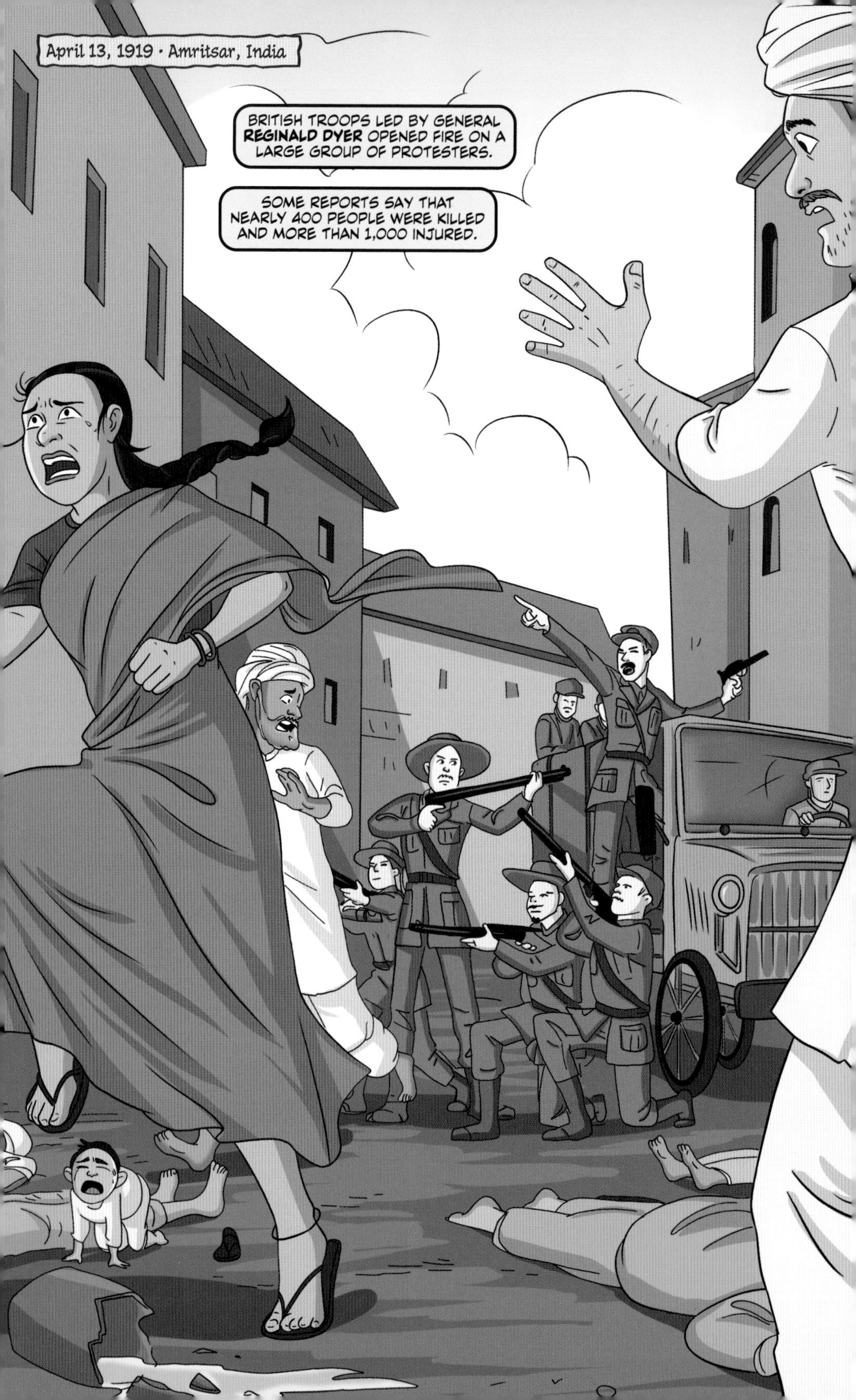
April 13, 1919 • Amritsar, India
BRITISH TROOPS LED BY GENERAL REGINALD DYER OPENED FIRE ON A LARGE GROUP OF PROTESTERS.
SOME REPORTS SAY THAT NEARLY 400 PEOPLE WERE KILLED AND MORE THAN 1,000 INJURED.

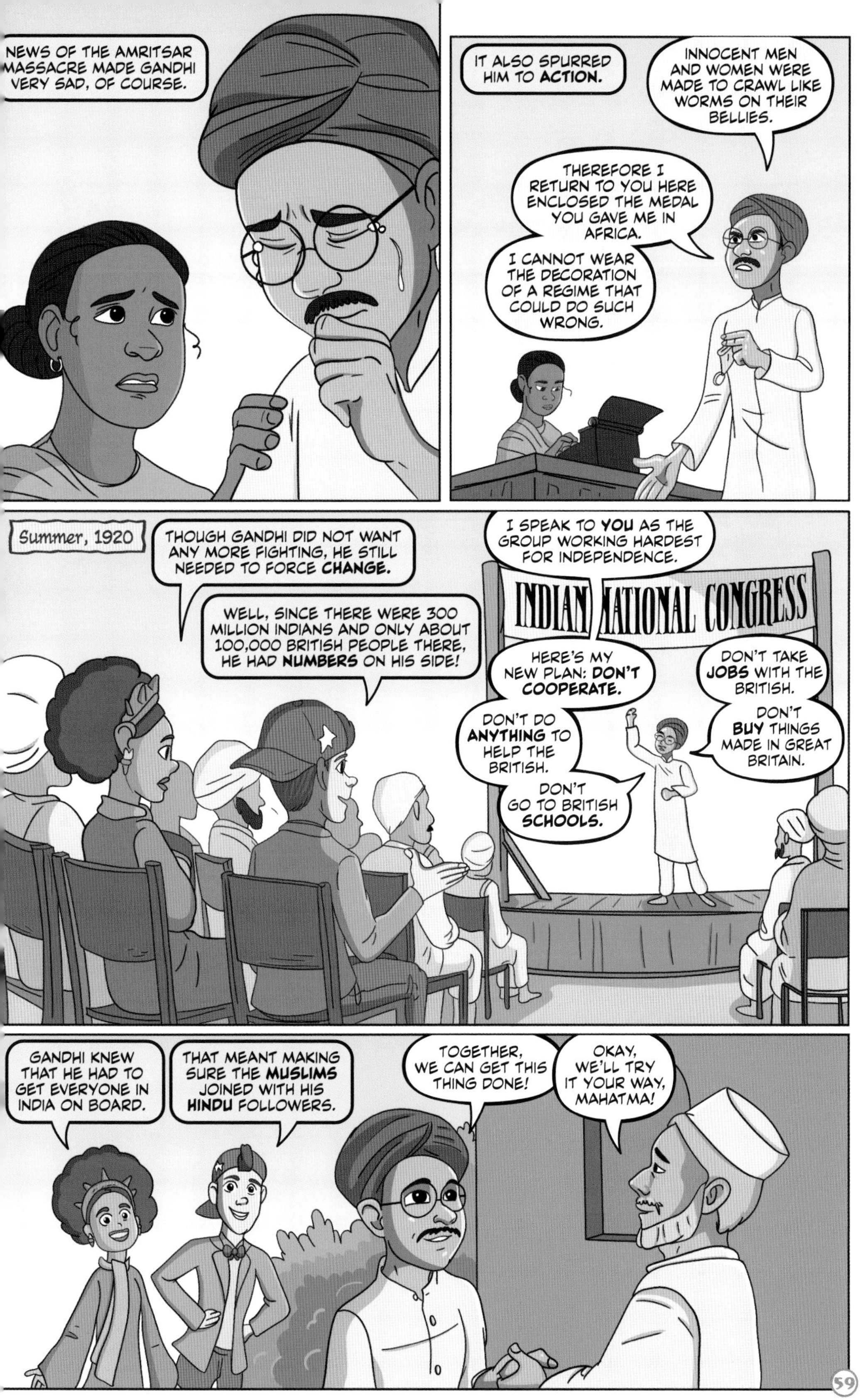

NEWS OF THE AMRITSAR MASSACRE MADE GANDHI VERY SAD, OF COURSE.
IT ALSO SPURRED HIM TO **ACTION.**
INNOCENT MEN AND WOMEN WERE MADE TO CRAWL LIKE WORMS ON THEIR BELLIES.
THEREFORE I RETURN TO YOU HERE ENCLOSED THE MEDAL YOU GAVE ME IN AFRICA.
I CANNOT WEAR THE DECORATION OF A REGIME THAT COULD DO SUCH WRONG.
Summer, 1920
THOUGH GANDHI DID NOT WANT ANY MORE FIGHTING, HE STILL NEEDED TO FORCE **CHANGE.**
WELL, SINCE THERE WERE 300 MILLION INDIANS AND ONLY ABOUT 100,000 BRITISH PEOPLE THERE, HE HAD **NUMBERS** ON HIS SIDE!
I SPEAK TO **YOU** AS THE GROUP WORKING HARDEST FOR INDEPENDENCE.
HERE'S MY NEW PLAN: **DON'T COOPERATE.**
DON'T TAKE **JOBS** WITH THE BRITISH.
DON'T DO **ANYTHING** TO HELP THE BRITISH.
DON'T **BUY** THINGS MADE IN GREAT BRITAIN.
DON'T GO TO BRITISH **SCHOOLS.**
GANDHI KNEW THAT HE HAD TO GET EVERYONE IN INDIA ON BOARD.
THAT MEANT MAKING SURE THE **MUSLIMS** JOINED WITH HIS **HINDU** FOLLOWERS.
TOGETHER, WE CAN GET THIS THING DONE!
OKAY, WE'LL TRY IT YOUR WAY, MAHATMA!

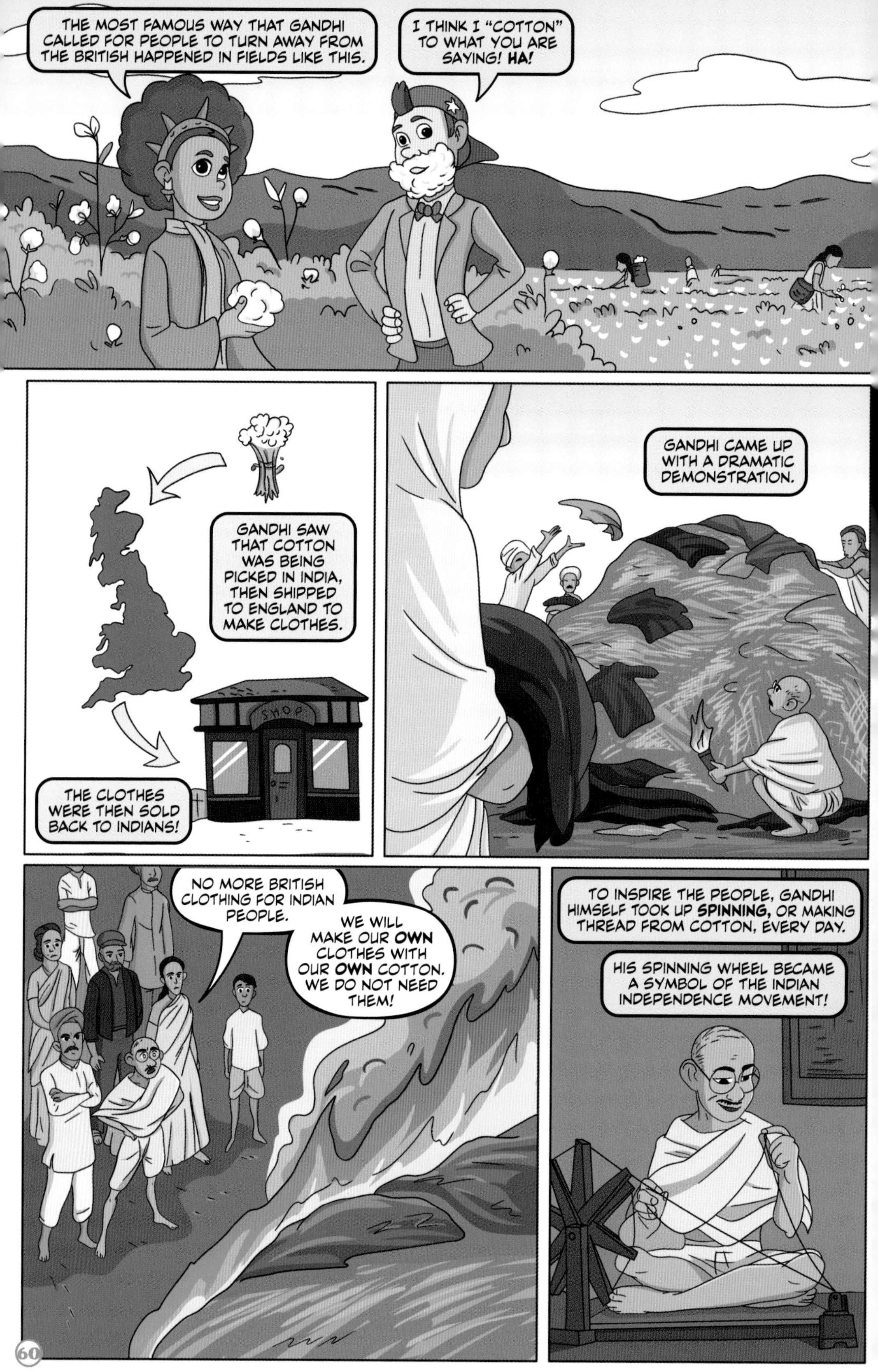
THE MOST FAMOUS WAY THAT GANDHI CALLED FOR PEOPLE TO TURN AWAY FROM THE BRITISH HAPPENED IN FIELDS LIKE THIS.
I THINK I "COTTON" TO WHAT YOU ARE SAYING! **HA!**
GANDHI SAW THAT COTTON WAS BEING PICKED IN INDIA, THEN SHIPPED TO ENGLAND TO MAKE CLOTHES.
SHOP
THE CLOTHES WERE THEN SOLD BACK TO INDIANS!
GANDHI CAME UP WITH A DRAMATIC DEMONSTRATION.
NO MORE BRITISH CLOTHING FOR INDIAN PEOPLE.
WE WILL MAKE OUR **OWN** CLOTHES WITH OUR **OWN** COTTON. WE DO NOT NEED THEM!
TO INSPIRE THE PEOPLE, GANDHI HIMSELF TOOK UP **SPINNING,** OR MAKING THREAD FROM COTTON, EVERY DAY.
HIS SPINNING WHEEL BECAME A SYMBOL OF THE INDIAN INDEPENDENCE MOVEMENT!

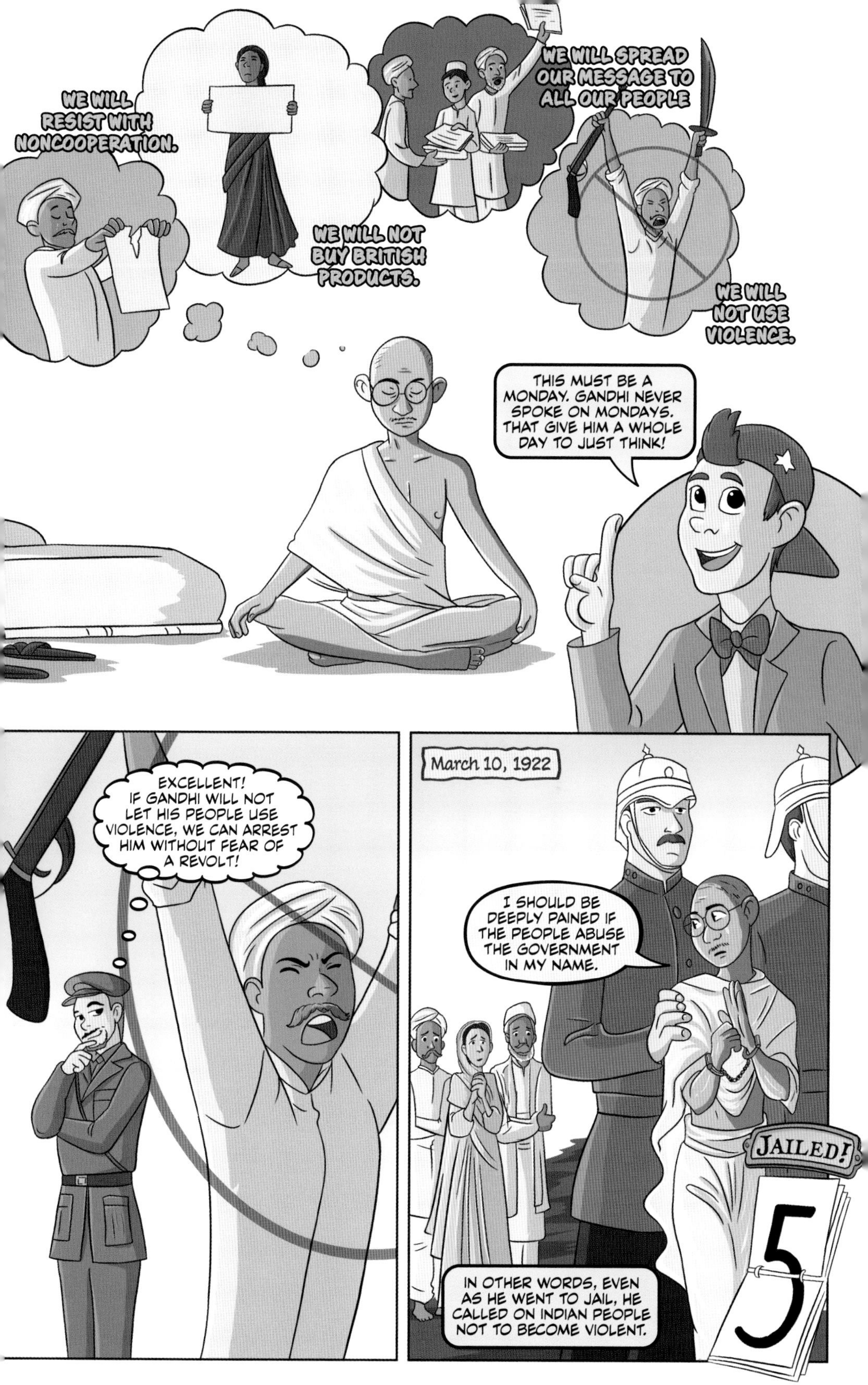
WE WILL RESIST WITH NONCOOPERATION.
WE WILL NOT BUY BRITISH PRODUCTS.
WE WILL SPREAD OUR MESSAGE TO ALL OUR PEOPLE
WE WILL NOT USE VIOLENCE.
THIS MUST BE A MONDAY. GANDHI NEVER SPOKE ON MONDAYS. THAT GIVE HIM A WHOLE DAY TO JUST THINK!
EXCELLENT! IF GANDHI WILL NOT LET HIS PEOPLE USE VIOLENCE, WE CAN ARREST HIM WITHOUT FEAR OF A REVOLT!
March 10, 1922
I SHOULD BE DEEPLY PAINED IF THE PEOPLE ABUSE THE GOVERNMENT IN MY NAME.
JAILED!
5
IN OTHER WORDS, EVEN AS HE WENT TO JAIL, HE CALLED ON INDIAN PEOPLE NOT TO BECOME VIOLENT.

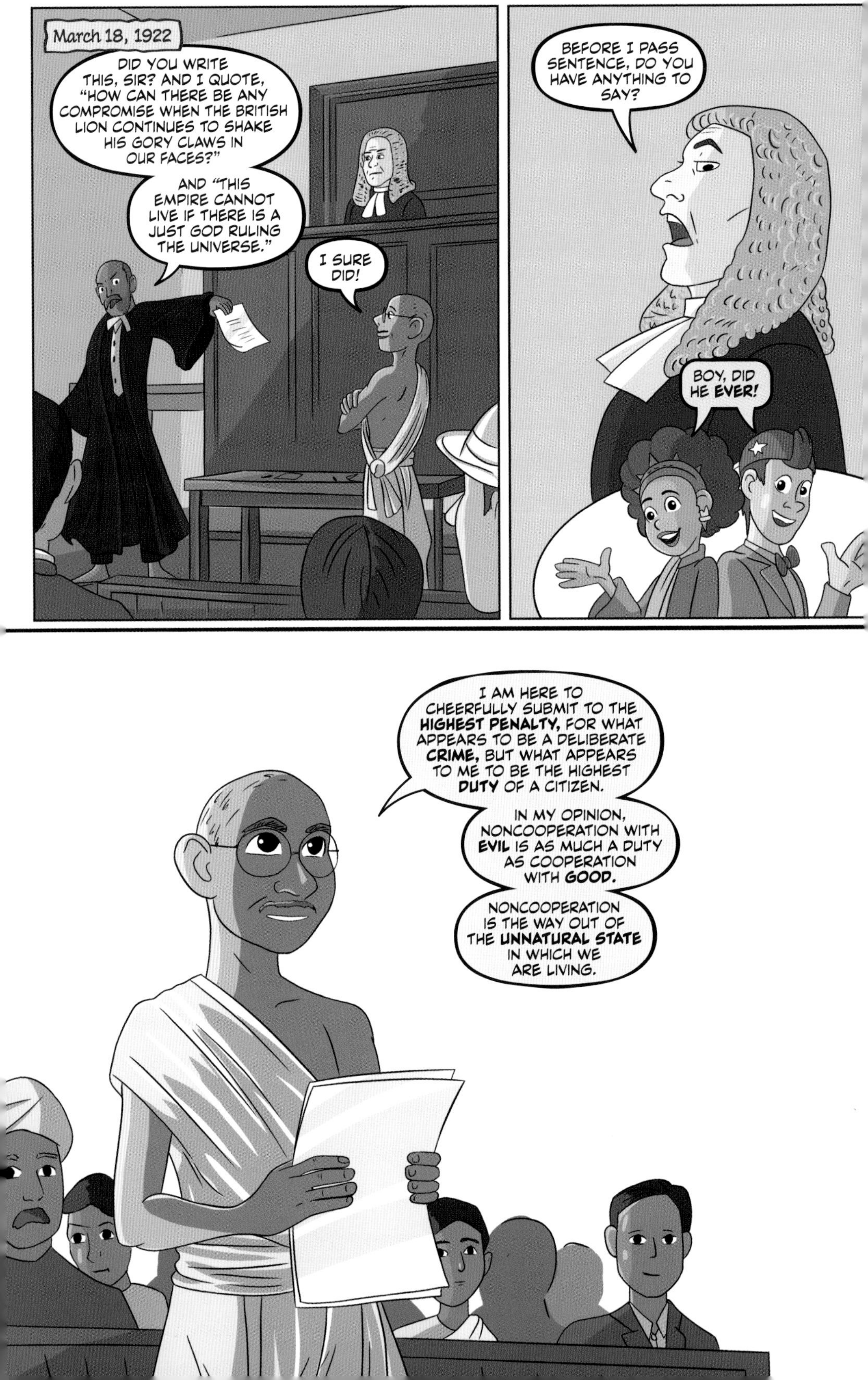
March 18, 1922
DID YOU WRITE THIS, SIR? AND I QUOTE, "HOW CAN THERE BE ANY COMPROMISE WHEN THE BRITISH LION CONTINUES TO SHAKE HIS GORY CLAWS IN OUR FACES?"
AND "THIS EMPIRE CANNOT LIVE IF THERE IS A JUST GOD RULING THE UNIVERSE."
I SURE DID!
BEFORE I PASS SENTENCE, DO YOU HAVE ANYTHING TO SAY?
BOY, DID HE **EVER!**
I AM HERE TO CHEERFULLY SUBMIT TO THE **HIGHEST PENALTY,** FOR WHAT APPEARS TO BE A DELIBERATE **CRIME,** BUT WHAT APPEARS TO ME TO BE THE HIGHEST **DUTY** OF A CITIZEN.
IN MY OPINION, NONCOOPERATION WITH **EVIL** IS AS MUCH A DUTY AS COOPERATION WITH **GOOD.**
NONCOOPERATION IS THE WAY OUT OF THE **UNNATURAL STATE** IN WHICH WE ARE LIVING.

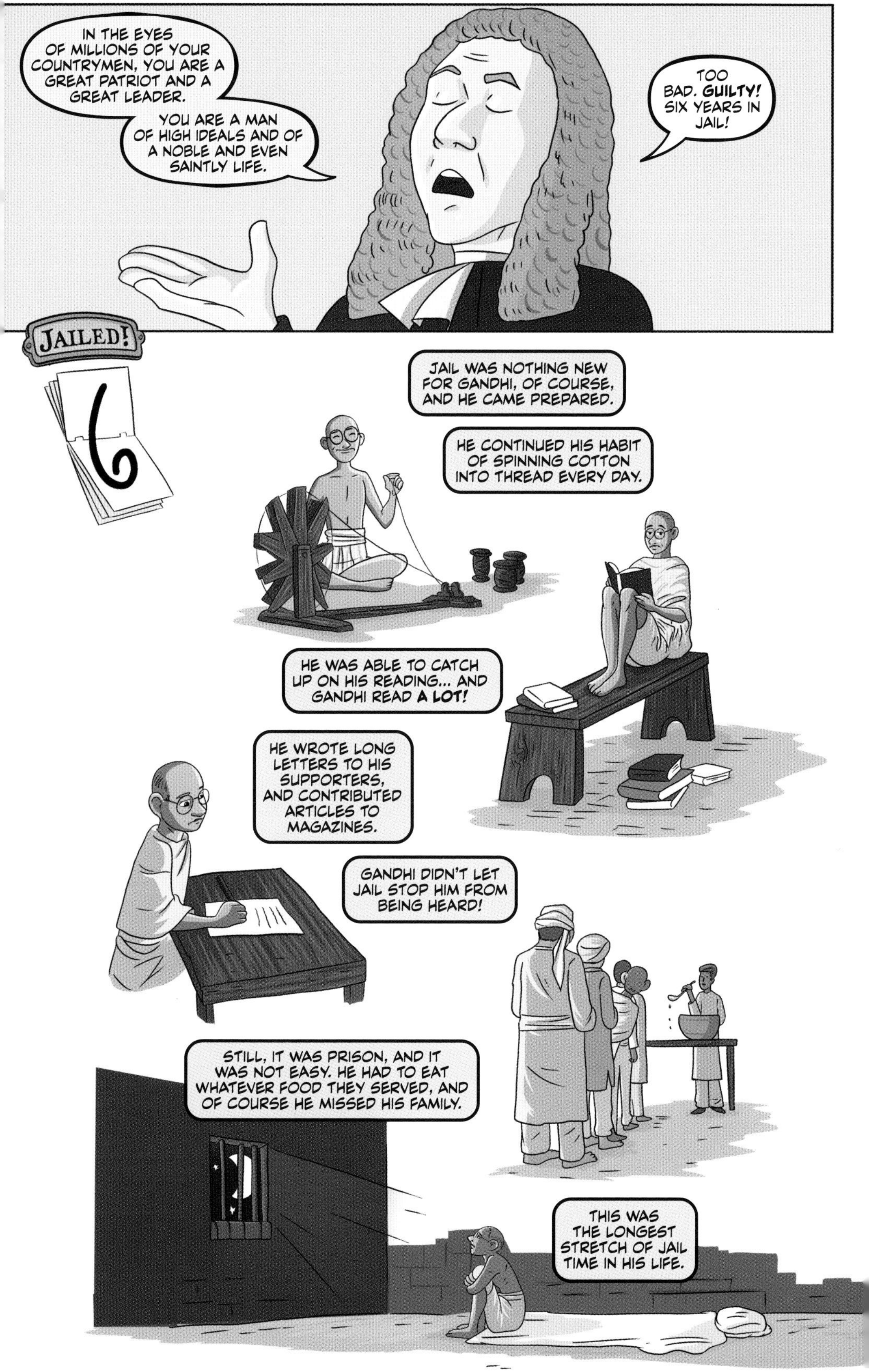
IN THE EYES OF MILLIONS OF YOUR COUNTRYMEN, YOU ARE A GREAT PATRIOT AND A GREAT LEADER.
YOU ARE A MAN OF HIGH IDEALS AND OF A NOBLE AND EVEN SAINTLY LIFE.
TOO BAD. GUILTY! SIX YEARS IN JAIL!
JAILED!
6
JAIL WAS NOTHING NEW FOR GANDHI, OF COURSE, AND HE CAME PREPARED.
HE CONTINUED HIS HABIT OF SPINNING COTTON INTO THREAD EVERY DAY.
HE WAS ABLE TO CATCH UP ON HIS READING... AND GANDHI READ A LOT!
HE WROTE LONG LETTERS TO HIS SUPPORTERS, AND CONTRIBUTED ARTICLES TO MAGAZINES.
GANDHI DIDN'T LET JAIL STOP HIM FROM BEING HEARD!
STILL, IT WAS PRISON, AND IT WAS NOT EASY. HE HAD TO EAT WHATEVER FOOD THEY SERVED, AND OF COURSE HE MISSED HIS FAMILY.
THIS WAS THE LONGEST STRETCH OF JAIL TIME IN HIS LIFE.

January 1924

IT'S **APPENDICITIS.** WE HAVE TO OPERATE RIGHT AWAY.

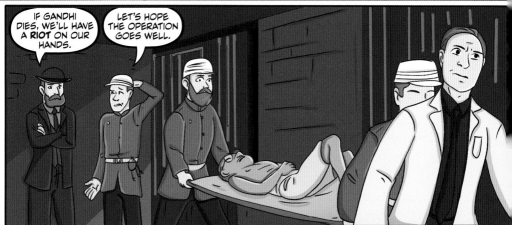

IF GANDHI DIES, WE'LL HAVE A **RIOT** ON OUR HANDS.

LET'S HOPE THE OPERATION GOES WELL.

WITH THE MOST IMPORTANT PERSON IN INDIA ON THE TABLE, THE OPERATION BEGAN.

THEN THE POWER FAILED AND THE LIGHTS WENT OUT!

THE SURGEON HAD TO FINISH BY LANTERN LIGHT!

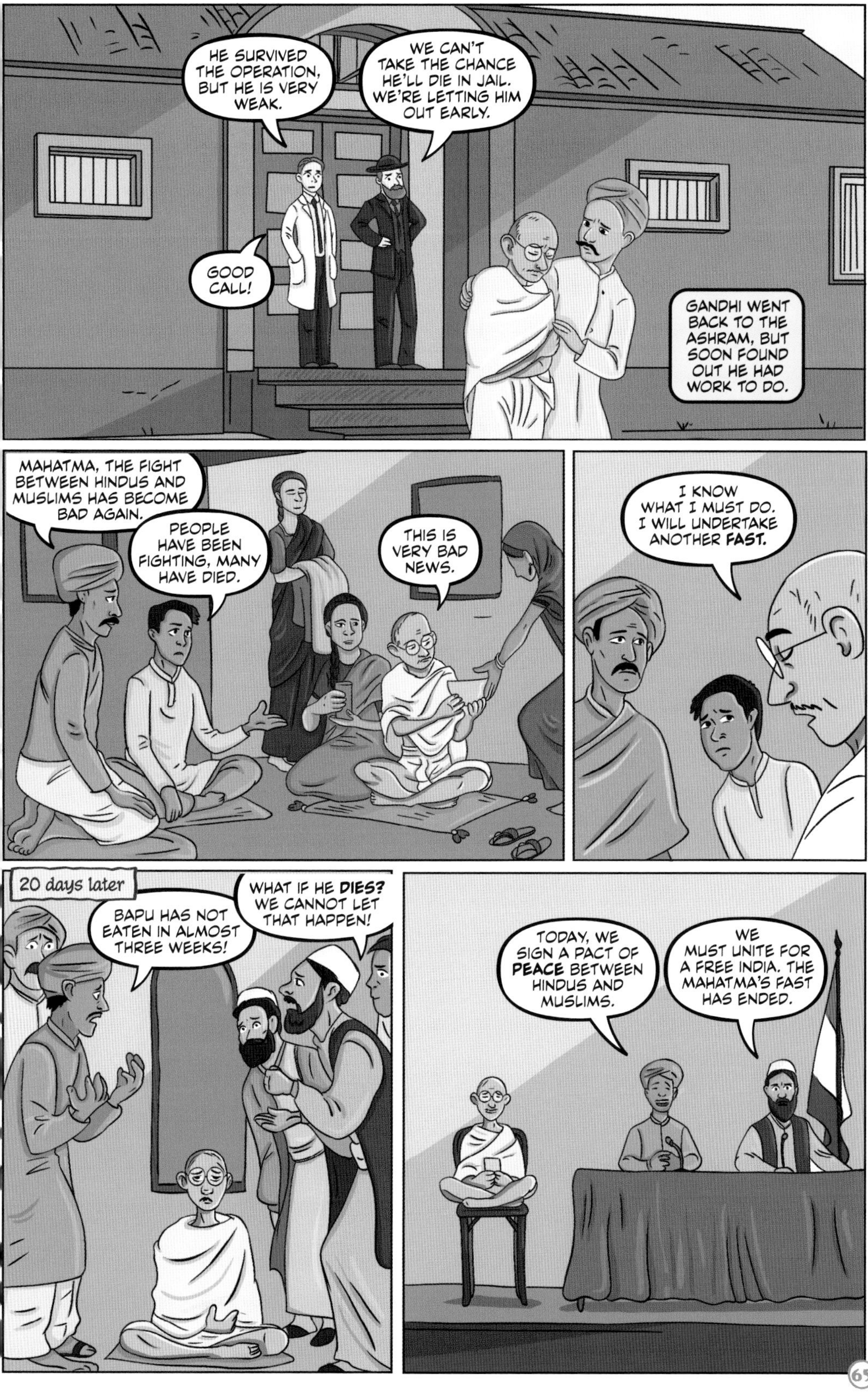
HE SURVIVED THE OPERATION, BUT HE IS VERY WEAK.
WE CAN'T TAKE THE CHANCE HE'LL DIE IN JAIL. WE'RE LETTING HIM OUT EARLY.
GOOD CALL!
GANDHI WENT BACK TO THE ASHRAM, BUT SOON FOUND OUT HE HAD WORK TO DO.
MAHATMA, THE FIGHT BETWEEN HINDUS AND MUSLIMS HAS BECOME BAD AGAIN.
PEOPLE HAVE BEEN FIGHTING, MANY HAVE DIED.
THIS IS VERY BAD NEWS.
I KNOW WHAT I MUST DO. I WILL UNDERTAKE ANOTHER **FAST.**
20 days later
BAPU HAS NOT EATEN IN ALMOST THREE WEEKS!
WHAT IF HE **DIES?** WE CANNOT LET THAT HAPPEN!
TODAY, WE SIGN A PACT OF **PEACE** BETWEEN HINDUS AND MUSLIMS.
WE MUST UNITE FOR A FREE INDIA. THE MAHATMA'S FAST HAS ENDED.

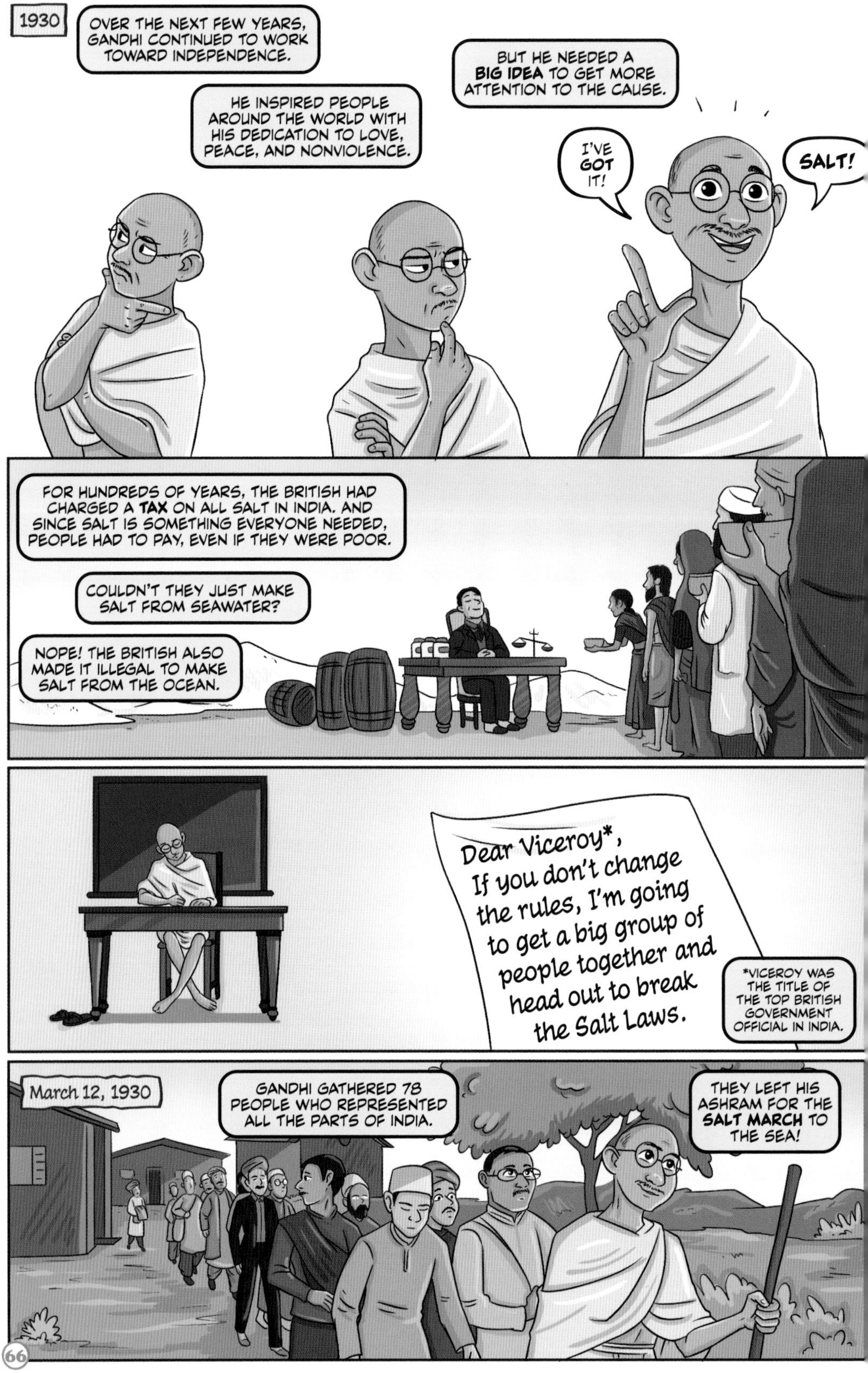

1930
OVER THE NEXT FEW YEARS, GANDHI CONTINUED TO WORK TOWARD INDEPENDENCE.
HE INSPIRED PEOPLE AROUND THE WORLD WITH HIS DEDICATION TO LOVE, PEACE, AND NONVIOLENCE.
BUT HE NEEDED A BIG IDEA TO GET MORE ATTENTION TO THE CAUSE.
I'VE GOT IT!
SALT!
FOR HUNDREDS OF YEARS, THE BRITISH HAD CHARGED A TAX ON ALL SALT IN INDIA. AND SINCE SALT IS SOMETHING EVERYONE NEEDED, PEOPLE HAD TO PAY, EVEN IF THEY WERE POOR.
COULDN'T THEY JUST MAKE SALT FROM SEAWATER?
NOPE! THE BRITISH ALSO MADE IT ILLEGAL TO MAKE SALT FROM THE OCEAN.
Dear Viceroy*, If you don't change the rules, I'm going to get a big group of people together and head out to break the Salt Laws.
*VICEROY WAS THE TITLE OF THE TOP BRITISH GOVERNMENT OFFICIAL IN INDIA.
March 12, 1930
GANDHI GATHERED 78 PEOPLE WHO REPRESENTED ALL THE PARTS OF INDIA.
THEY LEFT HIS ASHRAM FOR THE SALT MARCH TO THE SEA!

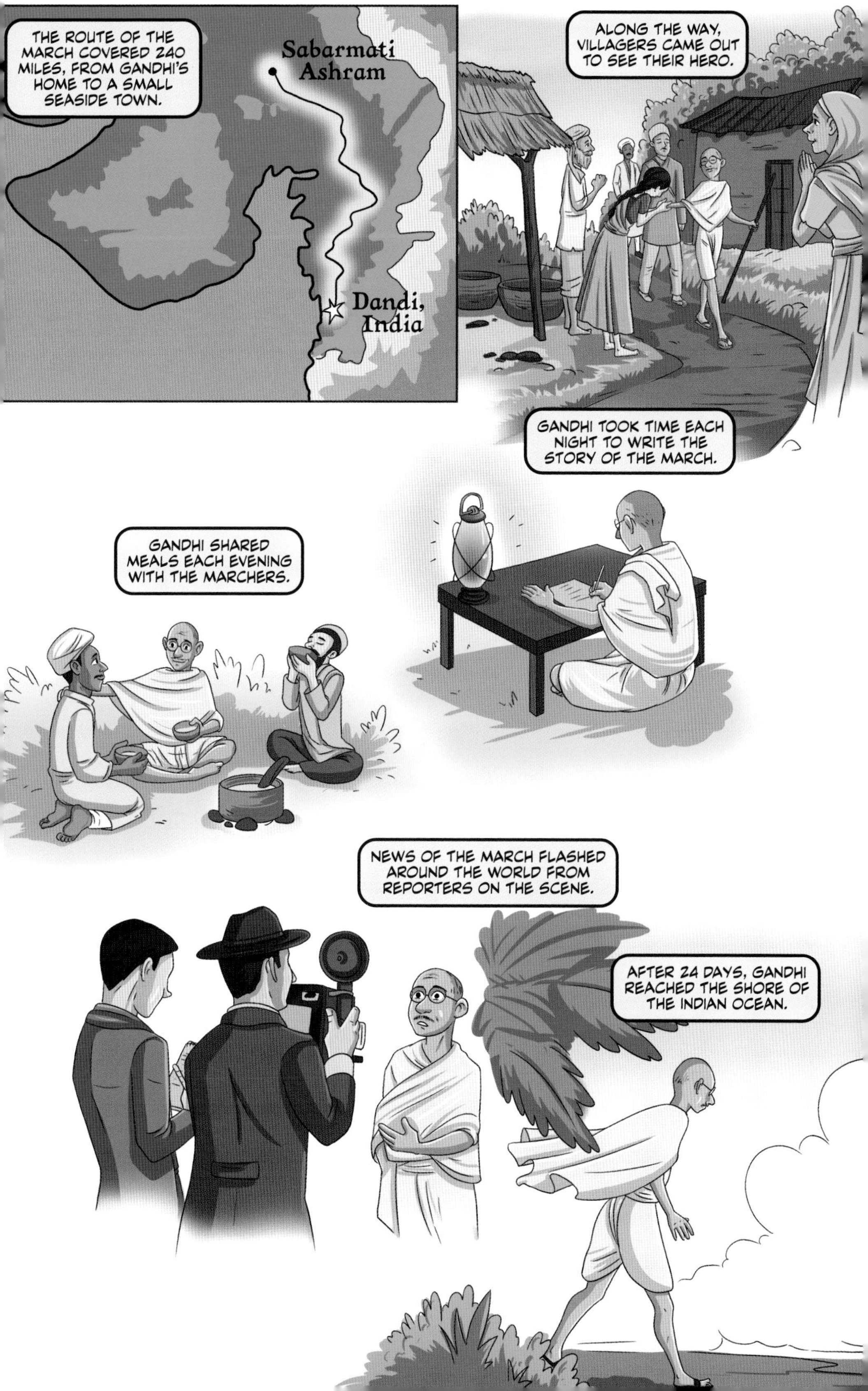
THE ROUTE OF THE MARCH COVERED 240 MILES, FROM GANDHI'S HOME TO A SMALL SEASIDE TOWN.
Sabarmati Ashram
Dandi, India
ALONG THE WAY, VILLAGERS CAME OUT TO SEE THEIR HERO.
GANDHI TOOK TIME EACH NIGHT TO WRITE THE STORY OF THE MARCH.
GANDHI SHARED MEALS EACH EVENING WITH THE MARCHERS.
NEWS OF THE MARCH FLASHED AROUND THE WORLD FROM REPORTERS ON THE SCENE.
AFTER 24 DAYS, GANDHI REACHED THE SHORE OF THE INDIAN OCEAN.

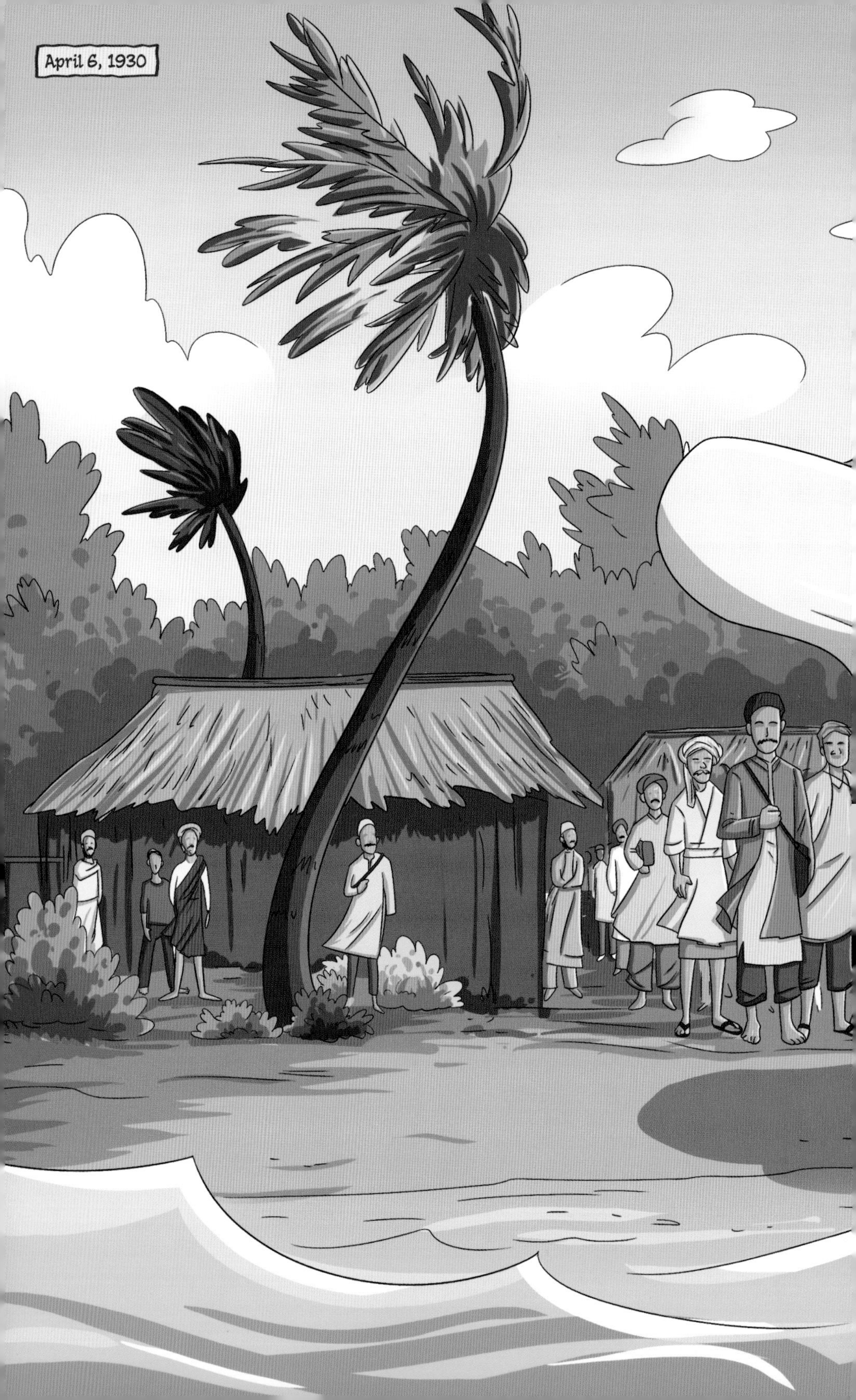
April 6, 1930

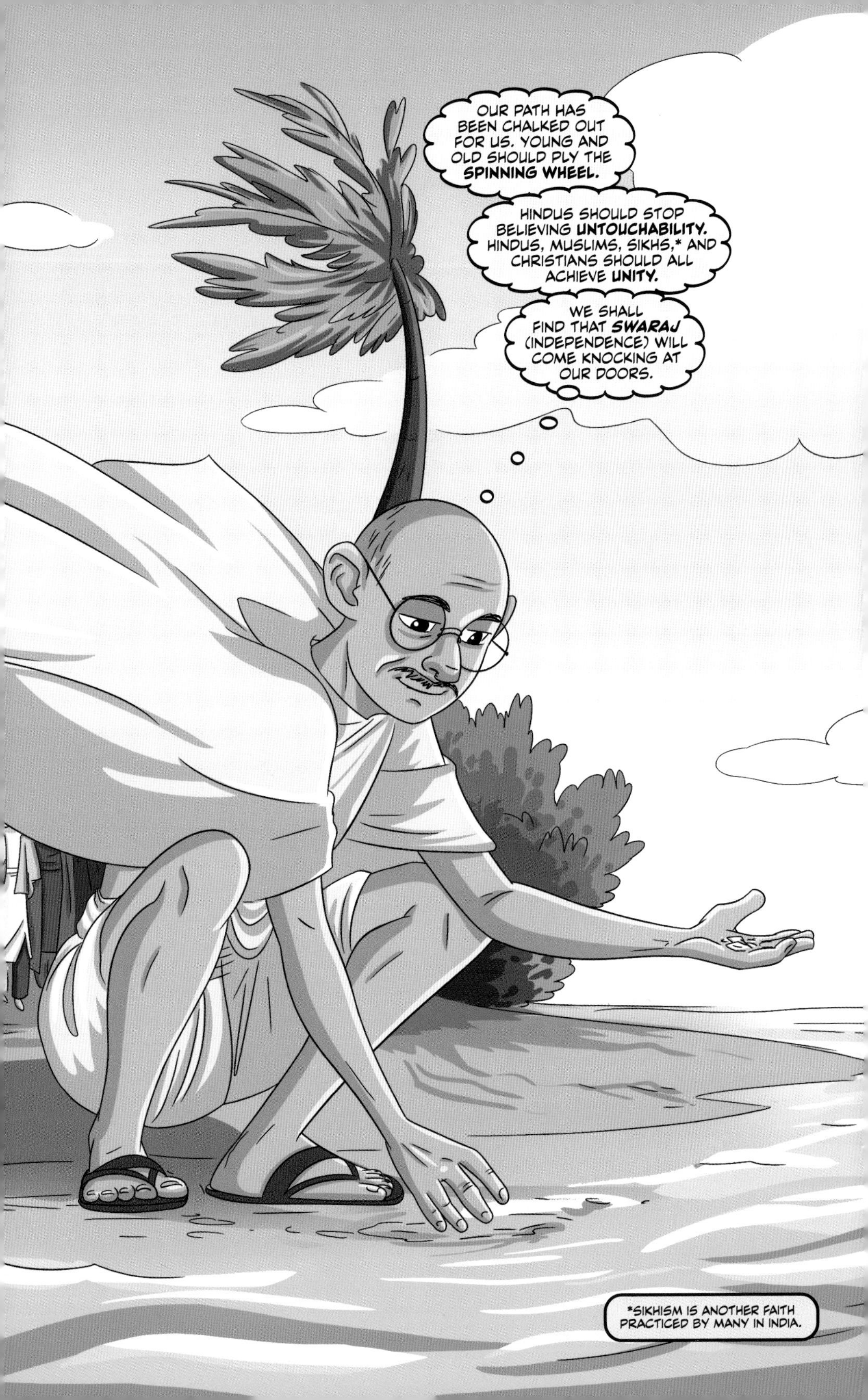
OUR PATH HAS BEEN CHALKED OUT FOR US. YOUNG AND OLD SHOULD PLY THE SPINNING WHEEL.
HINDUS SHOULD STOP BELIEVING UNTOUCHABILITY. HINDUS, MUSLIMS, SIKHS,* AND CHRISTIANS SHOULD ALL ACHIEVE UNITY.
WE SHALL FIND THAT SWARAJ (INDEPENDENCE) WILL COME KNOCKING AT OUR DOORS.
*SIKHISM IS ANOTHER FAITH PRACTICED BY MANY IN INDIA.

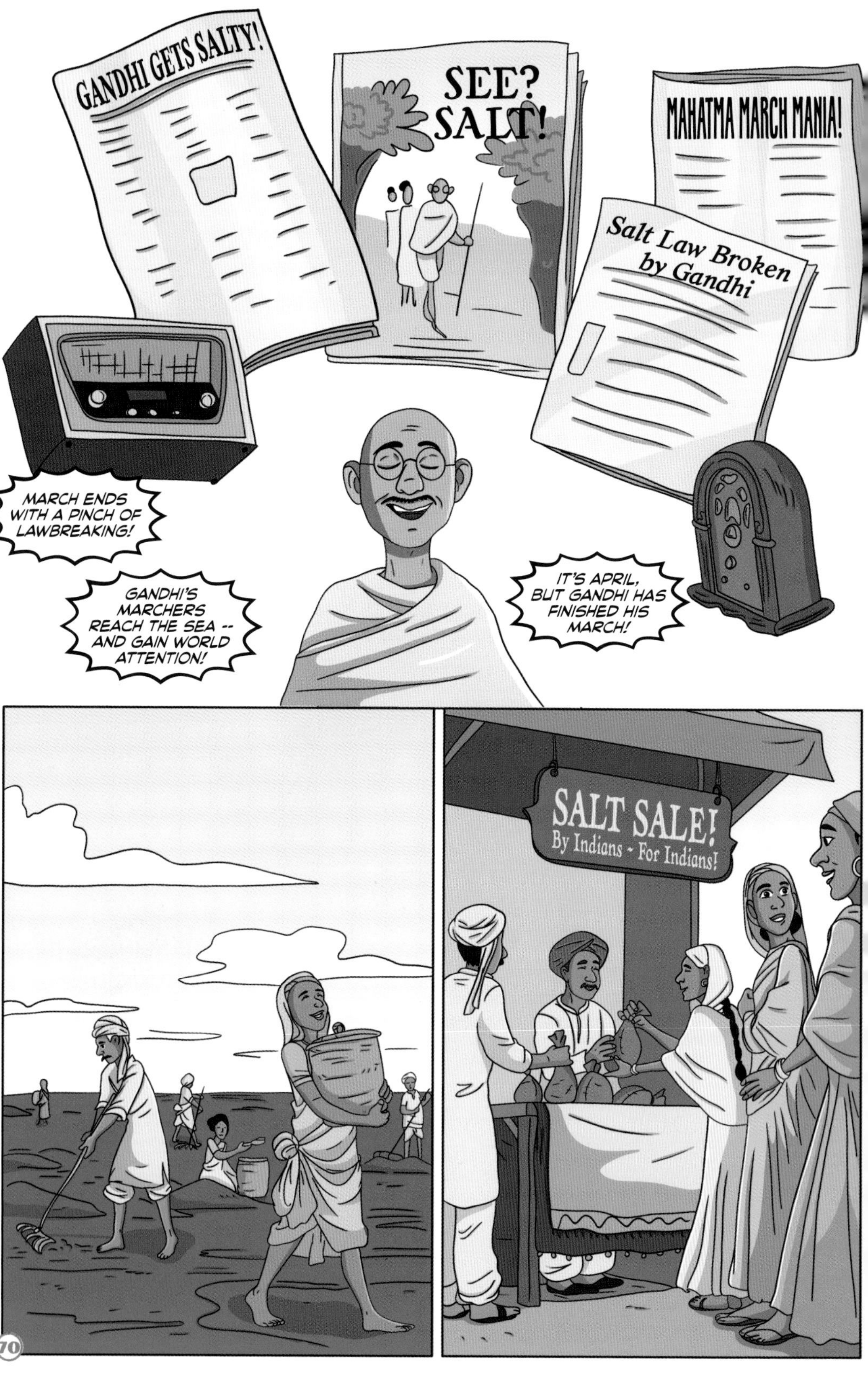
GANDHI GETS SALTY!
SEE? SALT!
MAHATMA MARCH MANIA!
Salt Law Broken by Gandhi
MARCH ENDS WITH A PINCH OF LAWBREAKING!
GANDHI'S MARCHERS REACH THE SEA -- AND GAIN WORLD ATTENTION!
IT'S APRIL, BUT GANDHI HAS FINISHED HIS MARCH!
SALT SALE!
By Indians ~ For Indians!

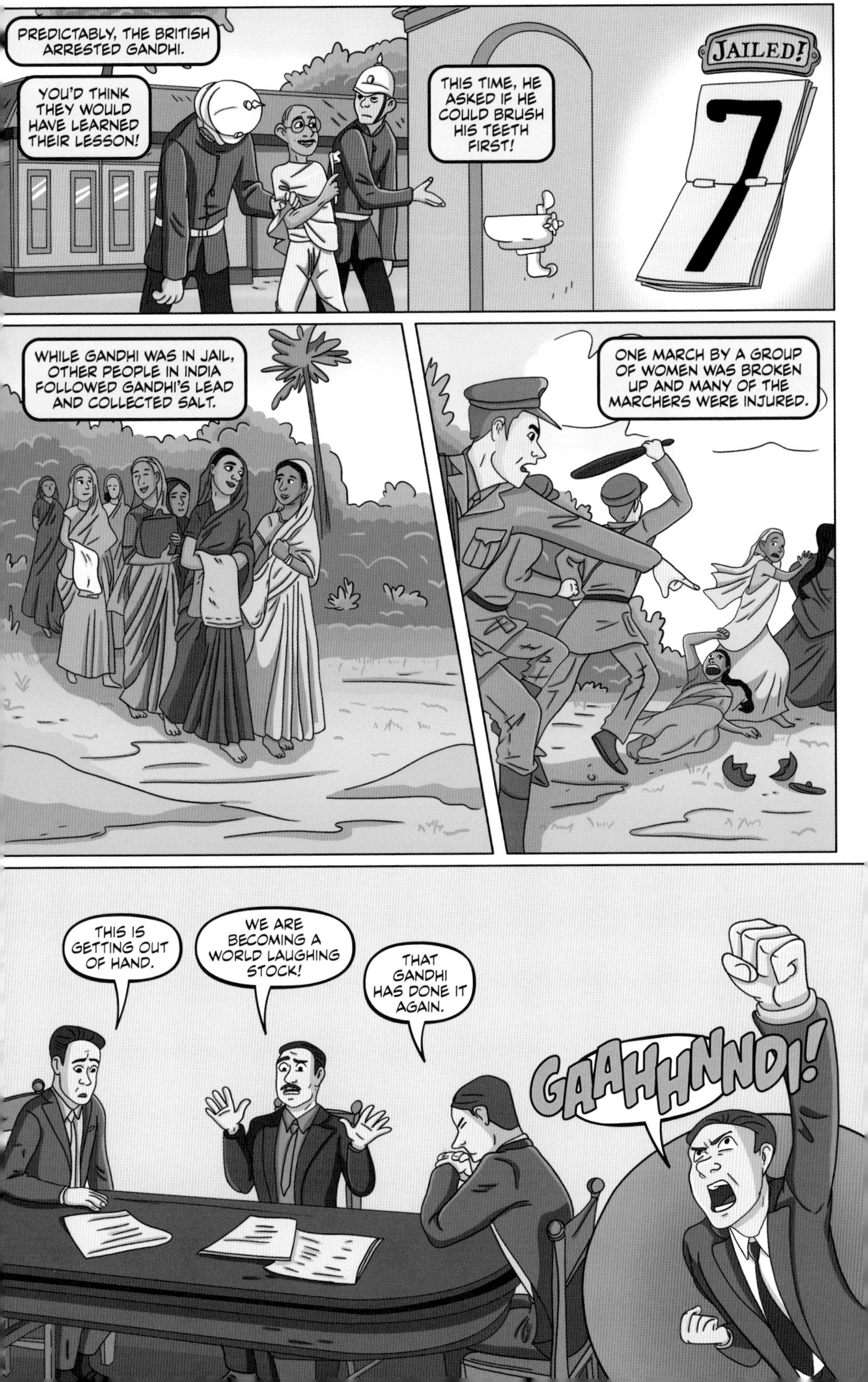
PREDICTABLY, THE BRITISH ARRESTED GANDHI.
YOU'D THINK THEY WOULD HAVE LEARNED THEIR LESSON!
THIS TIME, HE ASKED IF HE COULD BRUSH HIS TEETH FIRST!
JAILED!
7
WHILE GANDHI WAS IN JAIL, OTHER PEOPLE IN INDIA FOLLOWED GANDHI'S LEAD AND COLLECTED SALT.
ONE MARCH BY A GROUP OF WOMEN WAS BROKEN UP AND MANY OF THE MARCHERS WERE INJURED.
THIS IS GETTING OUT OF HAND.
WE ARE BECOMING A WORLD LAUGHING STOCK!
THAT GANDHI HAS DONE IT AGAIN.
GAAHHNNDI!

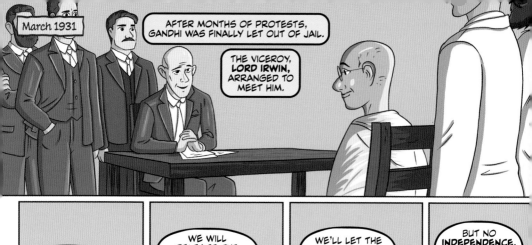

March 1931

AFTER MONTHS OF PROTESTS, GANDHI WAS FINALLY LET OUT OF JAIL.

THE VICEROY, **LORD IRWIN,** ARRANGED TO MEET HIM.

MAHATMA, WE WILL CHANGE THE **SALT LAWS.**

EXCELLENT! NOW WE WILL MAKE OUR OWN SALT.

WE WILL RELEASE THE **PRISONERS** JAILED FOR PROTESTING.

GREAT! WE WILL STOP MOST OF THE BOYCOTTS!

WE'LL LET THE **INDIAN NATIONAL CONGRESS** STAY IN BUSINESS.

WELL, WE ACTUALLY NEVER STOPPED!

BUT NO **INDEPENDENCE.** THAT'S UP TO THE LEADERS IN ENGLAND.

OKAY, I'LL GO **ASK** THEM!

WHILE I'M IN ENGLAND TALKING TO THE GOVERNMENT, DO NOT MAKE TROUBLE.

WE MUST KEEP DOING WHAT WE ARE DOING.

I HOPE TO COME BACK WITH WONDERFUL NEWS!

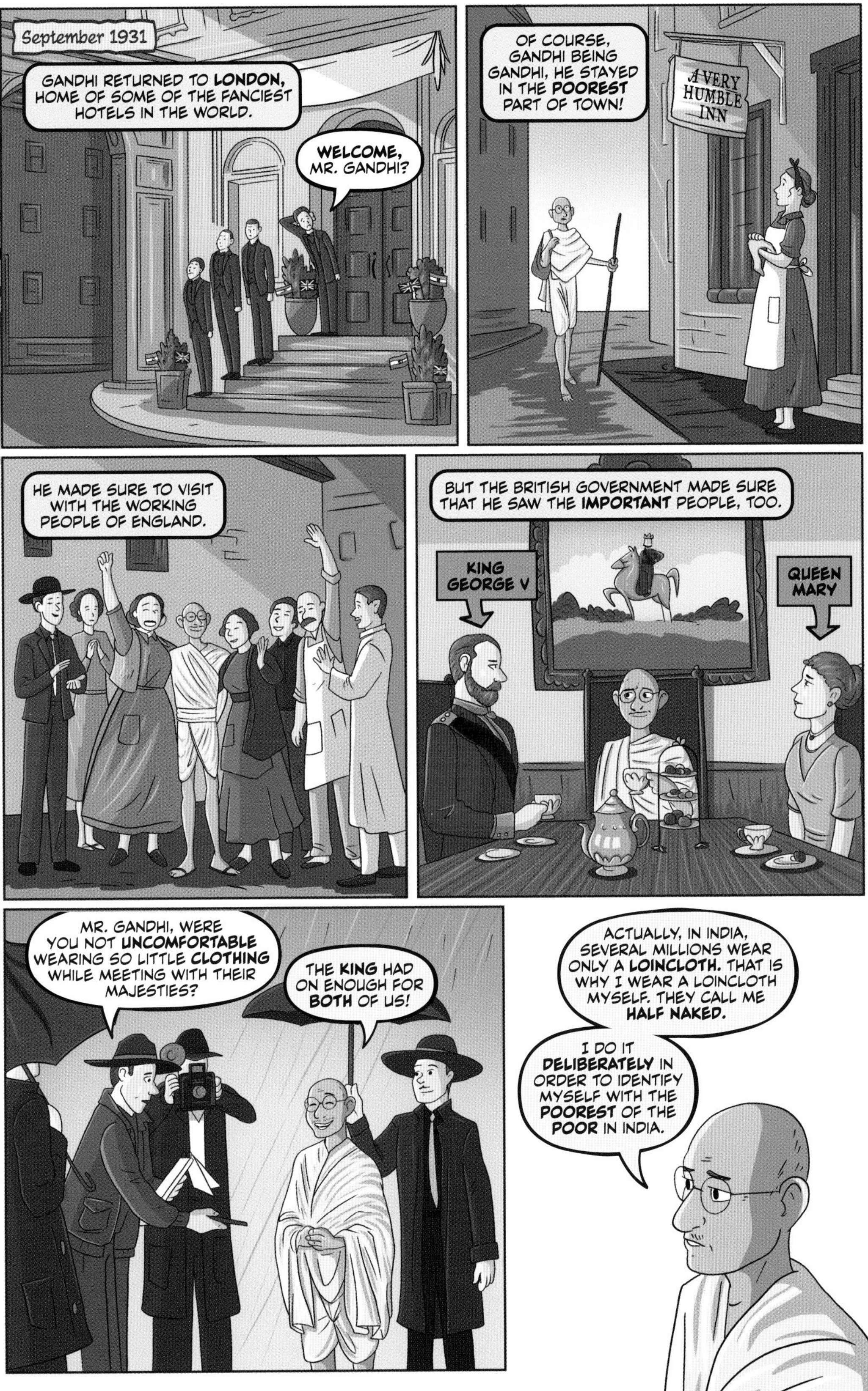
September 1931
GANDHI RETURNED TO **LONDON,** HOME OF SOME OF THE FANCIEST HOTELS IN THE WORLD.
WELCOME, MR. GANDHI?
OF COURSE, GANDHI BEING GANDHI, HE STAYED IN THE **POOREST** PART OF TOWN!
A VERY HUMBLE INN
HE MADE SURE TO VISIT WITH THE WORKING PEOPLE OF ENGLAND.
BUT THE BRITISH GOVERNMENT MADE SURE THAT HE SAW THE **IMPORTANT** PEOPLE, TOO.
KING GEORGE V
QUEEN MARY
MR. GANDHI, WERE YOU NOT **UNCOMFORTABLE** WEARING SO LITTLE **CLOTHING** WHILE MEETING WITH THEIR MAJESTIES?
THE **KING** HAD ON ENOUGH FOR **BOTH** OF US!
ACTUALLY, IN INDIA, SEVERAL MILLIONS WEAR ONLY A **LOINCLOTH.** THAT IS WHY I WEAR A LOINCLOTH MYSELF. THEY CALL ME **HALF NAKED.**
I DO IT **DELIBERATELY** IN ORDER TO IDENTIFY MYSELF WITH THE **POOREST** OF THE **POOR** IN INDIA.

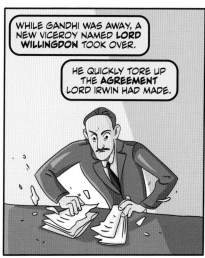

WHILE GANDHI WAS AWAY, A NEW VICEROY NAMED **LORD WILLINGDON** TOOK OVER.

HE QUICKLY TORE UP THE **AGREEMENT** LORD IRWIN HAD MADE.

January 4, 1932

NOT LONG AFTER RETURNING FROM ENGLAND, GANDHI WAS **ARRESTED AGAIN!**

JAILE

GANDHI WAS IN JAIL FOR MOST OF THE YEAR.

WHILE HE WAS INSIDE, HE READ SOME NEWS THAT SPURRED HIM TO ACTION.

ONCE AGAIN, BOTH INDIANS AND BRITISH MAKE LIFE IMPOSSIBLE FOR THE **DALIT.**

WE MUST STOP THIS. WE MUST NOT SEE **ANYONE** AS "UNTOUCHABLE."

NO, THANK YOU.

UNTIL WE FIND A WAY TO HELP UNTOUCHABLES, I WON'T BE EATING.

HE'S DOING IT **AGAIN!** WE CAN'T LET HIM DIE!

QUICK, LET'S CHANGE THE RULES!

YES, MAHATMA, DALIT CAN NOW SHARE **WELLS** AND **TEMPLES** WITH THE REST OF US.

AND THE BRITISH WILL LET THEM **VOTE**, TOO.

I WISH I DIDN'T HAVE TO **FAST** SO OFTEN TO MAKE THEM DO THE RIGHT THING!

74

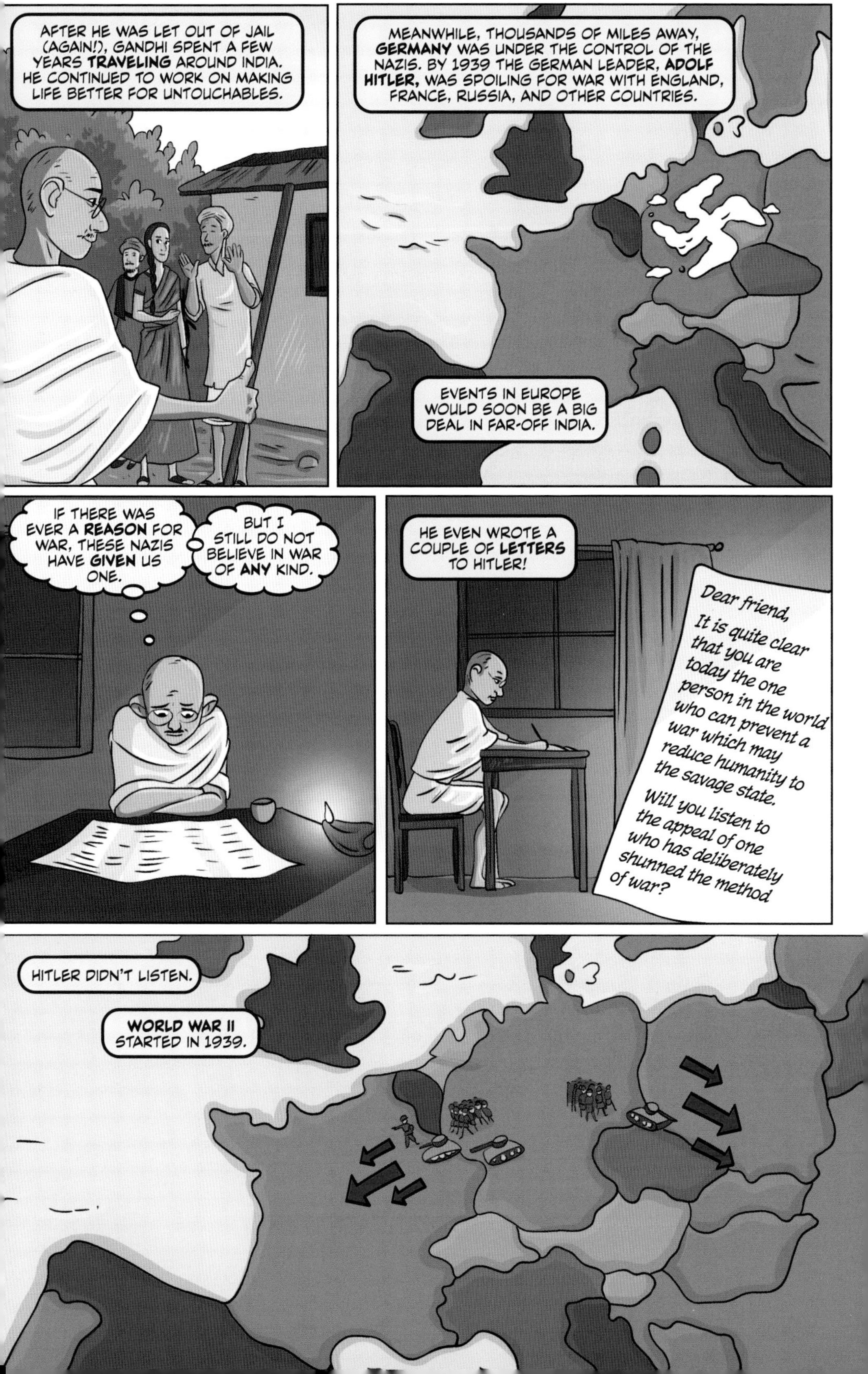
AFTER HE WAS LET OUT OF JAIL (AGAIN!), GANDHI SPENT A FEW YEARS TRAVELING AROUND INDIA. HE CONTINUED TO WORK ON MAKING LIFE BETTER FOR UNTOUCHABLES.
MEANWHILE, THOUSANDS OF MILES AWAY, GERMANY WAS UNDER THE CONTROL OF THE NAZIS. BY 1939 THE GERMAN LEADER, ADOLF HITLER, WAS SPOILING FOR WAR WITH ENGLAND, FRANCE, RUSSIA, AND OTHER COUNTRIES.
EVENTS IN EUROPE WOULD SOON BE A BIG DEAL IN FAR-OFF INDIA.
IF THERE WAS EVER A REASON FOR WAR, THESE NAZIS HAVE GIVEN US ONE.
BUT I STILL DO NOT BELIEVE IN WAR OF ANY KIND.
HE EVEN WROTE A COUPLE OF LETTERS TO HITLER!
Dear friend,
It is quite clear that you are today the one person in the world who can prevent a war which may reduce humanity to the savage state.
Will you listen to the appeal of one who has deliberately shunned the method of war?
HITLER DIDN'T LISTEN.
WORLD WAR II STARTED IN 1939.

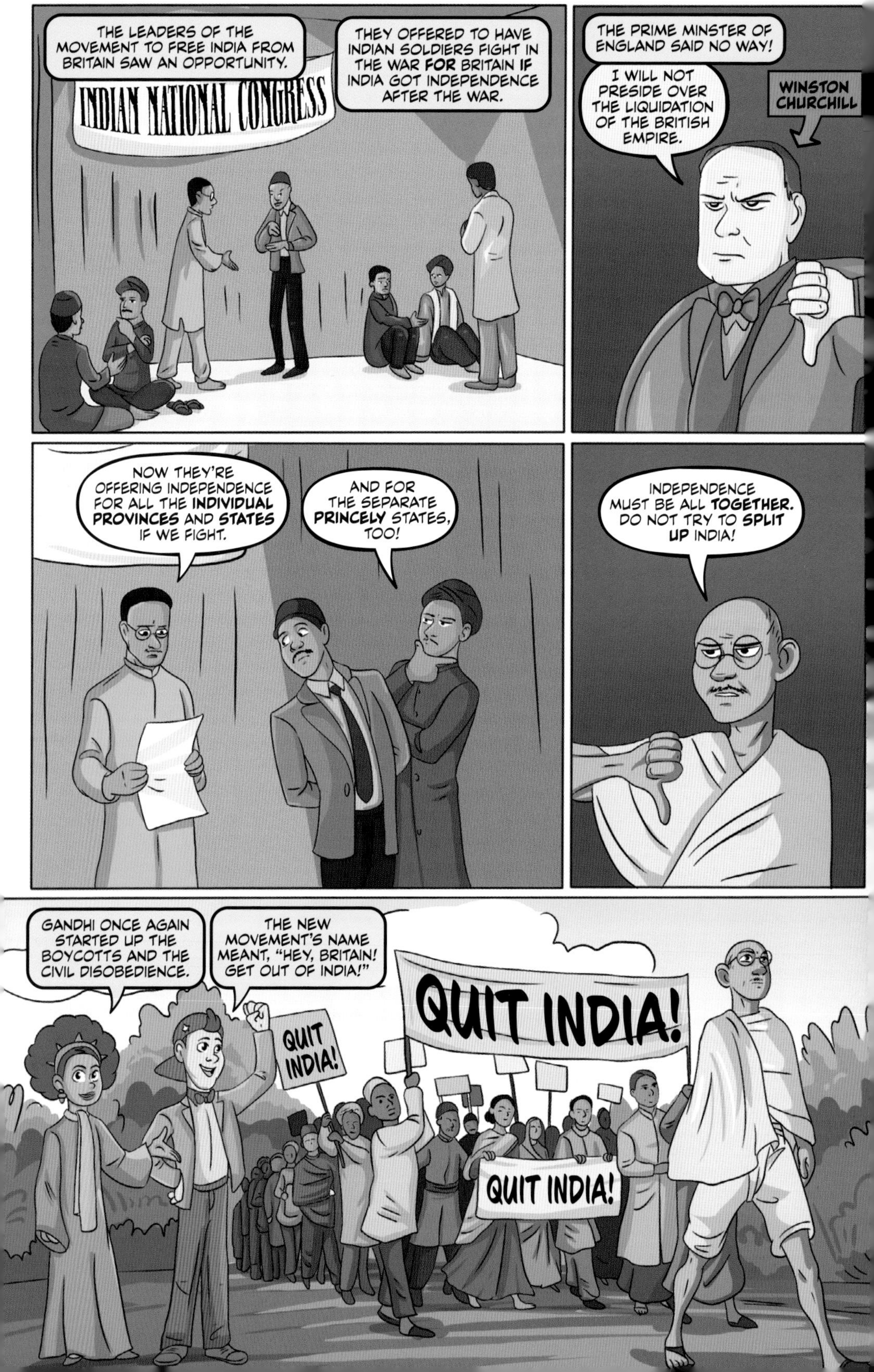
THE LEADERS OF THE MOVEMENT TO FREE INDIA FROM BRITAIN SAW AN OPPORTUNITY.
INDIAN NATIONAL CONGRESS
THEY OFFERED TO HAVE INDIAN SOLDIERS FIGHT IN THE WAR FOR BRITAIN IF INDIA GOT INDEPENDENCE AFTER THE WAR.
THE PRIME MINSTER OF ENGLAND SAID NO WAY!
I WILL NOT PRESIDE OVER THE LIQUIDATION OF THE BRITISH EMPIRE.
WINSTON CHURCHILL
NOW THEY'RE OFFERING INDEPENDENCE FOR ALL THE INDIVIDUAL PROVINCES AND STATES IF WE FIGHT.
AND FOR THE SEPARATE PRINCELY STATES, TOO!
INDEPENDENCE MUST BE ALL TOGETHER. DO NOT TRY TO SPLIT UP INDIA!
GANDHI ONCE AGAIN STARTED UP THE BOYCOTTS AND THE CIVIL DISOBEDIENCE.
THE NEW MOVEMENT'S NAME MEANT, "HEY, BRITAIN! GET OUT OF INDIA!"
QUIT INDIA!
QUIT INDIA!
QUIT INDIA!

I WANT **FREEDOM** THIS VERY NIGHT, BEFORE **DAWN** IF IT CAN BE HAD!

THE BRITISH, OF COURSE, DID WHAT THEY ALWAYS DID.

JAILED!

SADLY, WHILE GANDHI WAS IN JAIL, MANY PEOPLE IN INDIA CAUSED **TROUBLE.**

THEY WERE MAD GANDHI WAS IN JAIL, AND THEY WERE MAD THAT BRITAIN REFUSED TO SET INDIA FREE.

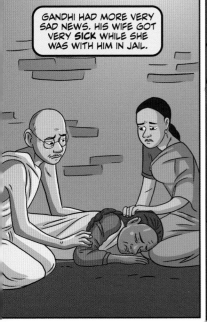

GANDHI HAD MORE VERY SAD NEWS. HIS WIFE GOT VERY **SICK** WHILE SHE WAS WITH HIM IN JAIL.

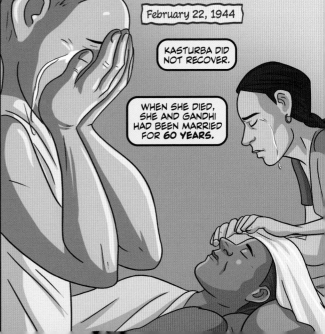

February 22, 1944

KASTURBA DID NOT RECOVER.

WHEN SHE DIED, SHE AND GANDHI HAD BEEN MARRIED FOR **60 YEARS.**

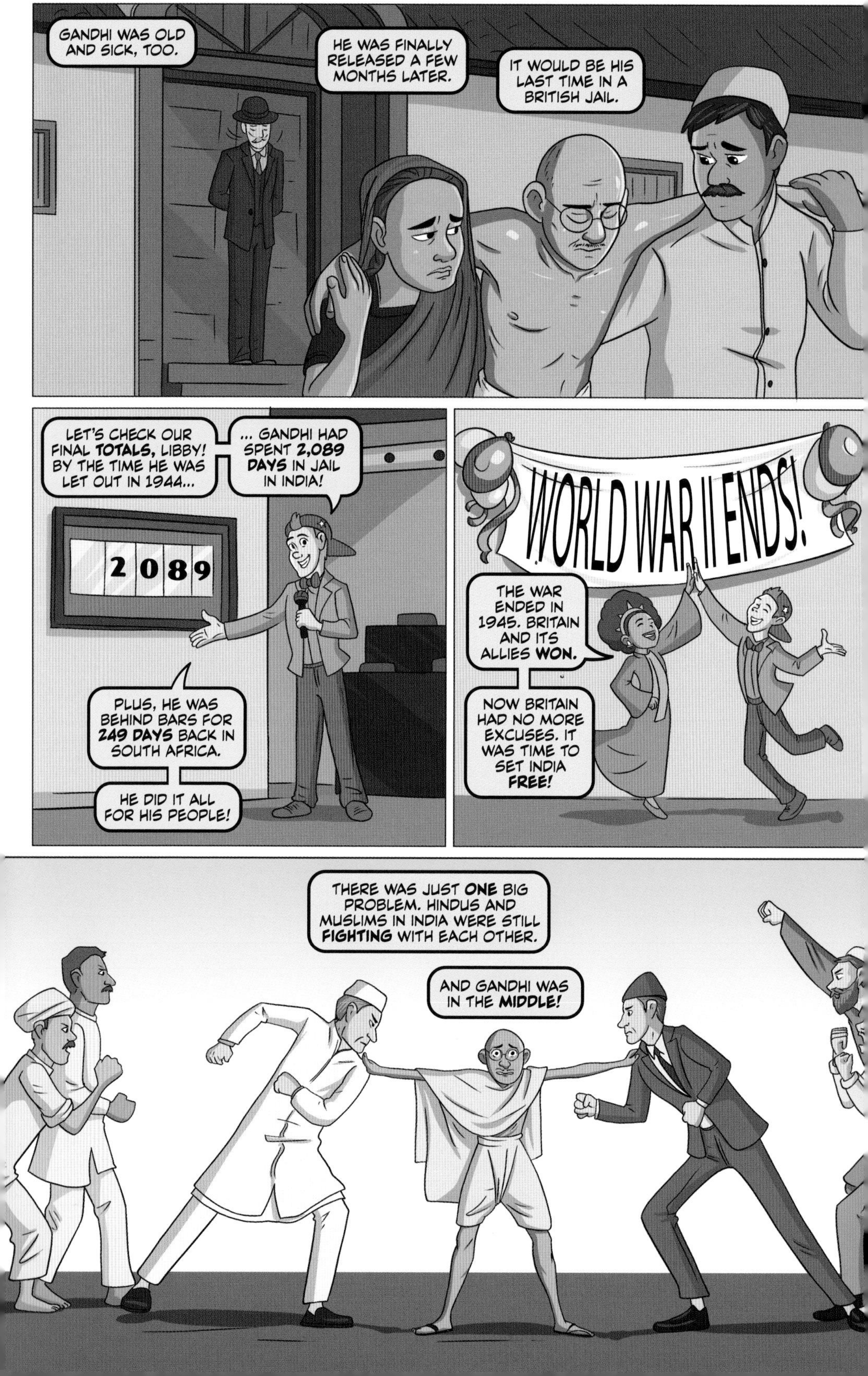
GANDHI WAS OLD AND SICK, TOO.
HE WAS FINALLY RELEASED A FEW MONTHS LATER.
IT WOULD BE HIS LAST TIME IN A BRITISH JAIL.
LET'S CHECK OUR FINAL **TOTALS,** LIBBY! BY THE TIME HE WAS LET OUT IN 1944...
... GANDHI HAD SPENT **2,089 DAYS** IN JAIL IN INDIA!
2089
PLUS, HE WAS BEHIND BARS FOR **249 DAYS** BACK IN SOUTH AFRICA.
HE DID IT ALL FOR HIS PEOPLE!
WORLD WAR II ENDS!
THE WAR ENDED IN 1945. BRITAIN AND ITS ALLIES **WON.**
NOW BRITAIN HAD NO MORE EXCUSES. IT WAS TIME TO SET INDIA **FREE!**
THERE WAS JUST **ONE** BIG PROBLEM. HINDUS AND MUSLIMS IN INDIA WERE STILL **FIGHTING** WITH EACH OTHER.
AND GANDHI WAS IN THE **MIDDLE!**

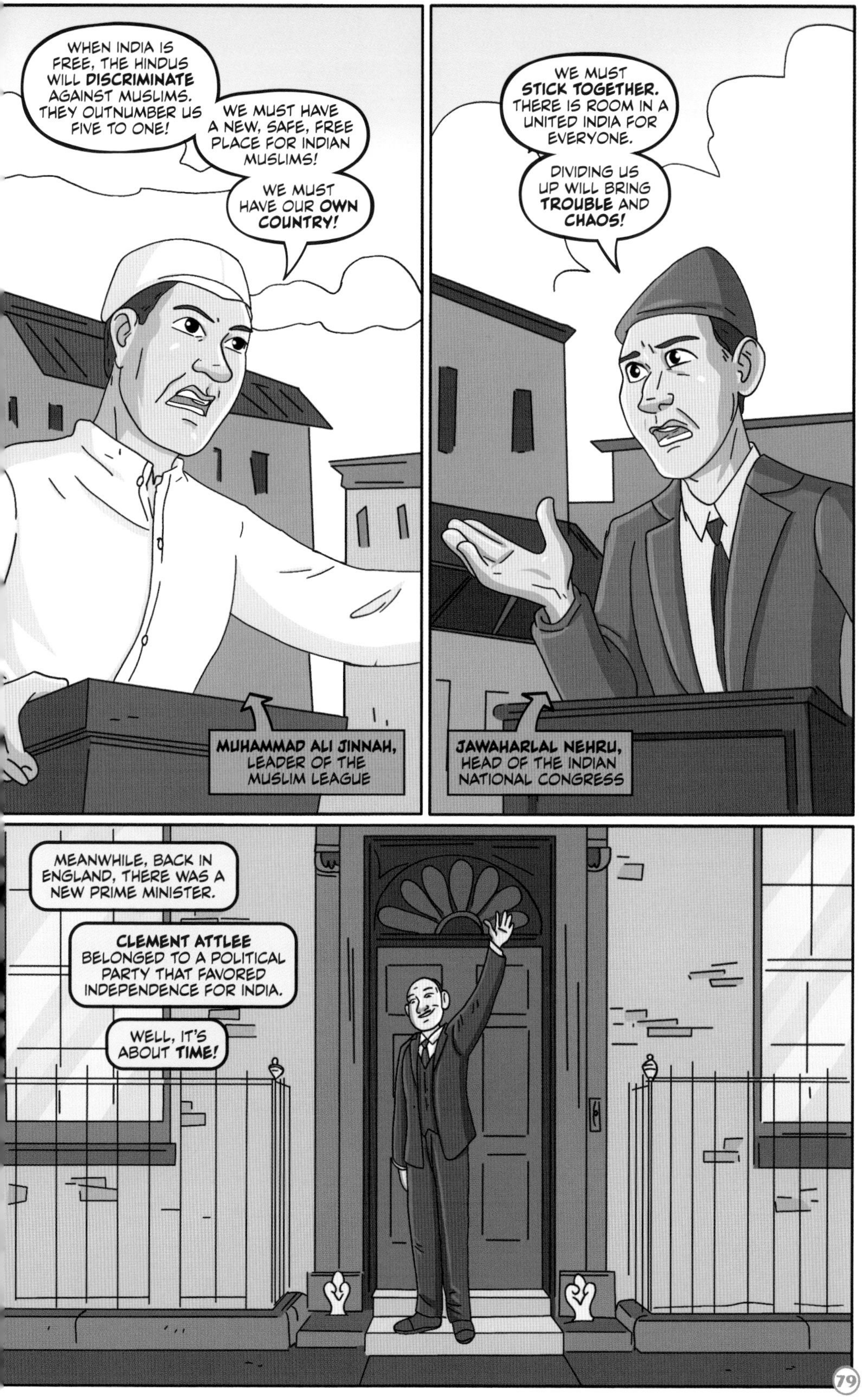
WHEN INDIA IS FREE, THE HINDUS WILL **DISCRIMINATE** AGAINST MUSLIMS. THEY OUTNUMBER US FIVE TO ONE!
WE MUST HAVE A NEW, SAFE, FREE PLACE FOR INDIAN MUSLIMS!
WE MUST HAVE OUR **OWN COUNTRY!**
MUHAMMAD ALI JINNAH, LEADER OF THE MUSLIM LEAGUE
WE MUST **STICK TOGETHER.** THERE IS ROOM IN A UNITED INDIA FOR EVERYONE.
DIVIDING US UP WILL BRING **TROUBLE** AND **CHAOS!**
JAWAHARLAL NEHRU, HEAD OF THE INDIAN NATIONAL CONGRESS
MEANWHILE, BACK IN ENGLAND, THERE WAS A NEW PRIME MINISTER.
CLEMENT ATTLEE BELONGED TO A POLITICAL PARTY THAT FAVORED INDEPENDENCE FOR INDIA.
WELL, IT'S ABOUT **TIME!**

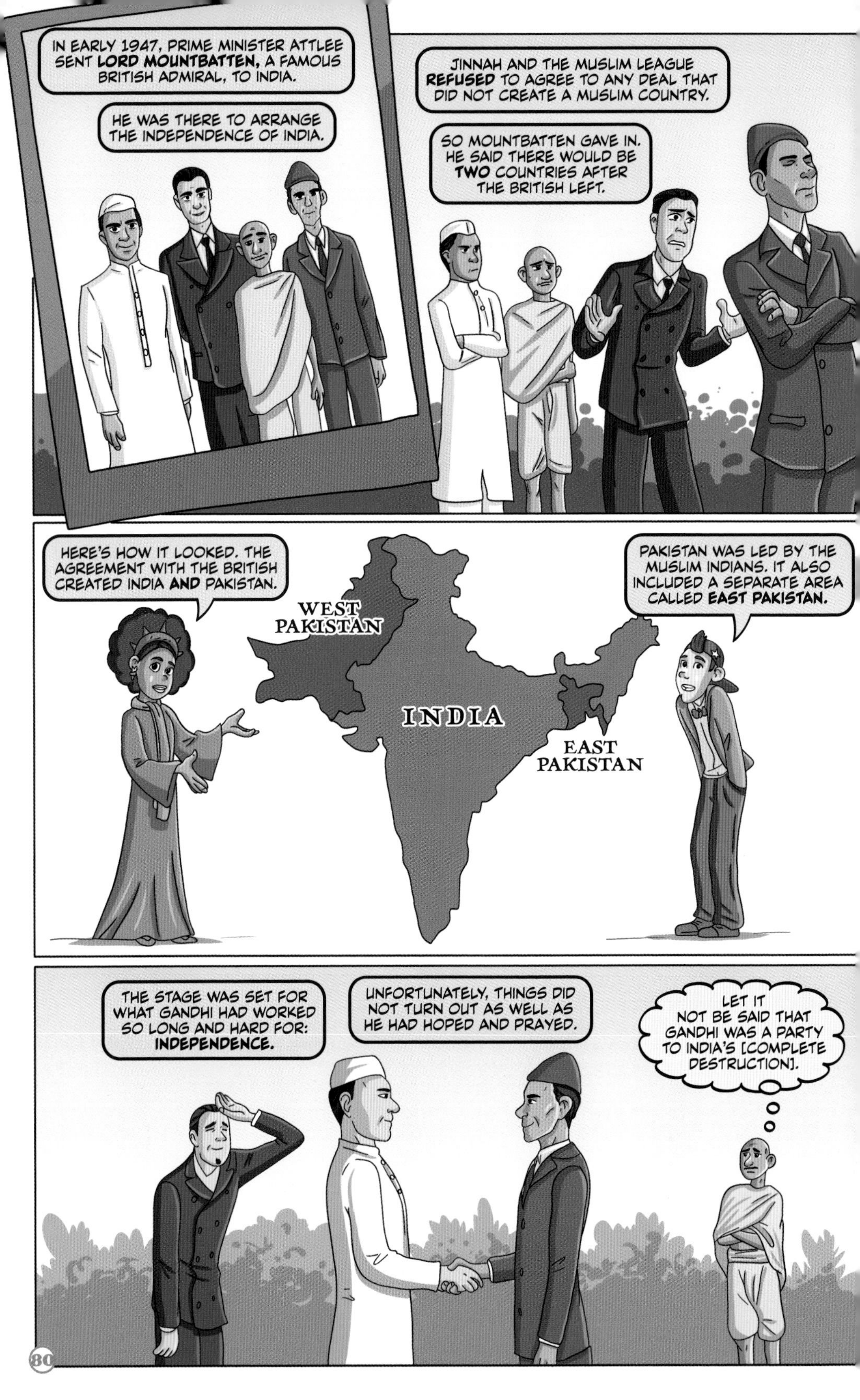
IN EARLY 1947, PRIME MINISTER ATTLEE SENT **LORD MOUNTBATTEN,** A FAMOUS BRITISH ADMIRAL, TO INDIA.
HE WAS THERE TO ARRANGE THE INDEPENDENCE OF INDIA.
JINNAH AND THE MUSLIM LEAGUE **REFUSED** TO AGREE TO ANY DEAL THAT DID NOT CREATE A MUSLIM COUNTRY.
SO MOUNTBATTEN GAVE IN. HE SAID THERE WOULD BE **TWO** COUNTRIES AFTER THE BRITISH LEFT.
HERE'S HOW IT LOOKED. THE AGREEMENT WITH THE BRITISH CREATED INDIA **AND** PAKISTAN.
WEST PAKISTAN
INDIA
EAST PAKISTAN
PAKISTAN WAS LED BY THE MUSLIM INDIANS. IT ALSO INCLUDED A SEPARATE AREA CALLED **EAST PAKISTAN.**
THE STAGE WAS SET FOR WHAT GANDHI HAD WORKED SO LONG AND HARD FOR: **INDEPENDENCE.**
UNFORTUNATELY, THINGS DID NOT TURN OUT AS WELL AS HE HAD HOPED AND PRAYED.
LET IT NOT BE SAID THAT GANDHI WAS A PARTY TO INDIA'S [COMPLETE DESTRUCTION].

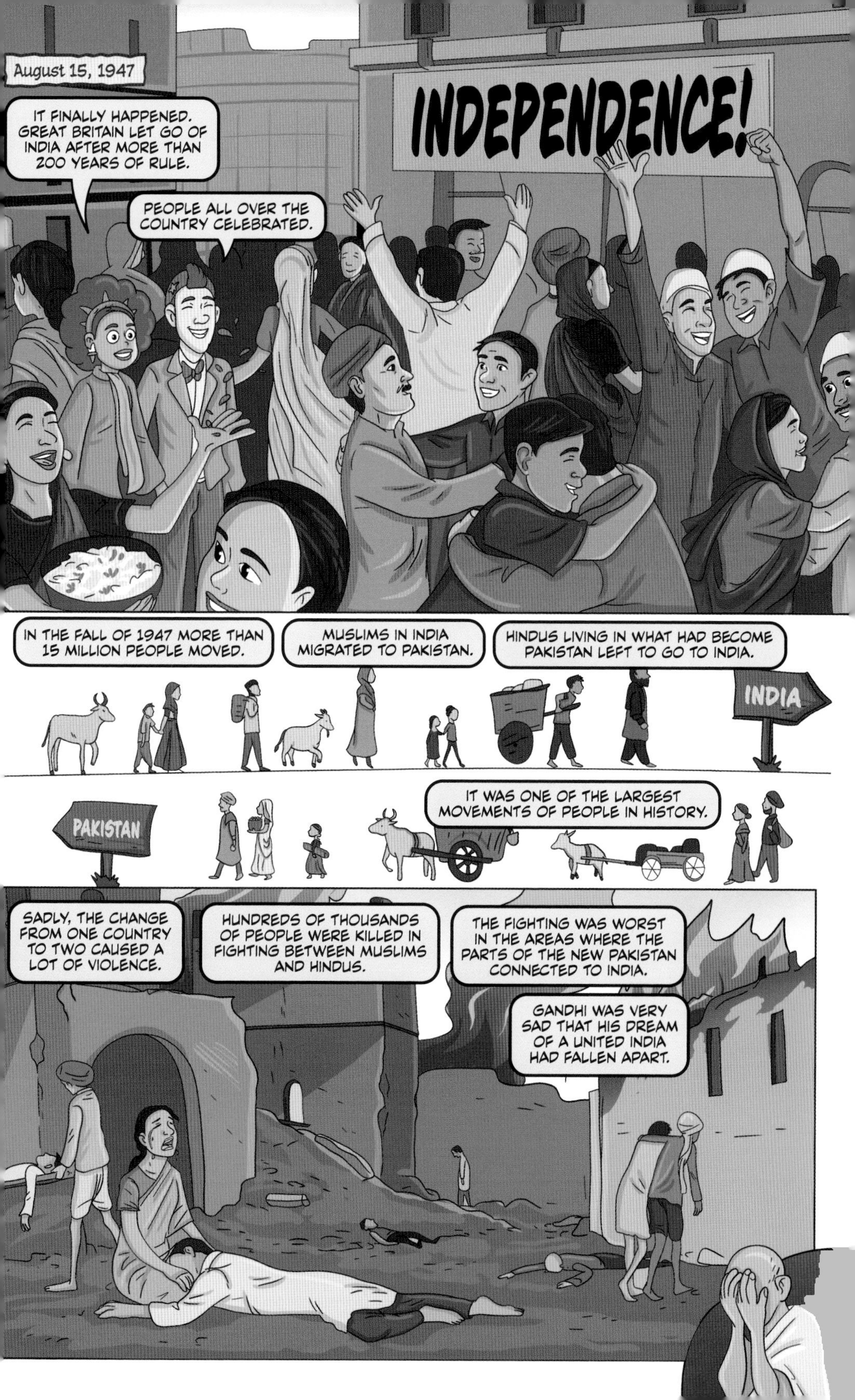

August 15, 1947
IT FINALLY HAPPENED. GREAT BRITAIN LET GO OF INDIA AFTER MORE THAN 200 YEARS OF RULE.
INDEPENDENCE!
PEOPLE ALL OVER THE COUNTRY CELEBRATED.
IN THE FALL OF 1947 MORE THAN 15 MILLION PEOPLE MOVED.
MUSLIMS IN INDIA MIGRATED TO PAKISTAN.
HINDUS LIVING IN WHAT HAD BECOME PAKISTAN LEFT TO GO TO INDIA.
INDIA
PAKISTAN
IT WAS ONE OF THE LARGEST MOVEMENTS OF PEOPLE IN HISTORY.
SADLY, THE CHANGE FROM ONE COUNTRY TO TWO CAUSED A LOT OF VIOLENCE.
HUNDREDS OF THOUSANDS OF PEOPLE WERE KILLED IN FIGHTING BETWEEN MUSLIMS AND HINDUS.
THE FIGHTING WAS WORST IN THE AREAS WHERE THE PARTS OF THE NEW PAKISTAN CONNECTED TO INDIA.
GANDHI WAS VERY SAD THAT HIS DREAM OF A UNITED INDIA HAD FALLEN APART.

AS 1947 WENT ON, MANY MUSLIM PEOPLE WERE MAD AT GANDHI FOR OPPOSING THE IDEA OF PAKISTAN AND FOR THE VIOLENCE.

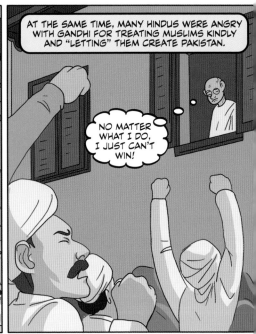

AT THE SAME TIME, MANY HINDUS WERE ANGRY WITH GANDHI FOR TREATING MUSLIMS KINDLY AND "LETTING" THEM CREATE PAKISTAN.

NO MATTER WHAT I DO, I JUST CAN'T WIN!

AS HE HAD BEFORE, GANDHI TRIED TO FAST IN PROTEST OF THE VIOLENCE.

ALL MY LIFE I HAVE STOOD, AS EVERYONE SHOULD STAND, FOR MINORITIES AND THOSE IN NEED.

HINDUS OUGHT TO PROTECT THE LIVES OF MUSLIMS.

GANDHI ENDED HIS FAST WHEN THE TWO SIDES SAID THEY WOULD STOP FIGHTING.

IT DIDN'T WORK.

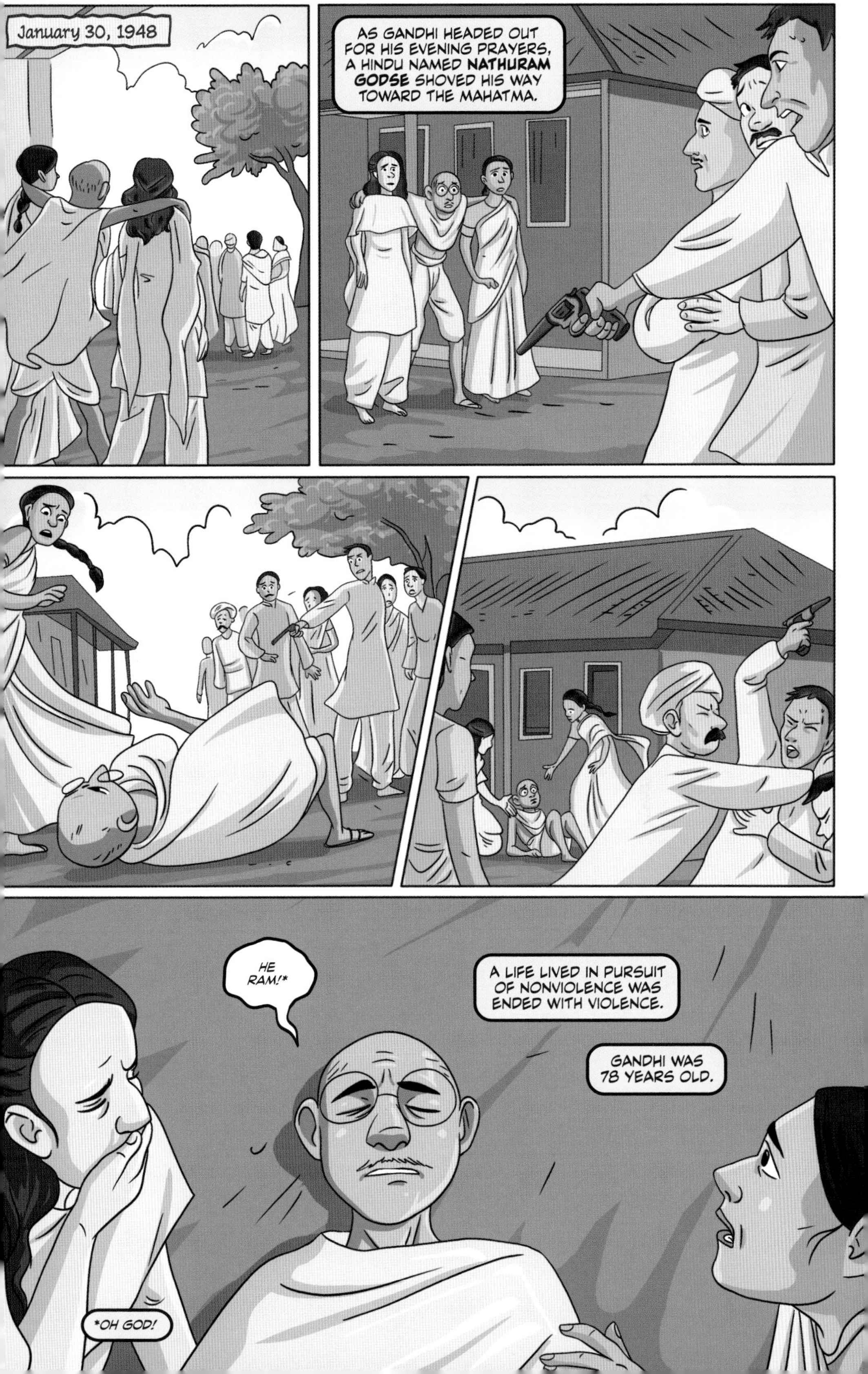
January 30, 1948
AS GANDHI HEADED OUT FOR HIS EVENING PRAYERS, A HINDU NAMED **NATHURAM GODSE** SHOVED HIS WAY TOWARD THE MAHATMA.
HE RAM!*
A LIFE LIVED IN PURSUIT OF NONVIOLENCE WAS ENDED WITH VIOLENCE.
GANDHI WAS 78 YEARS OLD.
*OH GOD!

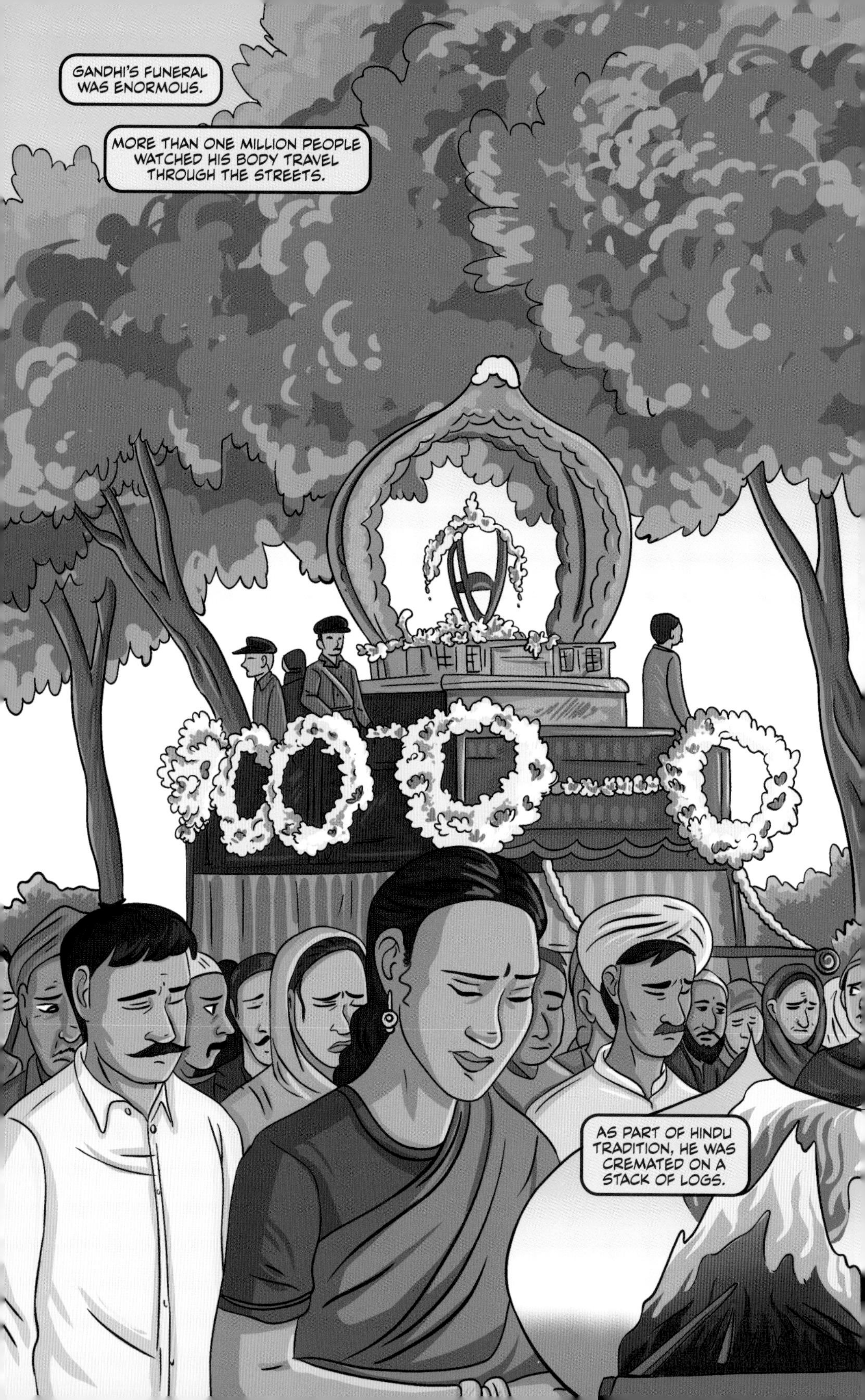
GANDHI'S FUNERAL WAS ENORMOUS.
MORE THAN ONE MILLION PEOPLE WATCHED HIS BODY TRAVEL THROUGH THE STREETS.
AS PART OF HINDU TRADITION, HE WAS CREMATED ON A STACK OF LOGS.

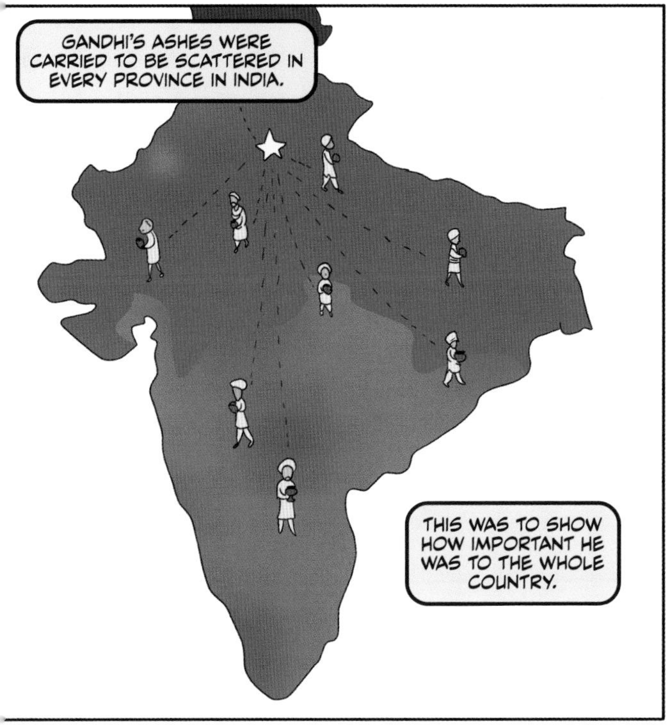
GANDHI'S ASHES WERE CARRIED TO BE SCATTERED IN EVERY PROVINCE IN INDIA.
THIS WAS TO SHOW HOW IMPORTANT HE WAS TO THE WHOLE COUNTRY.

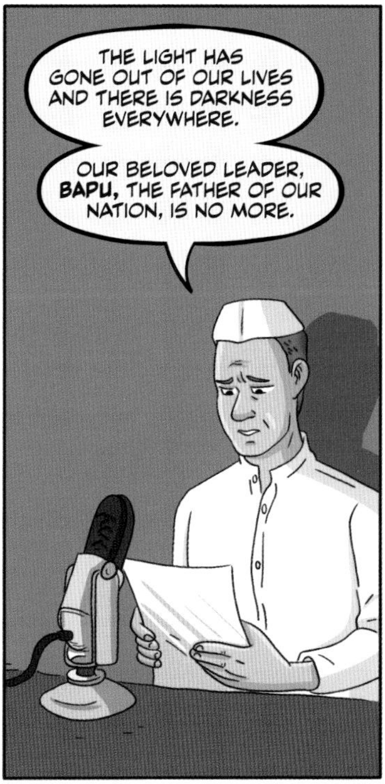
THE LIGHT HAS GONE OUT OF OUR LIVES AND THERE IS DARKNESS EVERYWHERE.
OUR BELOVED LEADER, **BAPU,** THE FATHER OF OUR NATION, IS NO MORE.

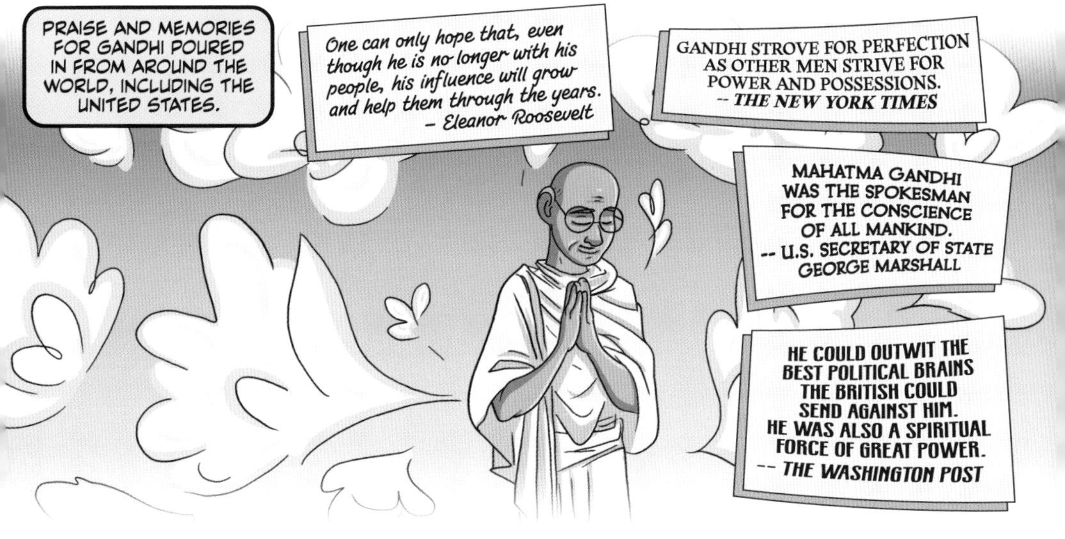
PRAISE AND MEMORIES FOR GANDHI POURED IN FROM AROUND THE WORLD, INCLUDING THE UNITED STATES.
One can only hope that, even though he is no longer with his people, his influence will grow and help them through the years. – Eleanor Roosevelt
GANDHI STROVE FOR PERFECTION AS OTHER MEN STRIVE FOR POWER AND POSSESSIONS. -- *THE NEW YORK TIMES*
MAHATMA GANDHI WAS THE SPOKESMAN FOR THE CONSCIENCE OF ALL MANKIND. -- U.S. SECRETARY OF STATE GEORGE MARSHALL
HE COULD OUTWIT THE BEST POLITICAL BRAINS THE BRITISH COULD SEND AGAINST HIM. HE WAS ALSO A SPIRITUAL FORCE OF GREAT POWER. -- *THE WASHINGTON POST*

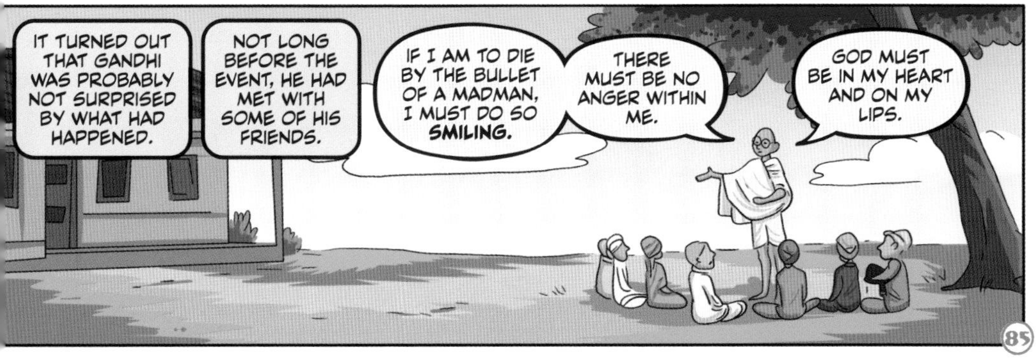
IT TURNED OUT THAT GANDHI WAS PROBABLY NOT SURPRISED BY WHAT HAD HAPPENED.
NOT LONG BEFORE THE EVENT, HE HAD MET WITH SOME OF HIS FRIENDS.
IF I AM TO DIE BY THE BULLET OF A MADMAN, I MUST DO SO **SMILING.**
THERE MUST BE NO ANGER WITHIN ME.
GOD MUST BE IN MY HEART AND ON MY LIPS.

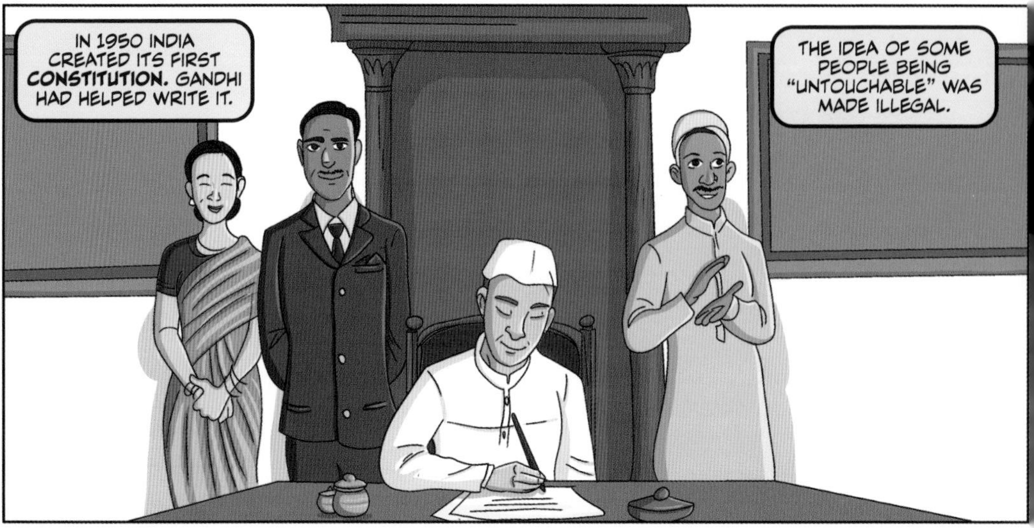
IN 1950 INDIA CREATED ITS FIRST **CONSTITUTION.** GANDHI HAD HELPED WRITE IT.
THE IDEA OF SOME PEOPLE BEING "UNTOUCHABLE" WAS MADE ILLEGAL.

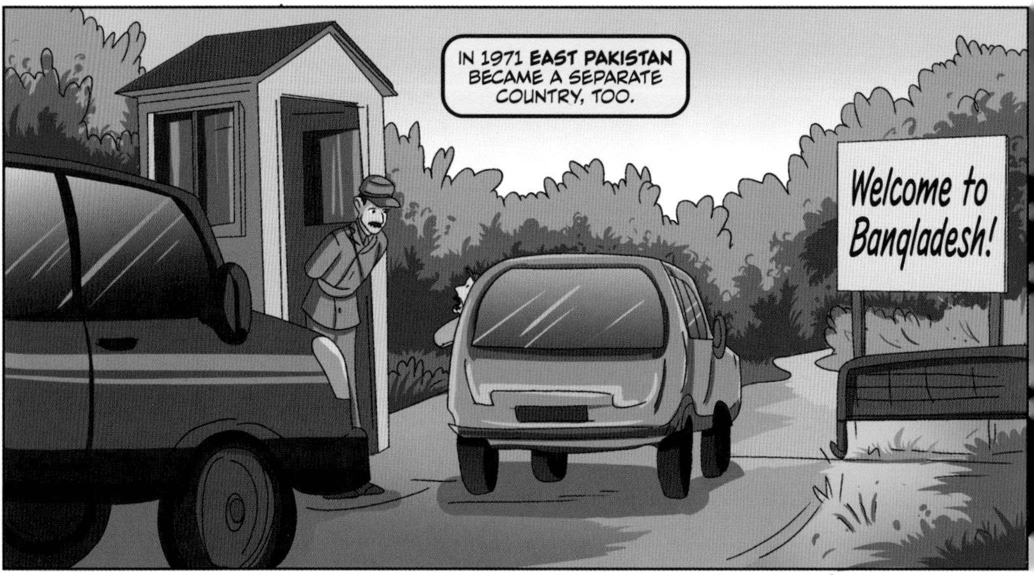
IN 1971 **EAST PAKISTAN** BECAME A SEPARATE COUNTRY, TOO.
Welcome to Bangladesh!

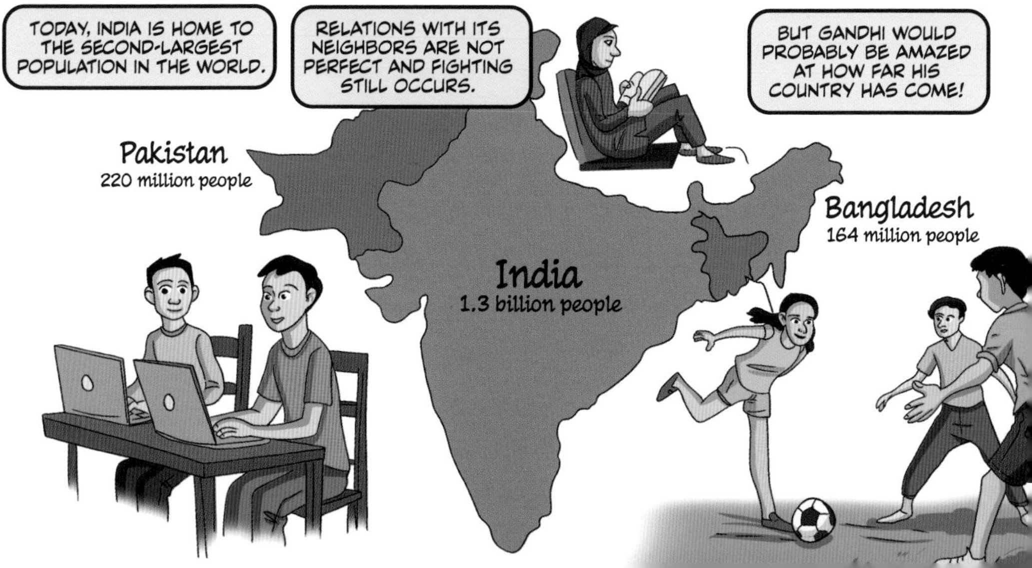
TODAY, INDIA IS HOME TO THE SECOND-LARGEST POPULATION IN THE WORLD.
RELATIONS WITH ITS NEIGHBORS ARE NOT PERFECT AND FIGHTING STILL OCCURS.
BUT GANDHI WOULD PROBABLY BE AMAZED AT HOW FAR HIS COUNTRY HAS COME!
Pakistan
220 million people
Bangladesh
164 million people
India
1.3 billion people

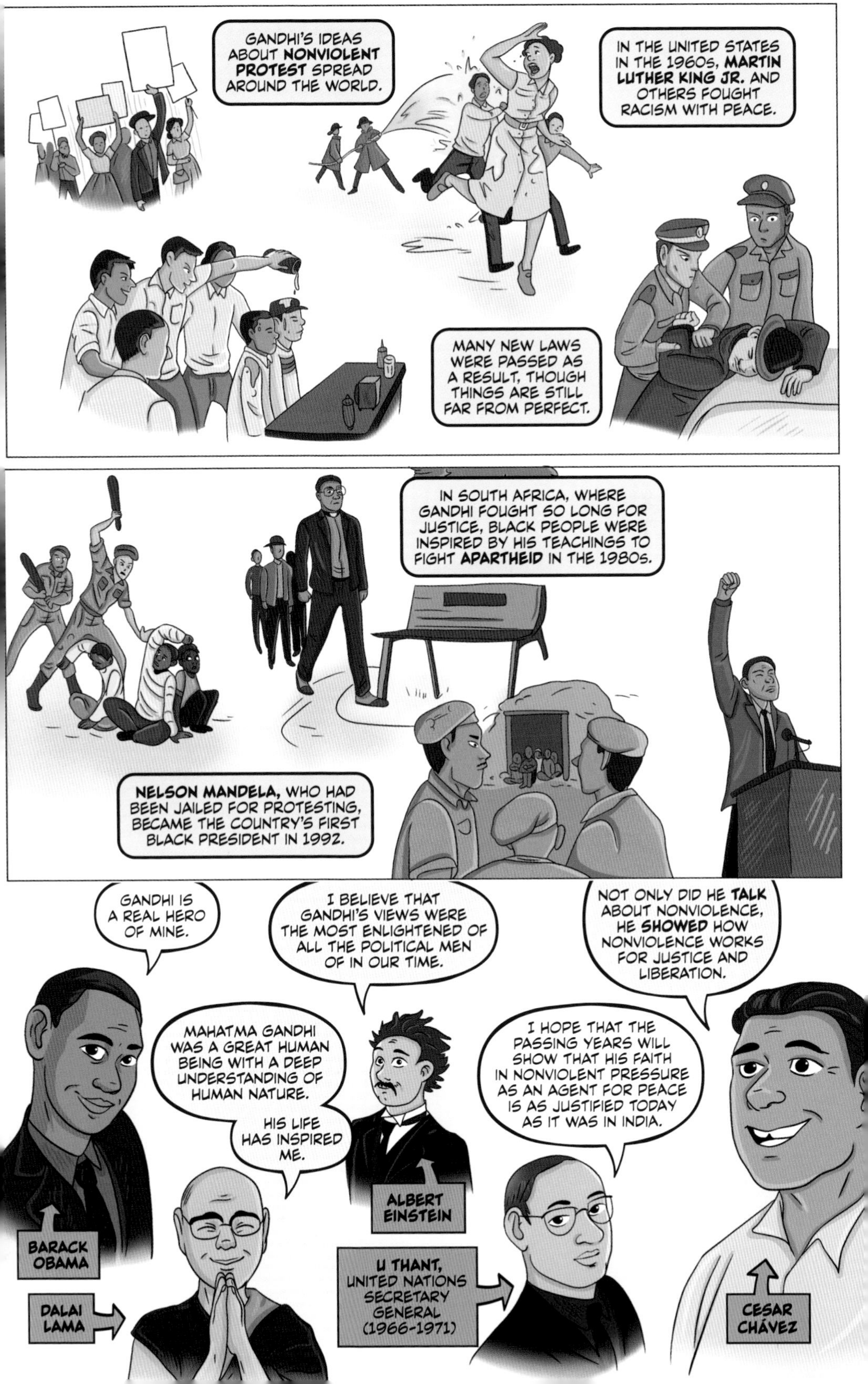
GANDHI'S IDEAS ABOUT **NONVIOLENT PROTEST** SPREAD AROUND THE WORLD.
IN THE UNITED STATES IN THE 1960s, **MARTIN LUTHER KING JR.** AND OTHERS FOUGHT RACISM WITH PEACE.
MANY NEW LAWS WERE PASSED AS A RESULT, THOUGH THINGS ARE STILL FAR FROM PERFECT.
IN SOUTH AFRICA, WHERE GANDHI FOUGHT SO LONG FOR JUSTICE, BLACK PEOPLE WERE INSPIRED BY HIS TEACHINGS TO FIGHT **APARTHEID** IN THE 1980s.
NELSON MANDELA, WHO HAD BEEN JAILED FOR PROTESTING, BECAME THE COUNTRY'S FIRST BLACK PRESIDENT IN 1992.
GANDHI IS A REAL HERO OF MINE.
I BELIEVE THAT GANDHI'S VIEWS WERE THE MOST ENLIGHTENED OF ALL THE POLITICAL MEN OF IN OUR TIME.
NOT ONLY DID HE **TALK** ABOUT NONVIOLENCE, HE **SHOWED** HOW NONVIOLENCE WORKS FOR JUSTICE AND LIBERATION.
MAHATMA GANDHI WAS A GREAT HUMAN BEING WITH A DEEP UNDERSTANDING OF HUMAN NATURE.
HIS LIFE HAS INSPIRED ME.
I HOPE THAT THE PASSING YEARS WILL SHOW THAT HIS FAITH IN NONVIOLENT PRESSURE AS AN AGENT FOR PEACE IS AS JUSTIFIED TODAY AS IT WAS IN INDIA.
BARACK OBAMA
ALBERT EINSTEIN
DALAI LAMA
U THANT, UNITED NATIONS SECRETARY GENERAL (1966-1971)
CESAR CHÁVEZ

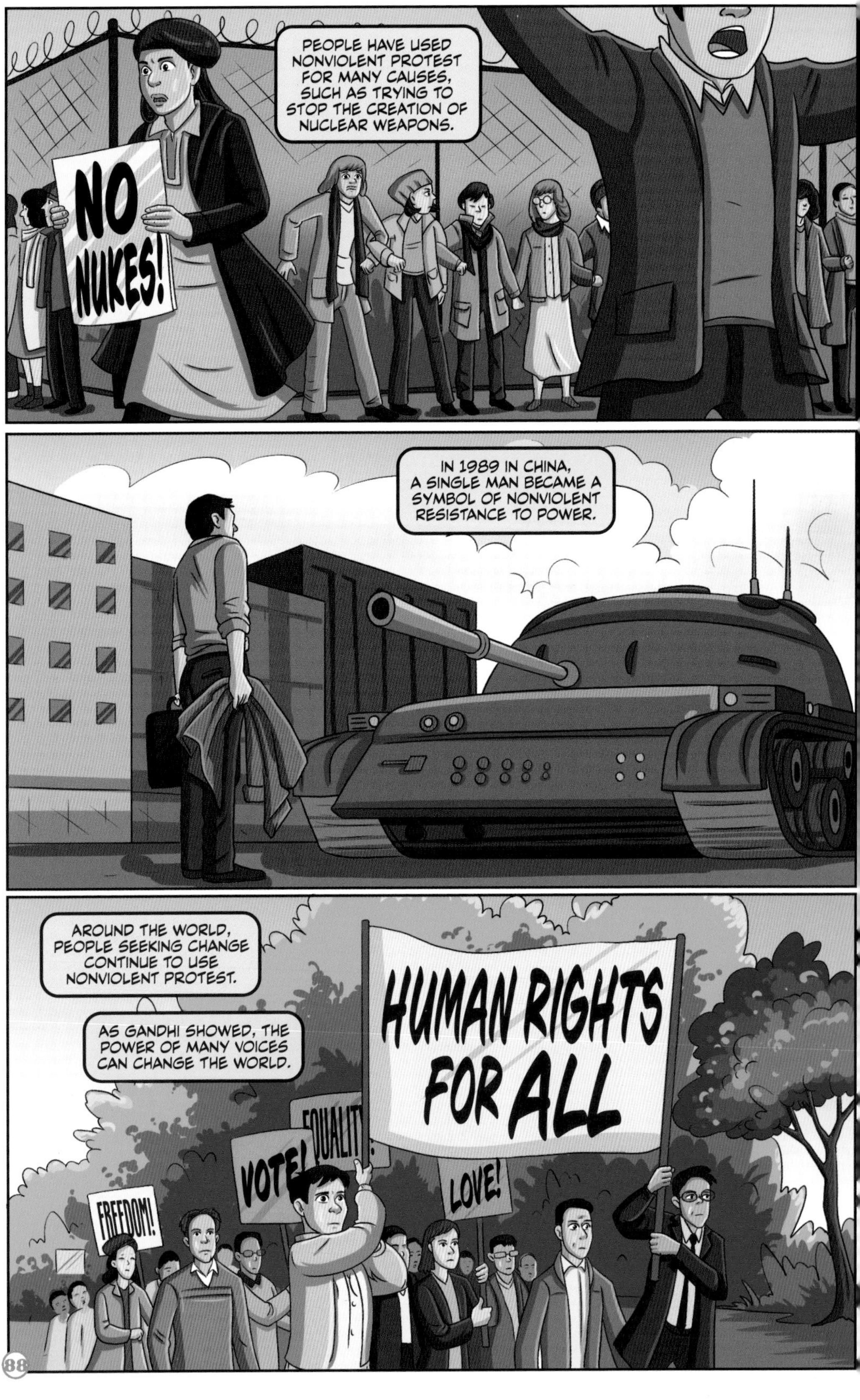

NO NUKES!
PEOPLE HAVE USED NONVIOLENT PROTEST FOR MANY CAUSES, SUCH AS TRYING TO STOP THE CREATION OF NUCLEAR WEAPONS.
IN 1989 IN CHINA, A SINGLE MAN BECAME A SYMBOL OF NONVIOLENT RESISTANCE TO POWER.
AROUND THE WORLD, PEOPLE SEEKING CHANGE CONTINUE TO USE NONVIOLENT PROTEST.
AS GANDHI SHOWED, THE POWER OF MANY VOICES CAN CHANGE THE WORLD.
HUMAN RIGHTS FOR ALL
VOTE!
LOVE!
FREEDOM!

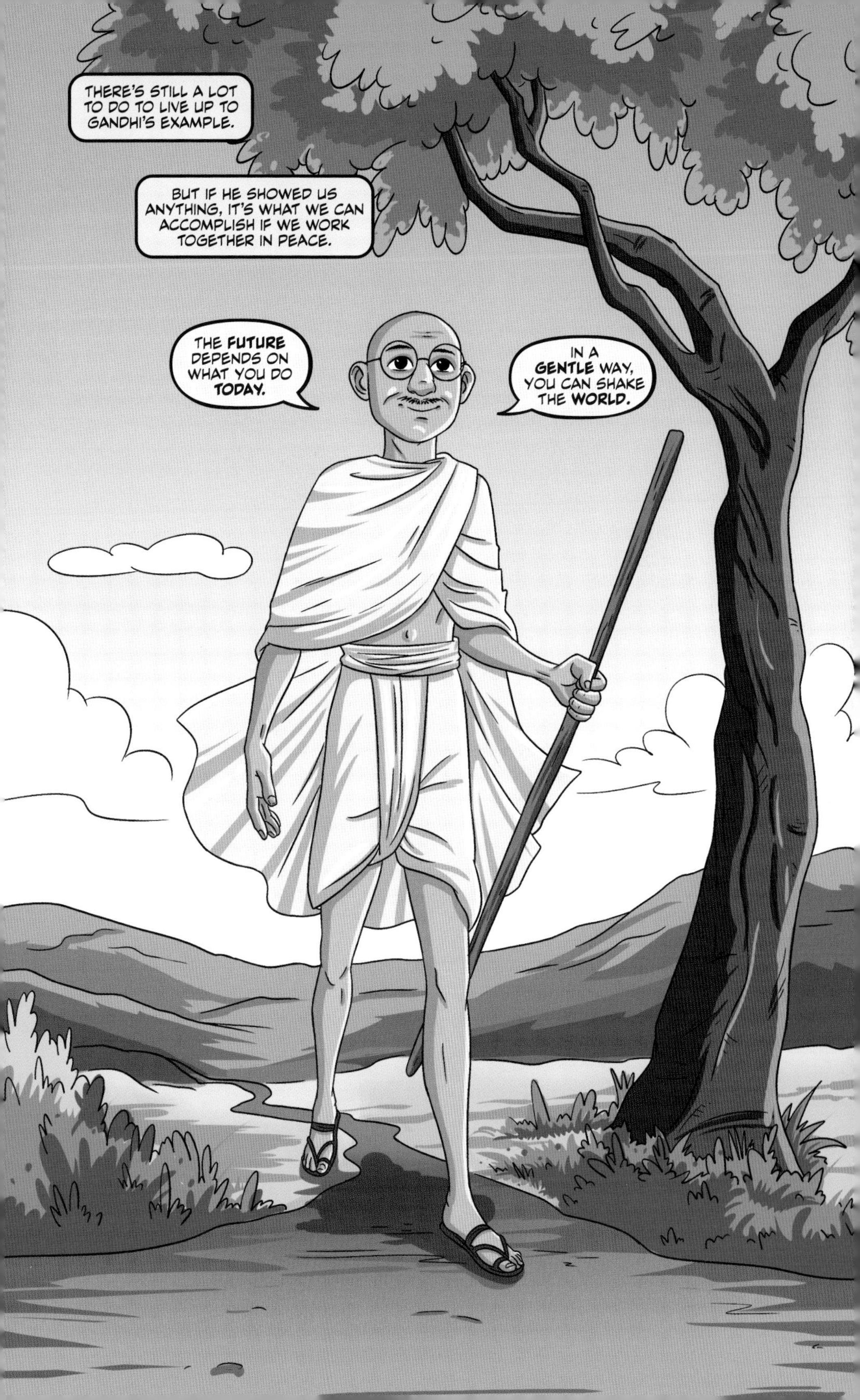
THERE'S STILL A LOT TO DO TO LIVE UP TO GANDHI'S EXAMPLE.
BUT IF HE SHOWED US ANYTHING, IT'S WHAT WE CAN ACCOMPLISH IF WE WORK TOGETHER IN PEACE.
THE **FUTURE** DEPENDS ON WHAT YOU DO **TODAY.**
IN A **GENTLE** WAY, YOU CAN SHAKE THE **WORLD.**

INSPIRATIONAL WORLD LEADERS

SINCE **GANDHI'S** TIME, PEOPLE HAVE STEPPED UP TO LEAD AND INSPIRE CITIZENS AROUND THE WORLD THROUGH PEACE AND NONVIOLENCE. HERE ARE JUST A FEW YOU CAN TRY TO FIND OUT MORE ABOUT.

CESAR CHAVEZ (1927-1993) was inspired by Gandhi to use nonviolence and fasting to fight for the rights of migrant farm workers in the United States.

The Black civil rights leader **DR. MARTIN LUTHER KING JR.** (1929-1968) inspired millions to use nonviolent protest in the U.S. during the 1960s. Sadly, he, too, was assassinated for his beliefs.

As the world leader of Tibetan Buddhism, the **DALAI LAMA** (b. 1935) spreads a message of peace and personhood.

NELSON MANDELA (1918-2013) was jailed for 27 years as a leader in the fight against apartheid (racial segregation) in South Africa. He later became the country's first Black president.

ELEANOR ROOSEVELT (1884-1962) used her position as the first lady of the United States from 1932 to 1944 to call for change in America's policies on race and women's rights.

Born in Albania, **MOTHER TERESA** (1910-1997) spent most of her life in India, starting an organization that took care of the poorest of the poor.

Shot by terrorists for being a female who dared to go to school, **MALALA YOUSAFZAI** (b. 1997) of Pakistan has become a worldwide leader for women's rights and a winner of the Nobel Peace Prize.

GANDHI TIMELINE

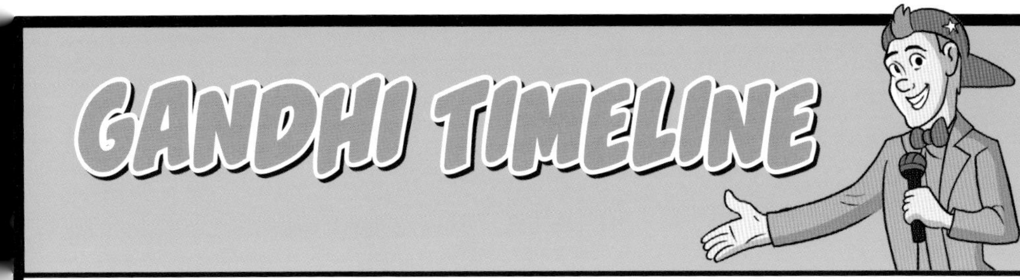

1869 Mohandas Karamchand Gandhi is born in Porbandar, India, on October 2.

1883 Gandhi marries Kasturba when both are only 13.

1891 After studying for three years in England, Gandhi becomes a barrister, a type of lawyer.

1893 He moves to South Africa and soon becomes involved in a fight for the rights of Indians living there.

1906 After much study, he develops the philosophy of nonviolence for civil disobedience that he calls *satyagraha*.

1914 After many years of struggle in South Africa, Gandhi and his followers force a change to some laws to make life better for Indians there.

1920 Back in India, following the passage of discriminatory laws by British rulers, Gandhi starts a national noncooperation movement to force the British out.

1922 Gandhi is arrested and sentenced to six years in jail for his actions against the British rulers.

1930 Gandhi leads the Salt March to break British laws; the Indian independence movement gains worldwide attention.

1942 During World War II, Gandhi starts the Quit India movement.

1947 Hindu-majority India becomes independent of Great Britain on August 15; the Muslim country of Pakistan is formed the same day from part of what was India.

1948 Gandhi is assassinated by an angry Hindu gunman on January 30.

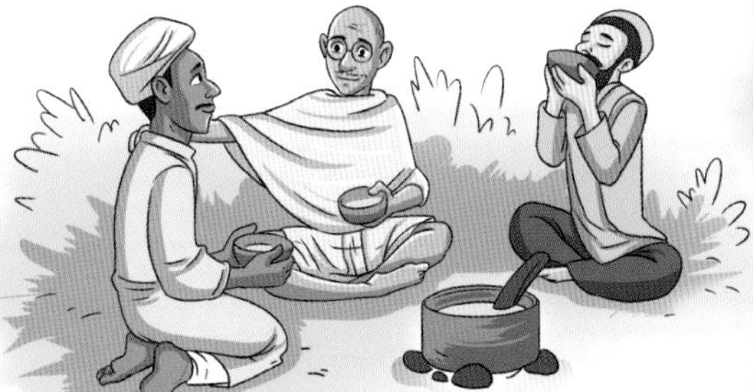

GLOSSARY

APARTHEID: The racist system of separation by race used in South Africa in the 20th century.

ASHRAM: A collective residence based on all members living spiritual lives.

BOYCOTT: Refusing to buy goods or use services in protest of something.

CASTE: One of the class divisions in Hindu India.

DEVOUT: Very faithful and holy.

DISCRIMINATE: Favor one group over another for the wrong reasons.

FASTING: The process of refusing to eat or drink as a form of protest.

FLOGGED: Whipped.

LIQUIDATION: Total destruction.

MIGRATE: Move from one area to another.

MUTTON: Form of lamb meat.

PASSIVE RESISTANCE: Refusing to comply with orders by taking no action.

QUARANTINE: A place or period of time in which sick people are separated from healthy people.

SATYAGRAHA: Gandhi's name for "soul-force," or the power of nonviolent resistance.

SUBJECTS: The name for people who live under a king or queen.

UNTOUCHABLES: The lowest-ranked members in the Indian caste system,.

WORLDLY: Knowledgeable about many things.

FIND OUT MORE

BOOKS

Bailey, Diane. *Gandhi.* DK Life Stories. New York: DK Publishing, 2019.

Chadha, Yogesh. *Gandhi: A Life.* New York: John Wiley, 1997.

Fischer, Louis. *Gandhi: His Life and Message for the World.* New York: New American Library, 1954.

Rau, Dana Meachen. *Who Was Gandhi?* Who Was Series. New York: Penguin Workshop, 2014.

Soundar, Chitra. *The Extraordinary Life of Mahatma Gandhi.* New York: Puffin Books, 2019.

Wilkinson, Philip. *Gandhi: The Young Protester Who Founded a Nation.* Washington, D.C.: National Geographic Kids, 2007.

WEBSITES

The M. K. Gandhi Institute for Nonviolence
www.gandhiinstitute.org

The Gandhi Heritage Portal
www.gandhiheritageportal.org

SHOW ME HISTORY!

COLLECT EVERY BOOK IN THE SERIES AND FIND THE *STORY* IN HISTORY!

ABRAHAM LINCOLN
DEFENDER OF THE UNION!

ALBERT EINSTEIN
GENIUS OF SPACE AND TIME!

ALEXANDER HAMILTON
THE FIGHTING FOUNDING FATHER!

AMELIA EARHART
PIONEER OF THE SKY!

ANNE FRANK
WITNESS TO HISTORY!

BABE RUTH
BASEBALL'S ALL-TIME BEST!

BENJAMIN FRANKLIN
INVENTOR OF THE NATION!

FRIDA KAHLO
THE REVOLUTIONARY PAINTER!

GANDHI
THE PEACEFUL PROTESTER!

GEORGE WASHINGTON
SOLDIER AND STATESMAN!

HARRIET TUBMAN
FIGHTER FOR FREEDOM!

HELEN KELLER
INSPIRATION TO EVERYONE!

JESUS
MESSENGER OF PEACE!

MARTIN LUTHER KING JR.
VOICE FOR EQUALITY!

MUHAMMAD ALI
THE GREATEST OF ALL TIME!

NEIL ARMSTRONG
FIRST MAN ON THE MOON!

SACAGAWEA
COURAGEOUS TRAILBLAZER!

SUSAN B. ANTHONY
CHAMPION FOR VOTING RIGHTS!

WALT DISNEY
THE MAGICAL INNOVATOR!

PARENTS AND TEACHERS: VISIT OUR WEBSITE FOR MORE *SHOW ME HISTORY!* FUN...

SHOWMEHISTORY.COM

... WHERE YOU CAN LEARN MORE ABOUT THE AUTHORS, SIGN UP FOR OUR EMAIL NEWSLETTER, AND DOWNLOAD OUR READING GUIDES!

ALSO FOLLOW US ON **SOCIAL MEDIA!**

 @showmehistorybooks **f** www.facebook.com/ portablepress   www.pinterest.com/ portablepress   @portablepress

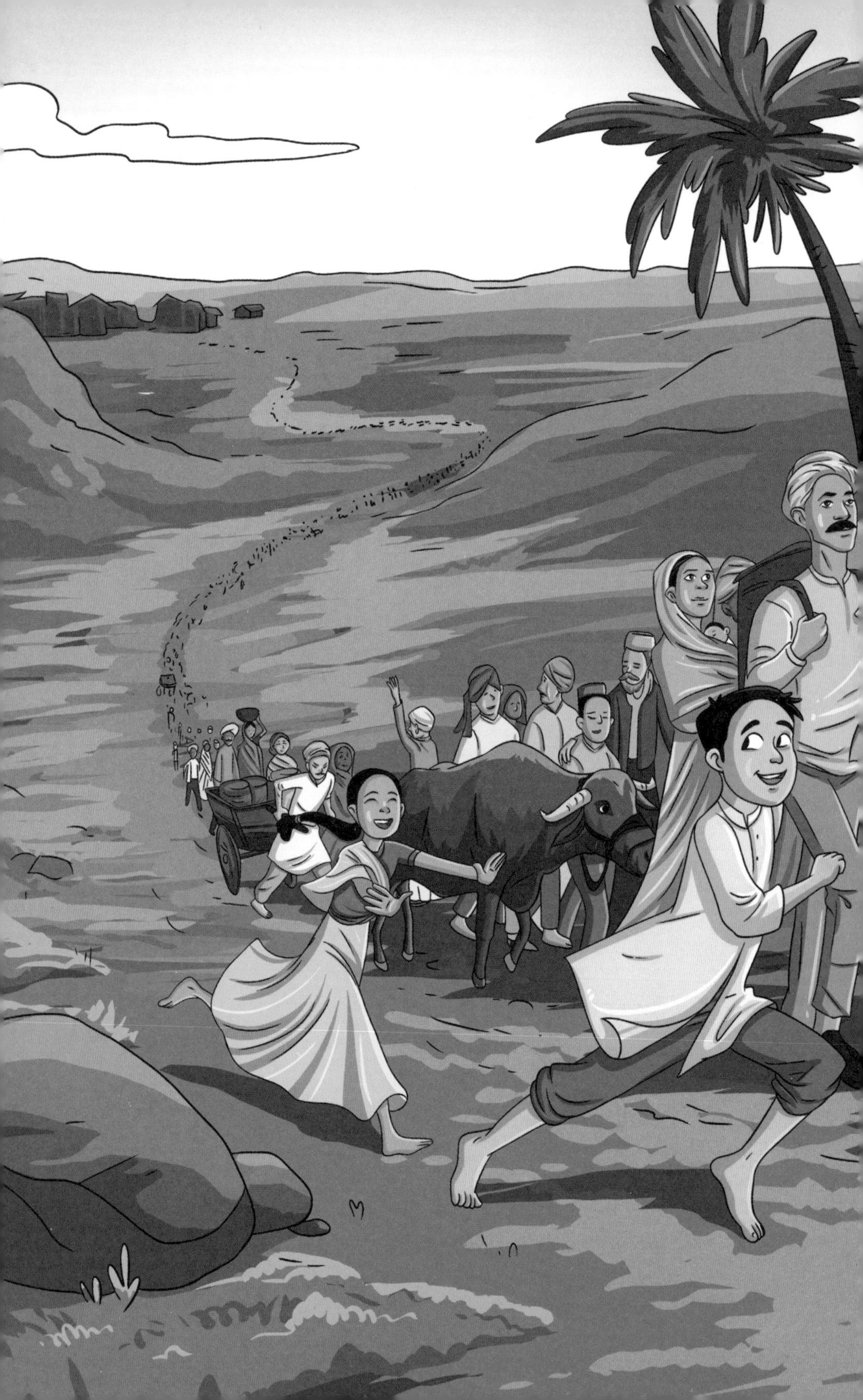